Community work and the state

This volume has been edited by Gary Craig, Nick Derricourt and
Martin Loney in co-operation with the Editorial Board appointed by
the Association of Community Workers:

Gary Craig
Marjorie Mayo
Laurie Bidwell
Anne Wright
Ian Kirkaldy
Chris Johnson
Ashok Ohri
Anne Lamming

It is no. 8 in the Community Work Series

Community work and the state

edited by
Gary Craig
Nick Derricourt
Martin Loney

Routledge & Kegan Paul

London, Boston, Melbourne and Henley

First published in 1982
by Routledge & Kegan Paul Ltd
39 Store Street,
London WC1E 7DD,
9 Park Street,
Boston, Mass. 02108, USA,
296 Beaconsfield Parade, Middle Park,
Melbourne 3206, Australia, and
Broadway House, Newtown Road,
Henley-on-Thames, Oxon RG9 1EN
Printed in Great Britain by
St Edmundsbury Press, Bury St Edmunds, Suffolk

ISBN 0 7100 9305 5

jwe   6-27-83

Contents

Contributors

PETER BALDOCK worked with voluntary organisations in Paris, Sheffield and Manchester before taking up his present post as leader of a small community work team in Sheffield's Family and Community Services Department.

GIDEON BEN-TOVIM lectures in sociology at the University of Liverpool.

HARRY BLAGG is a lecturer in the Social Administration Department of Lancaster University.

The COVENTRY WORKSHOP is a collectively organised, independent trade union and community research, educational and advisory centre, established in 1975 and still going strong. It is accountable to the groups it works with.

GARY CRAIG was a community worker in Chesterfield and Stoke-on-Trent before working in Newcastle for the Benwell CDP and the West End Resource Centre for ten years. He is a NUPE shop steward and currently editor of the Community Development Journal.

NICK DERRICOURT is a lecturer in the Social Administration Department of Lancaster University and is Chairman of the Editorial Advisory Board of the Community Development Journal.

GILL DIXON worked in Cleveland for two years as a neighbourhood worker with the County Social Services Department and is now employed by Lady Margaret Hall Settlement working on women's employment issues in Lambeth, London.

ELIZABETH FILKIN is a lecturer in social studies at Liverpool University providing courses for inner city residents. Previously she was a community worker and residential worker in Birmingham and London and lectured at the National Institute of Social Work and Birmingham University.

MIKE FLEETWOOD lives and works in Cardiff and is active in the South Wales Association of Tenants.

JOHN GABRIEL lectures in sociology at Birmingham University.

CHRIS JOHNSON has been employed as a community worker since 1974, initially in Salford and currently with the Newcastle Family Service Unit.   She is an active trade unionist.

CHRIS JONES and TONY NOVAK are both active in community politics in Rochdale.   They print and produce the Bulletin on Social Policy, a socialist publication appearing three times a year.   Both earn a living through teaching.

ROBERT KRAUSHAAR lectures in the School of Architecture and Environmental Design at the State University of New York at Buffalo, USA.

JOHN LAMBERT lectures in the Department of Social Administration at University College Cardiff and is Reviews Editor of the Community Development Journal.

IAN LAW is a research assistant at Liverpool University.

SUE LEIGH is Inner City Officer for the Newcastle upon Tyne Council for Voluntary Service.   She has lived and worked in the north-east of England since 1974, previously as a neighbourhood community worker and then as a welfare rights worker.

MARTIN LONEY lectures in social policy at the Open University.   He is the author of 'Rhodesia: White Racism and Imperial Response', Penguin, 1975 and has co-edited books on inner city policy and on social and community work in multi-racial settings.

DAVID MARSDEN is a lecturer in development studies at University College Swansea.   He was formerly at the Centre for Endogenous Development, Tehran.   He is an anthropologist with research interests in social policy and rural development.

MARJORIE MAYO is currently working on a women's employment and training project in Haringey, London.   She has previously worked on the evaluation of Area Resource Centres in the EEC Anti-Poverty Programme and in the Central Research Unit of the CDP.

MICHAEL NAISH has worked as a probation officer and lecturer in social work, and as a community worker, during the last twelve years.

The NETWORK OF LABOUR, COMMUNITY RESEARCH AND RESOURCE CENTRES is a federation of research and resource centres working at the base of the trade union, community and women's movements.   There are currently fifteen member organisations.

PETER OAKLEY worked as a volunteer in Peru and as an Oxfam Field Director in Brazil and Ethiopia.   He is currently lecturing in Extension Methods at Reading University's Agricultural Extension Centre and undertaking research into community action in the Third World.

CHRIS PHILLIPSON is Senior Research Fellow in the Department of

Adult Education, University of Keele.   He is the author of 'Capitalism and the Construction of Old Age', Macmillan, 1982 and has
written many articles on retirement and ageing.

BARBARA SCHMIDT de TORRES is a graduate student in the School of
Architecture and Environmental Design at the State University of
New York at Buffalo.

KATHLEEN STREDDER is a staff tutor with the Open University in
Birmingham.

NICKY TURNBULL is a member of Wear Women, a collective of practising
community and youth workers in Sunderland.

1 Introduction: Towards a radical practice

Gary Craig, Nick Derricourt and Martin Loney

Community work is frequently seen as providing a radical alternative
to other forms of social intervention, an opportunity to tackle
causes rather than bandage symptoms.   In fact, community work like
social work is open to a variety of ideological perspectives;   from
conservative strategies for social control or schemes to off-load
statutory responsibilities onto deprived communities, through tech-
nocratic attempts to define a more sophisticated skill base for community work, to various strands of radicalism.   The latter range
from the co-operative self-help tradition to more overtly revolutionary strategies.

The development of a satisfactory theoretical base for radical
practice, and a clarification of goals, are long overdue.   Development has, in part, been hampered by mechanistic views of the state
which has been seen simplistically as an ultimately repressive
apparatus manipulated by the bourgeoisie.   Welfare is viewed as a
sop to the working class.   This view is reflected for example in
some of the contributions to 'Community or Class Struggle?'.   Kaye
and Thompson, for example, suggest that 'The increasing involvement
of the Home Office in "Community" affairs alongside their police
responsibility is no coincidence.' (1)   A less dramatic account
might rather focus on the Home Office's pre-Seebohm responsibilities
for children.   The Community Development Projects, to which Kaye
and Thompson refer, were in fact designed in the old Home Office
Children's Department.

We hope in this volume to offer a more critical understanding of
the relationship of community work to the state, an understanding
which allows for the development of a viable socialist practice.

The origins of British community work include the Charitable
Organisation Society, the University Settlement movement and the
British Colonial Office.   The first of these groups was concerned
with regulating the charitable activities of upper income groups,
lest the enthusiastic provision of uncontrolled largesse should
fail to distinguish between deserving and undeserving recipients.
The second was concerned to reform and improve the character of the
poor by example;   it was believed that the presence of upright,
articulate members of the more prosperous classes might simultaneously provide role models for the poor and help to engineer some
cautious social reforms.   For its part the Colonial Office was concerned to ensure the governability and modernisation of Britain's
far-flung empire, not, let it be said, from altruistic motives, but

in order better to maximise the financial rewards of the imperial
era and to ensure a successful transition to a pro-Western independence.

From any radical perspective these beginnings could only be described as inauspicious, yet by the late 1960s community work had
undoubtedly developed a radical aura.   Many activists from the CND
and the Committee of 100 turned from the single-issue focus of unilateral disarmament to the potential for protest which was thought
to lie in low-income communities.   The poor not only faced the
prospect of annihilation like everybody else, they also had more
than enough reason to revolt against the here and now.   The organisers of the Notting Hill Project, one of the militant projects
which emerged in this period, specifically sought to help 'the
struggles of the working class for survival in the North Kensington
Area and for control over the resources and decisions which determine their living conditions'. (2)   The scale of interest in relatively unstructured community work jobs during this period is demonstrated by the fact that when the Young Volunteer Force Foundation
advertised, in 1968, for twelve field workers it received 1,200
enquiries. (3)

In the 1960s community work became the focus for many differing
interests.   The Seebohm Committee recommended the expansion of
community work and advocated a strong community work dimension to
the new local authority social services departments. (4)   The Gulbenkian Foundation sponsored two influential reports on community
work and community work training. (5)   In the planning field, the
Skeffington Report recommended changes to increase public participation and encourage community work input. (6)   The reorganisation of
local government following the Maud Commission encouraged a re-
thinking of the appropriate relationship between local government
and the electorate. (7)

Community work remained open to embrace by both radicals and government, a fact which was to cause confusion and conflict for all
concerned.   Participation was variously seen as a way of improving
the performance and responsiveness of local government (which seemed
to spend more and more for less and less consumer satisfaction but
with a veritable explosion of urban blight), and as a way of legiti-
mating more radical demands for structural change and more egalitarian social policies.   Community work was supported by those who saw
in the poor a combination of moral and physical inadequacy, lack of
motivation and insufficient attention to modern child-rearing practices, and others who saw the same group as the victims of an inherently exploitative capitalist society - victims who might also be
the architects of the new social order.

Some radicals saw in community work's expansion, in this period,
a new extension of the state's social control activities.   Corrigan, for example, argued: 'Throughout the Western world states are
characterised by one of the two major symbols of control in capitalist society; the tank or the community worker.' (8)   The launch-
ing of the Community Development Projects (CDPs) by the Home Office
in 1969 not only focused attention on the purpose of community work,
it also provided an arena within which many of these conflicts would
be fought out.

Lee Bridges saw in the Urban Aid Programme and the CDPs a larger
strategy of domestic counter-insurgency:

The function of the Urban Aid Programme was to buy out community-
based organisations by giving them relatively small sums of money
for 'safe' activities such as adventure playgrounds and legal
advice centres.   The Community Development Projects had the same
function on a larger and more concentrated scale.   Of course,
the Home Office hoped for some feedback from these projects in
terms of research and intelligence on the urban poor, and, in the
case of the Community Development Projects, university-based research teams were appointed for this purpose. (9)
Others argued that the structure of the Projects and, in particular,
the power of the local authorities would, in any case, neutralise
the impact of the local workers.   Holman argued that the CDPs would
be forced to rely on consensual strategies: 'As institutionalised
bodies, like local authorities, will not countenance conflict, the
Community Development Project is unlikely to promote radical
improvement.' (10)

In fact the CDPs produced a series of radical critiques of central government policies. (11)   The projects engaged in a variety
of local actions which were frequently far removed from the cautious
intentions of their founders.   One of these, Joan Cooper, at that
time Chief Inspector of Social Work in the Children's Department at
the Home Office, was concerned to find a community dimension to
social work's social control concerns.   In a contemporary article
on delinquency she spelt out what she saw as the community dimension
of the treatment of delinquency; noting that preventative and reme-
dial work already included the family, she argued: 'The next stage
is to work with communities producing the socially disadvantaged ...
highly skilled treatment with the individual is wasted if he is re-
turned to a disordered community which can offer little support.' (12)

This social pathology approach to the problems of low-income communities was to be universally rejected by the CDPs, though not all
of them endorsed the explicitly Marxist stance of the Political
Economy Collective (PEC) formed by some local project workers.   A
number of members of the PEC argued the need to move beyond left re-
formism to the development of a revolutionary strategy: 'For PEC
members the key question is surely how we can engaged in community-
based action for revolutionary ends.' (13)

In fact, leaving aside the rhetorical flourishes, it is clear
that the CDPs did leave an important legacy of radical praxis which
began to offer a counter-pole of attraction to traditional community
development approaches.   This volume is intended to continue that
tradition and we hope to further inform a radical but realistic
socialist practice.

Others have been simultaneously seeking a new, technically
sophisticated approach to community work, whilst rejecting the explicit socialism of the left-wing CDP workers as 'all the blather of
a few radical poseurs.' (14)   Instead they sought to rescue from
the entrails of American sociology models which, elsewhere, had
proved rather difficult to import: functionalism and systems
theory.   These models are rooted in the explicitly anti-socialist
stance of mainstream American sociology which, when taking note of
Marx at all, did so to caution the reader against him.   Faced with
the more theoretically sophisticated European social science

tradition these models have recently had all the success of a
British Leyland product in the Japanese market.   However, one
notable breakthrough into the British market occurred in social
work, where the decline of the psychoanalytic perspective had left a
theoretical void, into which any new legitimation for social work's
increasingly ambitious claims could be poured.   We are referring
here to what is variously called the unitary or integrated approach
to social work, an approach which makes up in vocabulary what it
lacks in theoretical depth or day-to-day perspicacity.   Mesmerised
by 'client systems' and 'change agent systems' the hapless social
worker might indeed be forgiven for feeling that there must, after
all, be something to all this.   Indeed the advocates of the
approach are ever-eager to claim new territories.   No sooner is the
patch system announced than we find that this too is claimed by the
unitary approach.   'To prepare workers for entry into patch teams,
CQSW courses would need to teach the unitary approach as the framework for practice.' (15)

The main franchise for this transatlantic import appears to have
been given to the London-based National Institute for Social Work
and it is not, then, fortuitous to find that as this mish-mash of
conservative theory and linguistic abuse penetrate into community
work it should be launched from the same base.   It is from here
that we receive the insight of community work as interjacence, presented with an obscurity worthy of American sociology at its finest:
'The fact of interjacence necessarily introduces a transactive element into the evolution of community work as an occupation.' (16)
In another contribution to the new community work technology we
learn: 'The worker may, of course, take or be given more of a
leadership role at the interface but remain inside the boundary of
non-directiveness with his transactions with local people.' (17)

Blagg and Derricourt look in more detail at the theoretical
underpinning of this emerging community work school (Chapter 2).
For the moment we raise it only to distance ourselves from it.
This volume is not about community work technology.   Our intention
has been to tackle some of the theoretical questions involved in
radical community work practice, to examine particular facets of
contemporary social policy, to exemplify practice in a number of
areas and to review some of the relevant international developments
in community work.

Radical community workers have had, as we have already noted, an
ambivalent or hostile relationship to the state, yet it has provided
the major source of employment for workers and the main funding for
community projects.   For those who have viewed the state in Machia-
vellian or conspiratorial terms and have seen the development of
social welfare as no more than a ruling-class strategy to blunt the
revolutionary zeal of the workers, the possibility of an effective
community work practice and theory has been rather restricted.
Others, however, have recognised that the ambiguity of the relationship also provides scope for progressive gains.   Cockburn, review-
ing the changing role and strategies of the local state and the increasing attempts to reach out to the local community and incorporate it in the decision-making process, has argued:

  The potential control of the state increases the more closely the
  working population is knit to the state system.   We should think

for the moment not of overtly repressive control but simply of management of the working class, its 'families' and 'groups' in the business of reproduction of the labour force and of capitalist relations.   But this incorporation of the population is a two-edged sword for the state, and for the working class, because the closer working-class groups come into inclusion within the state system, the more dangerous is any disruptive behaviour to the equilibrium of the state. (18)

Community work is equally a two-edged sword: 'Community work does bring with it new situations and new opportunities for working-class gain, it also sometimes leads working-class groups into incorporation and impotence.' (19)

This analysis, whilst an advance over more mechanistic views of the state, remains incomplete in that it fails to confront adequately the issues raised where socialist councillors gain 'control' of local authorities.   It is true that such control remains limited by the nature of the authority which they inherit and the difficulties of making rapid radical innovations, as well as by the growing attempt by central government to transform local councils into agencies of indirect Whitehall rule.   None the less the issues raised by the attempts in London, Sheffield, the West Midlands and elsewhere to move beyond a traditional view of municipal socialism invite new responses from community workers and a more sophisticated approach to the role of the local state.

Blagg and Derricourt argue the case for a more theoretically informed community work practice (Chapter 2).   They suggest that contemporary developments in Western Marxism provide an alternative framework to the narrow economism which sees community conflicts as but a pale reflection of the 'real' struggle taking place in industry and seeks to view every struggle through the restricted prism of social class.   At a more immediate level Baldock critically examines the role of local social service departments as major community work employers (Chapter 3).   His proposals for a more professional and accountable community work practice and for closer links with social work will not be universally supported but the questions he confronts are not ones that can continue to be ignored.

Naish and Filkin argue that community workers need an explicit set of values and objectives which should be based on egalitarian and democratic principles (Chapter 4).   In general this means a commitment to work with deprived groups in the community to maximise their access to resources.   The political conflict attendant on this strategy obliges workers to clarify their job description and terms of employment from the outset.

The central role of women in any community work is now widely recognised and Dixon et al. explore the contribution of a socialist feminist perspective for community work practice (Chapter 6). Lambert and Fleetwood suggest that the rift and misunderstanding between community action and socialist politics cannot be overcome by simply reasserting the importance of 'party' or 'workplace' (Chapter 5).   Community activists in housing should not give up, but draw on contemporary developments in Western socialist theory to justify patient, well-founded work with local authority tenants; the authors contend that this may play a part in the development of new, popularly-based radical politics.

Many community workers have appeared to dismiss community work with the elderly as insufficiently glamorous.   The elderly have been ignored by community workers, in part because work in closed institutions has been seen as the prerogative of other groups.   No doubt the ageism which condemns many of the elderly to obscurity once their 'productive' lives are over has had its effect on community work practitioners.   Jones et al. argue that community workers can play a role both in working with organisations for the elderly and in making institutional and other provision more responsive (Chapter 7).   Loney provides a critical review of community care strategies which, he suggests, are primarily motivated by the desire of central government to cut the costs of social services and to mobilise the unemployed for 'voluntary' action (Chapter 8).   He suggests that, none the less, community workers can play a critical role in using the opportunities which community care initiatives provide to offer a counter-ideology of community care and welfare provision.

The experience of successful community campaigns is useful in illustrating models of practice which may have wider relevance. The analysis of the Coventry Temporary Tenants Campaign by Coventry Workshop (Chapter 10), and the campaigns in Liverpool and Wolverhampton to secure more equitable treatment for the black population (Chapter 9), also seek to draw some general conclusions about the conditions for effective campaigning, including the strategies used for building alliances and the role of research and publicity. These issues are further developed in the discussion of the Resource Centres Network which highlights an area of community work first explored by the CDPs (Chapter 11).   The provision of specialist research, publication and organising skills can go some way to offset the relative weakness of local trade union and community groups in confronting well-organised and well-resourced opponents.   The development of national links serves to reflect the national dimension of local issues, to provide a wider focus for local campaigns and to parallel the national (and even multi-national) frameworks of groups which oppose local community interests.

Community work, as we noted, has its origins partly in the colonial past.   More recently British community work was informed by American literature and experience whilst the British membership of the EEC has produced a new source of funding for domestic anti-poverty projects.   Mayo argues that the EEC programmes, although flawed in conception, have provided some worthwhile models for future community work practice (Chapter 12).   Marsden and Oakley show that in the Third World more radical models of community work are coming to the fore, often in situations of considerable repression (Chapter 14).   Kraushaar and Schmidt de Torres review the emergence of conflict-based community action strategies in the United States and the break-up of the hegemony previously held by models of practice based implicitly or explicitly on consensual assumptions (Chapter 13).

Our concern has been to offer a basis for a radical theoretical perspective, elaborated in several contexts, some familiar and some less so.   We hope that community workers equipped with this perspective will be able to resist retrenched conservative theory and then make sense of the need to act imaginatively and constructively

in confusing and difficult times.   We are aware that the practical
steps which follow from this perspective will need some working out
and that what is offered in these pages is but a small beginning.
Nevertheless to focus on technique is to risk stepping out in
totally the wrong direction.

NOTES

1 J. Cowley et al., 'Community or class struggle?', Stage 1, 1977,
   p. 106.
2 J. O'Malley, 'The politics of community action', Spokesman,
   1977, p. 7.
3 C. Allinson et al., 'Young Volunteers?', Community Projects
   Foundation, 1978, p. 24.
4 Report of the Committee on Local Authority and Allied Personal
   Social Services, HMSO, 1968.
5 Gulbenkian Study Group, 'Community Work and Social Change',
   Longman, 1968; 'Current Issues in Community work', Routledge
   & Kegan Paul, 1973.
6 People and Planning: The Report of the Committee on Public
   Participation in Planning, HMSO, 1969.
7 Report of the Royal Commission on the Reorganisation of Local
   Government, HMSO, 1969.
8 P. Corrigan, Community work and political struggle: what are
   the possibilities of working on the contradictions?, in P.
   Leonard (ed.), 'The Sociology of Community Action', Sociological
   Review, Monograph 21, Keele, 1975, p. 57.
9 L. Bridges, The Ministry of Internal Security: British urban
   social policy, 1968-74, 'Race and Class', vol. XVI, no. 4, 1975,
   p. 376.
10 R. Holman, The wrong poverty programme, 'New Society', 20 March
   1969, p. 444.
11 Notably 'Gilding the Ghetto' and 'The Costs of Industrial
   Change', Community Development Project Inter-project Editorial
   Team, 1977.
12 J. Cooper, Social Disadvantage and Social Help, 'Approved
   Schools Gazette', March 1969, p. 646.
13 J. Mitchell, in 'PEC Bulletin', June 1975.
14 D.N. Thomas, Letters, 'Community Care', 25 May 1977.
15 A. Vickery, Settling into patch ways, 'Community Care', 14
   January 1982, p. 26.
16 P. Henderson, D. Jones and D.N. Thomas, 'The Boundaries of
   Change in Community Work', Allen & Unwin, 1980, p. 16.
17 P. Henderson and D.N. Thomas, 'Skills in Neighbourhood Work',
   Allen & Unwin, 1980, p. 103.
18 C. Cockburn, 'The Local State, Management of Cities and People',
   Pluto Press, 1977, p. 101.
19 Ibid., p. 112.

Part I Thinking politically about practice

2 Why we need to reconstruct a theory of the state for community work

Harry Blagg and Nick Derricourt

Community work may lose its way in the 1980s.   Although it will be
comforting and partly true to blame reductions in public expenditure, it would be a cop-out to look no further.   We believe that
three interconnected problems should be looked at urgently:
- firstly, the over-simple attitudes of most community workers to
  the state;
- secondly, the shift of emphasis from community issues to workplace issues;
- thirdly, the re-emergence of consensual and functionalist theoretical guides for action.
We will argue that a crude anti-state view has dogged the development of community work practice, and that this view has given
impetus to a shift of interest away from community issues towards
workplace issues.   This shift has helped to produce a theoretical
vacuum.   If workers did not opt for work with shop stewards' committees, what radical theory was there to enable them to persist in
and think creatively about locality work now defined as 'secondary'?
   Recently, attempts have been made to fill the vacuum with resus-
citated forms of liberal theoretical perspectives which are similar
to those offered by the two Gulbenkian Reports of 1968 and 1973. (1)
There have been notable attempts (2) to draw attention to the ways
in which functionalist and systems theory have been used to promote
consensus-based community work practice, but the implications have
never been as exposed to scrutiny among community workers as they
have been among social work practitioners. (3)   For this reason we
fear that community work practitioners who wish to go on working in
localities will come to accept uncritically these functionalist prescriptions without realising how fundamentally conservative are the
assumptions upon which those prescriptions are based.   The message
which we want to put across in this chapter is: It's all right to
work in localities, but you don't have to adopt an unhelpfully pessimistic, monolithic (4) conception of the state, nor do you have to
rely on the community-work-as-LEGO prescriptions of functionalist
and systems theory.   We will argue that while making links between
the 'community' and the workplace is necessary and important, there
is a lot of work to be done 'in the community' (to use that mislead-
ing shorthand) which should be considered seriously by community
workers before they decide to give up community struggle as a bad
job.
   Not long ago community work conferences reflected people's

11

interest in linking community group activity to the muscle of the
labour movement; now, as we argue below, it is at least as true
that the labour movement must seek to link its programme with the
democratic aspirations of new movements of social protest if it is
to become the leading force in society, or even simply to pre-empt
'authoritarian populism'. (5)   We also hope that this book as a
whole will persuade readers that a narrow preoccupation with issues
which have come to be defined as the only strategically important
ones stifles creative thinking about progressive collective work
in other areas.

We will discuss each of the three problems referred to above in
turn, although they are so interconnected that it is difficult to
keep them neatly apart.   We begin by looking at the way a dominant
liberal ideology has proved difficult to root out from community
workers' theoretical frame of reference, how it has hindered the
development of a useful theory of the state, and finally how it may
be possible to reconstruct a useful theory.

Community workers, whether as liberals, anarchists, utopian
socialists or conservatives, have been too ready to accept a monolithic conception of the state.   If for the liberal a corporate
state machine is to be humanised (a dominant idea in the 1968 Gulbenkian Report), for the anarchist, the utopian socialist, and the
real conservative it is to be expunged from all social life.

There is little doubt that all these political perspectives were
visible in community work's 'heroic decade', but in so far as the
liberal ideology has been dominant in every Western industrialised
state since the Second World War, so have the liberal tradition and
a 'common sense' tradition in community work been dominant and gone
hand in hand ever since it became possible to speak of community
work as a broadly recognisable activity.   But this tradition has
never been unproblematic, even to its most willing followers.   For
there are a great number of reasons why the enterprise of community
work should, while appearing to a great number of its practitioners
as eminent 'common sense', be highly ambiguous and inexplicably difficult to do well.

The mere attempt to get people together to analyse the daily
problems they face in their locality, in the hope that people will
learn organisational skills, political acumen, and succeed in some
measure in solving those problems, quickly reveals the fragmentation
of social relationships in working-class residential areas.   The
profound alienation of residents, the dilatoriness of unyielding
resource-holders, the increasingly centralised nature of public provision, and above all, the problem of getting paid to do this work,
have been well documented.   What the apparently common-sense nature
of community work suggests is that where there is something wrong
you can do something practical about it if you get enough people
together.

Oscar Wilde once gave his opinion of a common-sense practical
enterprise: (6)

For what is a practical scheme?   A practical scheme is either a
scheme that is already in existence, or a scheme that could be
carried out under existing conditions.   But it is exactly the
existing conditions that one objects to; and any scheme that
could accept these conditions is wrong and foolish.

If one makes slight allowances for the tongue in cheek, he makes the
point: common sense takes for granted the essential nature of what
is.   Both liberal and conservative perspectives on social policy do
the same.   We want, at this point, to trace the recent antecedents
of these perspectives in community work, beginning with the first
Gulbenkian Working Party Report (1968), which illuminates the dominant philosophical perspectives on community work at the end of the
1960s. (7)

> Community work is essentially about the inter-relations between
> people and social change, how to help people and the providers of
> services to bring about a more comfortable 'fit' between them-
> selves and constant change, how to survive and grow as persons in
> relation to others.

This general perspective supported the idea that the increasing
scale of public services widened the gap between managers of services and consumers, and that as corporatisation of state services
proceeded, community workers should be established in the role of
go-between and interpreter.   We should not claim that the Gulbenkian Report represented everything that was going on in community
work at that time.·   There undoubtedly was a burgeoning anti-state
tendency and some stirrings of interest in constructing a socialist
practice of community work. (8)   But these stirrings were as yet an
interesting minority.   A growing number of community workers, while
seeking to avoid the more obvious traps inherent in go-between work,
became engaged in the common-sense task of encouraging marginal
groups to adopt a mixture of self-help and pressure-group policies,
and declared their opposition to a dehumanising scale of state
activity from whose bureaucratic insensitivities 'communities' had
to be protected.   The second Gulbenkian Report was more forthright
about this in the preface, where Lord Boyle spoke of the 'special
contribution to be made by rogue elephants who don't fit easily
within the accepted institutional framework, yet possess the secret
of gaining the confidence of those seeking to become more involved.' (9)   He was referring to the desirability of bringing marginal groups into the mainstream of a still relatively affluent and
optimistic society.   Even allowing for the fading by time of his
original meaning, the term 'rogue elephant' hardly seems likely to
endear itself nowadays to workers or employers.

It is interesting to reflect that among those community workers
who were engaged in that task of encouraging marginal groups to
criticise public provision, a debate stuttered along about the
strategic value of being based inside a statutory agency or a non-
statutory one.   Voluntary organisations were never of course
totally autonomous, although the extent to which the autonomy they
did offer could be used to advantage by determined and disciplined
workers was probably not explored as thoroughly as it could have
been simply because the myth of their autonomy was given wide cur-
rency.   This myth was the mirror image of the prevalent monolithic
conception of the state.

Before going on to discuss the relationship between functionalist
theory and liberal ideology, we ought to say what we mean by 'functionalist'.   This refers to a school of sociological thought which
conceptualises societies (or smaller units such as communities or
organisations) as systems.   Functionalists then attempt to explain

particular features of the social structure in terms of their contribution (i.e. the function they fulfil) in maintaining the system
as a viable entity. Consequently, functionalism consists of assuming that whatever is, is good, and trying to justify it instead of
stating the conditions under which particular arrangements exist.
So society does not need any particular arrangement. It simply
gets whatever the existing forces produce. Functionalism has been
criticised for asserting that social systems tend to persist without
saying why this is, for failing to account for social change and
even treating it as abnormal, and for minimising the importance of
social conflict. Functionalist theory therefore stresses conformity of the parts to the whole; lack of conformity calls for
adjustment. (10) As will become apparent below, for systems theory
also 'the basic principle is the preservation of the character of
the system'; (11) it is therefore also based on consensual assumptions.

It is clear, though, that liberal Gulbenkian-type community work
thinking is never far away; not only does it seep back into the
theoretical vacuum referred to earlier via common-sense notions
about how practical community work ought to be carried out, but it
has also lately been put forward again (12) in a 'neutral' functionalist and systems theory form as a way of rallying community
workers who wish to go on working in the locality.

Attempts to apply 'neutral' systems theory to community work are
not new. A surprisingly durable example is that by Lippitt, Watson
and Westley. (13) The same tradition is still alive in the recent
work of Brager and Specht, (14) and even more recently in the work
of Henderson and Thomas. (15) Both the last two books draw on the
general systems theory and the functionalist sociological tradition
to put forward a professional, value-neutral approach to community
work practice; the community work practitioner is advised to be
flexibly expert, but receives little encouragement to exercise moral
and political judgment. In Thomas and Henderson, the depoliticisa-
tion of community work practice is rendered as 'interjacence'. (16)
This term has some meaning when it is used to express the marginal
character of go-between work, but can easily be taken normatively in
a way which sanctifies marginality.

We want to pick up two issues arising from these depoliticised
prescriptions, to show that the alleged neutrality of the functionalist systems theory tradition is akin to the common-sense liberal
assumptions characteristic of the Gulbenkian Reports, and that to
place emphasis on skills and expertise, while it may be welcomed by
beleaguered community workers who would settle for a skilled professional identity, is putting the cart before the horse.

To take the skills point first, it may seem to be quite good
common sense for community workers to seek to restore community
work's reputation by brushing up its skills and enlarging upon an
identifiable repertoire of expertise. But there is a trap here.
To concentrate on skills may exclude moral and political discourse
and shift discussion from ends to means.

Harry Braverman, in discussing the use of systems thinking to
promote the de-skilling of the labour force, has described the
attempts of managers in industry to reduce work to a set of technical procedures, and workers to interchangeable operators of those

procedures. (17)   Community workers should notice a similar trend
in social work; some writers, notably Pincus and Minahan, (18) have
attempted to describe social work practice as a set of techniques,
to make it orderly and predictable, and to judge whether the social
work operatives are proficient.   Not only can such schematic meas-
urements be used as a management wants to define them, but there
follows an objectification of clients, as knowable things subject to
various forms of manipulation.   According to these prescriptions,
social work becomes a set of mechanical procedures.   Bill
Jordan (19) jokes about the use of systems theory in social work
practice, and captures the spirit of the approach when he cites an
induction course for new social workers in one department which
starts with a session named after a referral form: 'The APG 701 -
the basic tool of our trade'.   Social work can then end up being
technologised, sanitised, and not engaged with the mess of social
life.   Would it be going too far to suggest that this technological
mind-set risks actually becoming the real inherent political stance
of the worker?   An account of the rationalisation by a Taylorist
job study of social work in Texas would be hilarious if it was not
so sinister. (20)· Having treated clients as merely a form of input
in the production process, similar to any other form of raw materials or machinery, the consultants codified them by well-defined
'case-classification characteristics' and processing time.   One of
the work study engineers complained that 'presently workers show no
respect whatsoever for productivity', i.e. they spent more time than
the engineers thought was needed to take care of individual clients'
needs.

This should not be taken to mean that we believe social workers
should spend limitless amounts of time on each and every client nor
community workers idle extravagantly in the pub.   On the contrary,
we are arguing that positivistic drives to efficiency hinder workers
and their supervisors from making proper judgments about how to
balance the priorities of correct management (including form-
filling) with adequate client contact.   But by mechanical symbols
community work practice may also be reduced to allegedly politically
neutral components and moves; action systems, target systems,
client systems, seem scientific and impartial and avoid the problems
of political priorities and moral objectives.

We now turn to systems theory itself; Armstrong and Gill (21)
have given a good account of the reasons for attempts to use the
systems approach to incorporate community work into social work.
On close examination, the systems approach proves to be something
other than a middle-range, politically neutral framework into which
the worker can insert his own theories.   As Armstrong and Gill say,
'It is located in a particular culture and ideological base which
promotes values such as consensus and integration, and plays down
values such as class and conflict.' (22)   Peter Leonard has noticed
that systems theorists 'demonstrate a combination of sociological
naïveté and conservative ideology when they argue that 'some societal systems have been granted the authority to serve as agents of
social control for people whose behaviour deviates from societal
laws and norms and to protect people who may be harmed by the behaviour of others.'   None of these writers seriously question the use
of the term 'societal' in this monolithic way: their lack of a

class analysis of society reveals itself throughout their work.' (23)

Nevertheless, it has to be admitted that the systems approach helped social work to transcend the 'fossil paradigm' (24) and concern itself with 'sociological' reasons for a client's predicament as well as psychological reasons. By this means, community work or something like it became a more legitimate activity for social workers. By the same token, the systems approach must have encouraged some community workers to lift their noses out of a parochial concern for their neighbourhood, and explore the systematic effect of public agencies' policies on the 'collective consumers' (25) in their constituency.   So it can be seen that the systems approach cuts both ways.   The approach places primary emphasis on processes of integration and stability within social systems, and has a secondary interest, or no interest at all, in processes of change. Since the system is accepted as unproblematic, as a given entity, its underlying movements are not explored. As has been noted, proponents of the systems approach argue that one can invest the procedures they suggest with whatever political philosophy you wish. In fact, the procedures assume that the system's maintenance is high on the list of priorities. The dominant ideology of the organisation carries workers through busy days and weeks with little chance of support for reasoning over issues of value. Values, let alone the perpetual political issues of freedom and human rights, have no place in this scheme.

Far from allowing practitioners holding a wide range of moral and political views to use its framework with equal effectiveness, the systems approach has a normative capacity to relativise different perspectives and hitch them softly to the central consensual tenets of general systems theory. It therefore seeks to accommodate the perspective developed by the CDP Political Economy Collective, and also the typically liberal, reforming work. Rather like the second Gulbenkian Working Party Report, (26) this formulation seeks to accommodate conflict whilst holding on to a conservative theoretical base. So we can see the contemporary relevance of the use of functionalist and systems theory in Britain. Ultimately, it offers academic respectability to the idea that a theoretical or moral orientation should not dictate the purpose of community work and social work practice.

We now turn to the question: what theory of the state is helpful to community workers? As part of this discussion we will consider some of the causes and effects of the enthusiasms of the 1970s for an industrial focus for community work.

The present government's attack on the welfare state has exacerbated and intensified processes already well under way. The particular savageness of Thatcherism has severely dented the credibility of one of the more cherished catechisms of the British Marxist primer, that capitalism 'needs' welfare, and has stimulated a long overdue reassessment of the welfare state and social democracy. This reassessment has yet, we believe, to confront adequately the particularly acute problems of the city and its relationship with the state.

We want to focus upon a few of the popular theories by which writers have attempted to come to terms with local issues.

Firstly, we should mention the tendency to perceive the state as a simple instrument of the ruling class, and secondly, the type of theory which attaches overall determinacy to economic structure outside the locality and thereby shifts the field of struggle elsewhere.

Between the reforming epoch of the 1960s and the present urban crisis the problems of the city were low on the list of political priorities. The seemingly inexorable decline of the inner city areas and the increasing immiseration of the inhabitants was readily apparent. It was nevertheless obscured in political discourse by the immediate issues of industrial decline and recession. This industrial crisis posed acute dilemmas for community workers. For although conditions for inner city residents were declining, the primary causes seemed to lie somewhere at a distance, since the particular conjuncture was one of defensive industrial struggles against increasing attacks on union power and living standards. The response of radical community workers faced with these developments (political quietude and decline in the cities, militancy and decline in industry) was to accept the primacy of worker militancy, embrace shop stewards' committees, and forge links with industrial struggles.

This 'economistic' stance did not constitute an effective position from which to challenge the twin developments of the late 1970s: the rise of the New Right and the urban crisis. It may be significant that there has been little public response from community workers to the vigorous promotion of voluntarism by the Radical Right and its exploitation of consumer disillusionment with already decimated state services. That the Right has done so by employing anti-statist rhetoric uncomfortably close to the radical sloganising of the 1960s makes a developed critique and counter-strategy particularly difficult. What is obvious is that community workers have lacked a well-developed and articulated conception of the state and their own position on its margins. We believe that, on the whole, radical community work practice has been informed by a view of the state which tends either to divorce the state altogether from problems of the community or reduce it to its capitalist/repressive apparatus.

We wish to make clear that we are not discounting the excellent and important work undertaken by workers (e.g. the Coventry Community Workshop) who have sought to make sense of community-workplace links. Rather we suggest that there is work to be done within the community that cannot be collapsed into the problems of industry, that is specific to the structure and composition of the modern city, and cannot be reduced to the 'class struggle' as it is commonly defined.

Jerry Smith has correctly pointed out that the general conclusion reached about the Home Office CDPs was that neighbourhood community work was largely 'secondary'. (27) Such a depressing conclusion led many community workers to seek out positions from which they could focus on employment issues and link such strategically crucial areas as housing to the workplace. Community workers for whom such a transition was impossible (and it is by no means clear how available forms of sponsorship could support all those interested in such work) were made to feel guilty and compromised. We would contest

the necessity for such a wholesale transformation and we reject its
class reductionism, as we shall explain.   It remains to be added
that many community workers must have been eager to read the CDP
evidence in this manner since by no means all the material was open
to such an unambiguous reading.

We would contend that the variant of radicalism which seemed to
provide a path out of the tortuous labyrinth of local issues was
itself a form of diversion, because it removed the site of struggle
to another dimension altogether.   The perspective implied in this
removal tends to perceive the locality as an 'arena' within which
'class' struggle is acted out, because classes live out their class
position not only in the factory but also in the locality.   The
locality becomes the domain of 'reproduction', wherein class relationships and class ideologies are replenished; the locality therefore reflects the social relations of production.   Therefore the
personae in this drama - even the script itself - have been devised
elsewhere.   The important actors are the same, plus the now obligatory supporting roles for women, blacks and community workers - a
kind of 'left tokenism'.   This classic drama has its origins in a
reading of Marxist theory which inevitably reduces community politics to either an 'epiphenomenon' or 'superstructural reflex'; a
reflection of the 'real' class struggle out there somewhere.   It is
held to be 'epiphenomenal' because it possesses no real existence of
its own, but only reflects a deeper more fundamental set of processes, and it is superstructural because it responds inevitably, and
in a sense unconsciously, to the motions of an underlying base.
The mode of production and its immutable laws of motion constitute
the real dynamic of history.   Accompanying this dynamic is the real
working class occupying the centre of the historical stage because
of its fundamental antagonism to the existing productive form.
This perspective had obvious repercussions for community politics,
placing them in every sense subordinate to the real class struggle
taking place on the industrial front.

Socialist community work in its quest for a praxis unadulterated
by bourgeois ideology 'forged its links' with trades councils, shop
stewards' committees and other less suspect vehicles for revolutionary transformation.   The idealisation and reification of the community, typical of so much liberal and reformist literature, met its
mirror image in the idealisation of the working class by vanguard
Marxists.   In so doing the terrain was left open for intervention
by groups whose simplistic targeting of minorities seemed to explain
what abstract references to the declining rate of profit could not -
the destruction of their living space.

Jerry Smith has described this process: (28)
The clear signs are that while the left concentrates on industrial struggle and community work deserts the neighbourhood for
work on the wider issues, the right is stepping into the vacant
spaces.   The National Front is busy organising on council
estates neglected by community workers and is concentrating on
winning local government seats which the left sees as of a marginal relevance.

The engagement of the Front in local politics had the effect in
some instances of drawing socialists into local and cultural struggles. (29)   For others, one fears, the Front's success may well

have served only to reinforce the view that these areas were
'lumpen' and to intensify the Arthurian quest for a pure working
class.

We need now to move away from the topological formulations of
society such as the base/superstructure dichotomy with all its
inherent problems of linear causality and simple determinism.   The
kinds of theorisation that posit a simple correlation between the
'economic' and 'society' and affirm the necessary primacy of the
former over the latter are inadequate tools for grasping the complex
ensemble of relations and forces at work in the community.   These
forces have a materiality of their own and are not reducible in some
simple manner to the mode of production.   How best then can we con-
ceptualise the relatively autonomous nature of community struggles
without removing them altogether from their place in the general
social formation?   We may utilise some of the recent theoretical
constructs which have themselves arisen in opposition to mechanical
Marxism.   Althusser, for example, uses the concept of 'over-deter-
mination', derived from Freud, to illustrate how the particular
relationship of forces in a society is not the result of one single
contradiction, but is part of a complex multi-determinacy, a series
of contradictions not reducible to a simple 'class' determinacy.
Some forms of oppression, in particular women's oppression and
racism, do not have their derivation simply in the capitalist mode
of production and may actually outlive it.

Similarly we must expand and enrich our conception of the state
and its parameters.   This requires a twofold elaboration.
Firstly, we need to see the state as a far more complex and ambiguous formation than hitherto, not reducible either to its purely
repressive apparatus nor to a simple instrument of the ruling
class.   Secondly, we need to see the state as encompassing more
than just its administrative 'commanding heights'.

Gramsci has provided us with an invaluable means of analysing the
state.   He saw the political terrain as encompassing the whole
domain of social relations in society.   The state in the highly
complex and composite industrial formations of today attempts to
provide moral and ethical leadership by organising the consent of
the masses.   This involves more than just coercion and repression;
it also involves, critically, education and leadership and results
in what Gramsci called 'hegemony'. (30)   The state in this sense is
not a machine but a system of social relations, a moving fluid field
of intervention and resistance in which the ruling power bloc
attempts to incorporate the dominated as a subordinate entity.

The state is not, therefore, separate from us, a 'thing' remote
and monolithic, devoid of contradictions.   Rather in its 'extended
form' it penetrates into every possible sphere of social relations,
attempting to establish them as fields of its power.   The contemporary crisis of the city, the socio-political disaffiliation of so
many of its inhabitants, and the absence of hegemonic apparatus for
their incorporation, make it obligatory for the state to establish
authority - beyond purely repressive forms.   Both the parameters of
the state and the fields of struggle are extended.   The masses
become not just the subject of politics but are, crucially, *in* politics.   This is Gramsci's formulation of the 'war of position' which
involves more than just a 'reciprocal siege' within the parliamentary arena but the extension of this front into the social realm.

Laclau and Mouffe suggest that the extended nature of the state (the integral state) and the consequent expansion of forms of struggle (the war of position) have far-reaching implications for socialist strategy. (31)   Because, if the field of politics is extended throughout the social formation as a whole then a 'multiplicity of dimensions of struggle' will open up.   Power, and consequently forms of resistance, will not have a necessary or specific location (the economy or parliament), but will be present on a number of levels.   Also political subjects, such as blacks, young people and women, who cannot be placed within the relations of production come into prominence.   Their position may be profoundly over-determined by class struggle but is not simply reducible to it. It is necessary therefore that we perceive struggles and antagonisms within the community as possessing characteristics often different from class struggles and class antagonisms.   Therefore community politics should go beyond struggles over traditional forms of class reproduction in the locality (e.g. the social wage) and engage seriously with those who perceive their oppressor not as the hidden hand of the market but as the very visible hand of the state.

Cynthia Cockburn's invaluable study of the local state has greatly extended our perceptions of local struggle.   Nevertheless we believe that even her text is marked by a form of class reductionism.   Struggle in the locality is, for her, 'class struggle outside the job situation'; (32) similarly she restricts the reproduction process to capitalist reproduction and therefore to the reproduction of class relationships.   Cockburn treats dismissively conflicts over 'technology' and 'officialdom' as a diversion from class struggle in the localities.   Implicit in her theorisation is the old conspiracy theory in which the 'ruling class' continuously diverts the masses from their historic mission by shunting them up sidings and cul-de-sacs.   Indeed, surprisingly for someone who takes the local state so seriously, she remains circumspect with regard to its overall importance, saying that 'the mode of production is the real cause of exploitation', and rejecting the view which tends to 'give the state too much importance and apparent detachment from the economic base'. (33)

What she overlooks is the fact that the very problems of the 'economic base' (to adopt her problematic shorthand) make the autonomy and dominance of the state necessary for the maintenance of the present social divisions of labour.   The dominance of monopoly capital cannot be achieved without the dominance of the state. Also the monopolistic phase of capital has the effect of condensing and intensifying production, always leaving in its wake vast wastes of redundant productive modes and people.   The problem for many becomes not the 'economic base', but its disappearance from their horizons altogether.   The state has the task of organising those who have been ejected from the economic discourse.   The elderly, the young, and racial minorities in particular experience their exploitation in forms altogether separate from the rhythms of surplus value extractions, and experience them precisely in officialdom, bureaucracy, isolation, indifference and those other 'superstructures'.

Simon Frith has recently noted the effects of structural unemployment on the lives of young people in the cities. (34)   It has had the effect of rupturing traditional class patterns and cutting them off from mainstream class relationships.   What they experience is the state, from the law to the Manpower Services Commission, and they identify themselves not with the distant struggles of capital and labour but with friends, neighbours and families.   Their enemies are authority in most forms and, increasingly, easily scape-goated racial minorities who have 'taken the jobs' and generally destroyed the area.

To confront adequately the new antagonisms and the very real crisis of the inner cities requires a range of imaginative and varied interventions.   The more society in general becomes the sub-ject of politics the more it is necessary to engender a diversity of political struggles.   These struggles should include the very ideo-logical and cultural issues generally written off as 'bourgeois' ideology.

Such issues as democracy, authority, bureaucracy, technology, the environment, personal freedom, and sexual freedom, must be taken seriously.   As we have seen, the left, in its failure to take seriously the anti-bureaucratic and anti-authoritarian feelings of many people has handed them over to the intervention of right-wing populists, and even fascists.   (Liberal councillors in particular have been successful because they at least take seriously anti-bureaucratic feelings and Thatcherism has also latched on to the anti-statist and anti-bureaucratic currents.)   The mistake we have always made is to assume that because these elements occupy a promi-nent position in the discourse of the right then they 'belong' to them in some way.   These elements are not the property of a par-ticular class, but are taken up and articulated by the hegemonic class which then can really seem to represent 'the people'. (35)

The struggle for social transformation involves the appropriation of these neglected spheres.   It means engaging in precisely those messy, confused, ambiguous and painful issues which arise in every locality.   It means that we must learn some new lessons and face the new terrains of struggle inventively.   The problem-solving tool kit of functionalist theory depoliticises the social realm and is therefore an inadequate means of grasping the rich diversity of conflicts and antagonisms at work in society.   On the other hand a traditional Marxist analysis may, in its own fashion, confuse rather than clarify.   We realise that we ourselves have offered few alter-natives.   It is the task of this book as a whole to look at ways of finding new handholds in both familiar and potential areas of commu-nity work activity.

NOTES

We would like to thank John Lambert and Peter Baldock for reading the first draft of this chapter and making several valuable sugges-tions.
  1 Calouste Gulbenkian Foundation, 'Community Work and Social
     Change: A Report on Training', Longman, 1968.   Calouste Gul-
     benkian Foundation, 'Current Issues in Community Work', Rout-
     ledge & Kegan Paul, 1973.
  2 See, for instance, H. Rose and J. Hanmer, Community

participation and social change, in D. Jones and M. Mayo (eds), 'Community Work Two', Routledge & Kegan Paul, 1975.

3   W. Jordan, Against the unitary approach to social work, 'New Society', vol. 40, 2 June 1977, p. 448.   J. Armstrong and K. Gill, The unitary approach: what relevance for community work?, 'Social Work Today', vol. 10, no. 11, 7 November 1978. The term 'unitary' refers to attempts to unify, by means of systems theory, three methods of social work - casework, group work, and community work.

4   By monolithic we mean ... that it is perceived as being rather like a fortress, standing above and apart from the social formation.   It is the same from top to bottom, each layer moulded to the next to form a unified and homogenous entity without cracks or fissures.   Social contradictions exist only external to it; it lies in wait for them, and will consume them as surely as Kafka's Castle consumed the will of the land surveyor.

5   S. Hall, The great moving right show, in 'Marxism Today', January 1979.

6   O. Wilde, The soul of man under socialism, in 'Critical Writings of Oscar Wilde', R. Ellman (ed.), W.H. Allen, 1970, p. 284.

7   Op. cit., p. 29.

8   See Jan O'Malley, 'The politics of community action', Spokesman, 1977.   The Camden Community Workshop also produced an interesting manifesto in 1972 (mimeo by J. Cowley and M. Mayo).

9   Op. cit., preface, p. x.

10 For a longer explanation, see P.S. Cohen, 'Modern Social Theory', Heinemann, 1968, from which some of this paragraph is taken.

11 D. Katz and R.L. Kahn, Common characteristics of open systems, in F.E. Emery (ed.), 'Systems Thinking', Penguin, 1969, p. 97.

12 P. Henderson, D. Jones and D.N. Thomas, 'The Boundaries of Change in Community Work', Allen & Unwin, 1980.

13 R. Lippitt, J. Watson and B. Westley, 'The Dynamics of Planned Change', Harcourt Brace, 1958.

14 G. Brager and H. Specht, 'Community Organising', Columbia 1973.

15 Op. cit.

16 Ibid., p. 2 and passim.

17 H. Braverman, Labor and Monopoly capital, 'Monthly Review Press', 1974.

18 A. Pincus and A. Minahan, 'Social Work Practice: Model and Method', Peacock, 1973.

19 Op. cit., p. 448.

20 Bill Patry, Taylorism comes to the social services, 'Monthly Review', October 1978, p. 30.

21 Op. cit.

22 Ibid., p. 20.

23 Peter Leonard, A paradigm for radical practice, in 'Radical Social Work', Edward Arnold, 1975, p. 52.

24 G. Pearson, Prisons of love: the reification of the family in family therapy, in N. Armistead (ed.), 'Reconstructing Social Psychology', Penguin, 1974, p. 137:   '... the "fossil paradigm" of psychiatry: the idea that emotional problems are firmly rooted inside the patient's head, having nothing to do with what goes on between people'.

25   'The term "collective consumption" is used to mean that the
     financial (state) provision is no longer an individual and
     family responsibility' (council housing is an example of such
     provision), C. Cockburn, 'The Local State', Pluto Press, 1977,
     p. 64.   See also M. Castells, 'The Urban Question', Edward
     Arnold, 1979, p. 406.
26   Op. cit.
27   J. Smith, Hardlines and soft options, in P. Curno (ed.), 'Poli-
     tical Issues and Community Work', Routledge & Kegan Paul, 1978.
28   Ibid., p. 25; we should take little comfort from the Front's
     failure to gain respectability via the ballot box.   The less
     'respectable' British Movement has had some success in mobilis-
     ing sections of white working-class youth for racist purposes.
29   The Anti-Nazi League and in particular Rock Against Racism were
     inventive and (dare one say it) enjoyable movements.   The prob-
     lem with the former is that, as it was primarily concerned with
     election issues, a great many of its strategies are no longer
     applicable to fascist mobilisations less concerned with electo-
     ral respectability.   As Stuart Hall suggests, 'It is an experi-
     ence we can and must build on - not by imitating and repeating
     it, but by matching it in imaginativeness,' S. Hall, The whites
     of their eyes, in S. Bridges and R. Brunt (eds), 'Silver
     Linings: Some Strategies for the Eighties', Lawrence & Wishart,
     1981.
30   See A. Gramsci, 'Selections from Prison Notebooks', Lawrence
     & Wishart, 1978, particularly pp. 206-75; also C. Buci-Glucksman,
     'Gramsci and the State', Lawrence & Wishart, 1980, pp. 47-111.
31   E. Laclau and C. Mouffe, Socialist strategy: where next?,
     'Marxism Today', January 1981, pp. 17-22.
32   C. Cockburn, op. cit., p. 162.
33   Ibid., pp. 162-3.
34   S. Frith, Youth in the eighties: a dispossessed generation?,
     'Marxism Today', November 1981, pp. 12-15.
35   E. Laclau, 'Politics, Ideology and Marxist Theory', New Left
     Books, 1977.

3 Community work and the social services departments

Peter Baldock

INTRODUCTION

Much of the British community work literature that is currently influential came out of the ad hoc projects in the late 1960s and
early 1970s.   Such projects often generated critical writing on
community work because that was part of their remit.   Examples
include reports from the Home Office Community Development Project
and the books by Mitton and Morrison, Thomas, and Jacobs. (1)   One
unfortunate consequence of this feature of our home-grown literature
is the inadequate attention paid to the development of long-term
programmes in established agencies such as social services departments (SSDs).

This is a nuisance for people like me who work in them, but it is
of wider importance.   SSDs in particular are crucial to the past
history and the foreseeable future of community work in this country.   I have made this claim before and it has been challenged by
Smith, (2) but only on the basis of an exaggerated and distorted
version of the point I was making.   It is true (as she says) that
British thinking about community work has come overwhelmingly from
outside the social work profession.   But the creation of SSDs provided an organisational base for new employment opportunities without which the mid-seventies boom in community work would probably
not have happened.   Moreover, as an organised public service, community work can only develop within one or more of the established
agencies of the welfare state.   SSDs are not the sole candidates
for that role, but they are very important ones.

Between Smith and I there is, I think, a fundamental difference.
She sees community work as a set of ideas and consequential praxis.
The history of community work becomes, in her perspective, the history of a set of ideas: who had what notions, when and how did they
influence whom?   I view community work as part of the welfare state
and, therefore, wish to study its history (to understand its present) initially in institutional terms.   She sees community work as
a sort of social movement.   I see it as work, as a job people do,
paid labour.

The recognition that community work is work is crucial in the
formation of any socialist perspective on the subject.   Community
work did start life as a social movement (one that was, incidentally, self-consciously conservative for the most part until radicals, who took it up in the late 1960s, turned its value system

inside-out).   But, like other social movements of the late nineteenth century (social work, town planning etc.), it has sought to
achieve some of its objectives by becoming incorporated as a profession within the state.   Community workers do not like to face
this squarely, preferring to believe that, because they have rejected professionalism in principle, they can escape the consequences
of the professionalist compromise entailed in working for the state
(whether directly or in the shape of state-supported 'voluntary'
organisations).   Employing agencies are seen as important only to
the extent that they allow greater or less autonomy to the community
worker.   But this attitude is not especially radical or unprofes-
sional.   It is precisely how all welfare professionals tend to
regard their employing agencies.   Community work in Britain is
characterised by the covert nature of its professionalism rather
than by any real freedom from professionalsim as social status or
ideology.   As long as we are caught in this trap - as long as we
believe that there is something called 'community work' which we
ought to be trying to practise, rather than an area of public service as much subject to contradiction as other areas such as social
work - no theoretical perspective that is devised for community
workers can be described as socialist.   People may use Marxist or
libertarian categories in their depiction of the situation 'out
there'.   But the use of those categories will be a superficial one
if we appear only as the users of them and not as people to whom
they also refer.
   The theoretical struggle against 'covert professionalism' in community work requires study at a very fundamental and generalised
level.   We need an understanding of the state, including the local
state, as a product of capitalist organisation, not merely a tool
which happens to be used by businessmen in ways that can be empiri-
cally demonstrated.   We need an understanding of the role of local
government in servicing the reproduction of labour.   We need to
grapple with the dilemmas that arise for those working within the
local state structure (as, in a sense, everyone has to do), dilemmas
usefully examined in the recent book 'In and Against the State'. (3)
More specifically, we need to grasp that the 'bureaucracy' against
which community workers often range themselves is a mere symptom, is
the organisational form taken by the twin processes of the reification of class struggle in the form of the state and the alienation
of the state's own employees - community workers included.
   In describing 'bureaucracy' in such terms one has already begun
to move from the general to the particular and this needs to be
developed in an effort to understand the various agencies for which
community workers work, including SSDs.   In this chapter I shall
concentrate on two topics: what are SSDs like as places in which to
work and what areas of fieldwork are specially relevant to those
employed in them?

SOCIAL SERVICES DEPARTMENTS AS EMPLOYING AGENCIES

As an employing agency, an SSD poses in its own way the three types
of problem for community workers that any employing agency is likely
to pose: the ways in which it affects the relationship between the

community worker and those with whom he or she works, the ways in which it selects priorities for work and the ways open to the community worker to relate to the rest of the workforce.

Most community workers work for the state directly or indirectly. But the community worker in an SSD is more directly an agent of the state, and may be called upon as part of his or her work to exercise bureaucratic power over people.   Like other local government officers, they may generally exercise such power in one of two ways. Officers give or withhold permission for people to do things they want to do and they give or withhold the resources that people need to do things they want to do.   In many cases, of course, the officer's decision is not a final one, but is a recommendation, say, to a council committee or a court.   The power to recommend is still significant and often determines the outcome.

The idea of acquiring policing powers is likely to stick in community workers' gullets.   But already many community workers act as the agents for their local authorities in the registration and inspection of pre-school playgroups under the 1968 Public Health Act.   The community work team that I lead wanted to acquire those powers and responsibilities because we felt happier with them in our hands than in those of other people.   That tactical decision does not, of course, in itself resolve the associated dilemmas.   In the future it is conceivable that SSDs might acquire other statutory duties to license and inspect different kinds of community activity with a service delivery element.   If they did, community workers might feel that it would be better if they themselves were acting as the state's agents in the matter rather than leaving it to potentially less sympathetic officers.

Those who reject policing powers, even when responsibility for them might offer them opportunities to help people, often feel differently about power over resources.   It is common for community workers to argue for more resources to be made available to community groups.   It is also common for them to attempt to secure for themselves degrees of control over their own agencies' grant-aiding programmes in order to ensure, as far as possible, that resources are distributed to the best advantage of the organisations they most wish to promote and support.   Since the motive is to obtain resources for people, it is often forgotten that control over resources entails refusing them as well as granting them.   The community worker with a fund at his disposal or a key role in the determination of departmental grant-aiding is in a position of power over people whether he likes it or not.   This can affect the quality of the relationship between a community worker and a group just as much as the powers of social workers inevitably affect their relationships with clients.

If community workers in SSDs can acquire powers over those with whom they work, those people also have some control over them as public servants.   A few departments have now employed enough community workers for a sufficient period for some people at least to see community work as a public service and exercise their rights as citizens to complain about its defects.   This raises uncomfortable issues about our self-image.   Recently in Sheffield the local federation of single parents' groups complained that the willingness of community workers in different parts of the city to support their

member groups seemed to vary for no reason that they could understand.   The question was discussed at a meeting of the department's
community work staff.   There a number of things were said by different people about the setting of priorities and the need to ensure
that this was a rational process, not one subject to the whims of
outside groups with special interests.   I actually agreed with most
of what was said, but it was still disturbingly reminiscent of
things I have heard said at meetings of planning and housing officials.   And it would not be surprising if community groups that
felt that their special needs were being neglected by community
workers should choose to protest about us as they have about other
local government officers whose professional priorities were seen as
entailing injustice.

The covert professionalism of community workers has never come
out in to the open more clearly than when they have rejected departmental proposals that their skills be used for certain purposes on
the grounds that these do not constitute 'real' community work.
There have been several such sources of contention, but the most
common has been the suggestion that community workers should be involved in volunteer organising and 'community care'. (4)   Some community care programmes are objectionable in themselves.   But I do
not take very seriously the suggestion that there is a real threat
that an ideology of community care will play a major role in the
run-down of social services.   Politicians who decide to purchase
the survival of capitalism at the expense of the elderly and handicapped will do so whether or not they have some clap-trap at their
disposal to help salve their consciences.   Community care programmes may be objectionable in some cases, but this is not true of
every case and I can see no objection in principle to departments
employing community workers precisely in order to use their group-
work or organisational skills in this particular field.

The question of how the community work service fits in with other
services within the department leads naturally on to the question of
the relationships between community workers and other staff.   There
has been a certain amount of debate about the ways in which community workers ought to be located within departments.   The research
conducted in Scotland by Gallacher and Robertson (5) is likely to
aid this debate and the detailed case study by Thomas and Warburton (6) provides another kind of evidence.   Essentially, four patterns have emerged of the organisational placing of community
workers in SSDs.   Some departments have recruited small numbers of
community workers and located them in rather ad hoc ways, sometimes
in small project teams directly responsible to senior management
(e.g. Harlesden Community Project, (7)) sometimes somewhere in central middle management (as in some of the authorities in Greater
Manchester).   Others have placed community workers as members of
social work teams (e.g. the department studied by Thomas and Warburton).   Others have set up central sections of community workers
(as in Manchester, Cleveland and some of the London boroughs).
Sheffield is, as far as I know, unique in offering a fourth pattern,
a compromise between the previous two, in which teams of community
workers supervised by people who are themselves community workers
work in divisions (or area teams) alongside the social work teams
and the home help organisers.

Managers in SSDs tend to be suspicious of community work sections operating in their departments separately from the field social work service.   Most of the structures outlined are defended on the grounds that they make for the closer integration of community work and social work, something that is seen as good either because it makes social workers more radical or because it makes community workers more controllable.   From experience I would suggest that formal structures do little to help integrate community workers with the field social work service because of the existence of fundamental obstacles to that development.

Although area social workers are only a small minority of the work force of an SSD, they are in many ways the key sector of the staff.   The creation of the departments was seen as a major triumph for social work, it marked its arrival as an established profession and a major force in local government.   But, although the departments were set up in an atmosphere of increasing confidence in social work and their first three years were marked by escalating budgets, since the mid-1970s social workers have been under increasing attack in the mass media and in books such as the well-known polemic by Brewer and Lait. (8)   The reasons for this switch of opinion are varied, though the worsening economic situation has evidently been a determining factor.   The point here is that the change in public opinion has left social workers themselves in a state of nervous sensitivity to attack and lacking in confidence about their corporate identity.   Community workers by the very fact of their existence raise questions about the nature of social work, since - whatever community workers themselves may say about their own identity - social workers tend to see community work as 'radical social work'.   Under present conditions the challenge posed by our presence is rarely a welcome one and the tactless statements and callow self-assurance of some community workers (bolstered by culpable ignorance about the work situation of social workers) frequently aggravates the situation. (9)   Tensions that exist in any case are frequently made worse by the attempts of social work managers to force community workers to conform to the subculture of social work.   Arguments over supervision and record-keeping take on an occasionally destructive importance here, as does the insistence of some directors that community workers should hold the Certificate of Qualification in Social Work before they are recruited or properly paid.   But just as much ill feeling can be created when, for example, middle managers in charge of both groups of staff fail to appreciate that community workers with a youth work background and intermediate treatment officers with a social work background may bring different working assumptions to projects with the same groups of kids.

There is a basic problem here that is not going to be resolved by efforts to 'improve communication'.   If there is a solution, it lies in community workers seeking the best organisational and other arrangements to facilitate the service for which they undertake responsibility and in a critical appreciation of the things they do have in common with social workers (and other staff) as employees. Both of these in turn imply active membership of the appropriate trade union.

SOCIAL SERVICES DEPARTMENTS AND WORK IN THE FIELD

What I have said so far largely concerns the ways in which location within SSDs affects community workers personally.   Equally important is the way in which it offers new opportunities for work in the field.   This is not only because of the opportunities represented by many of the resources of the departments as organisations.   It is also because they offer particular opportunities for work with people with whom contact is difficult.

A disproportionate number of community workers operate in areas of extreme deprivation of the sort that generate a large number of referrals for social work services.   In this respect location in SSDs offers no special advantage.   But the extent to which social problems are geographically concentrated varies enormously.   While many long-term cases come to social workers from neighbourhoods that are stigmatised or suffer extreme material deprivation, referrals are not, for the most part, concentrated in this way.   The unhospitalised mentally ill, the physically handicapped, the isolated elderly in need of support, single parent families on low incomes - these and many other groups are found everywhere.   Unlike the poor in areas recognised as deprived, most of these people live in isolation from each other.   They are often partially or completely housebound by the physical problems of handicap or the necessity of looking after small children.   Many of the situations from which they suffer draw stigma upon their victims.   The services that are offered to them are offered to them as individuals and rarely organised in such a way as to bring them into useful contact with each other.   This is true of virtually all public services and the psychological impact of the 'housing queue' is a particular example that has received a lot of attention. (10)   But at least once people are housed on a council estate, there is a reasonable chance that they will be able to see clearly what they have in common and that is an important factor in the creation of tenants' associations.   In contrast, the woman who becomes a single mother may be overwhelmed by a sudden change in personal circumstances, suffer from guilt over the situation that led her to become a single mother and, perhaps above all in significance, feel that she is an oddity when, in fact, she is typical of at least one in ten people caring for children.   The isolation of people with problems such as those I have mentioned is the fundamental cause of their lack of organisation.   Most of them, even those that would like to be, are not in community groups that cater for their special needs and the organisations that do exist tend either to be weak or to be taken over by better educated or upwardly mobile members of the group and change from being primarily action groups to acting as agents of service provision.

Many of the areas in which community workers have become particularly involved - housing issues and children's play, for example - are ones where spontaneous community organisation happened before the community work boom and where one might expect some spontaneous activity even if community work had never been invented.   It is possible to exaggerate the strength behind such spontaneous activity and it is wrong to suggest that it proves that professional community work is superfluous.   To the extent that activity in such

areas is spontaneous, a policy of concentrating community work resources on them can be defended.   It makes sense to focus on those
areas where there are reasonable prospects of success.   Our work is
more about using opportunities than it is about solving problems.
Nevertheless, it is also true that by concentrating on areas where a
degree of spontaneity exists we tend to deprive of our assistance
precisely those people that most need it.   Location in SSDs offers
community workers a number of opportunities for contact with people
whose problems do not bring them together, but, if anything, force
them apart.

It is possible to justify this in relatively non-political terms
as a public service.   But a socialist community worker is going to
ask how this kind of work will contribute to significant social
change.   In terms of the building of political organisation, the
answer must be frankly that for the most part work with people such
as those described makes precious little contribution to social
change.   If there is a socialist justification for it, it is that
care for those whose own contribution to the struggle must be limited is essential to the labour movement because it aids the development of solidarity and because it demonstrates the real commitment
that exists to the long-term aims of the movement.

It is for reasons such as these that I feel that community care
activity (in which some people provide services for others) and
self-help groups (in which people with particular problems provide
moral and practical support to each other) are crucial parts of any
successful community action movement and those who attempt to assist
that movement in their jobs ought to be encouraging such work as
well as more straightforward political organisation.   I believe
this all the more strongly because my experience and that of many of
my colleagues proves to me that it is precisely where community care
and self-help activity are most successful that they lead on to
political organisation and activity.   A good deal of my work over
the past few years has been with single parent groups.   Of all the
groups with which I have worked it was the one in which mutual support became most highly developed that made political demands on the
local authority for a better deal for single parents.   As well as
demanding service improvements the group also developed a political
appreciation of the fact that the problems of its members had their
source in the fact that society was dealing with them as deviants
from normal family life.   I feel, though it would be difficult to
prove, that the limited effectiveness of the political initiatives
taken by the group was related to its limited ability to develop
mutual support and the tendency to place disproportionate responsibility for support of members on the leadership core.   In that particular group self-help did not distract from political consciousness and activity, it created it.   Most of the community groups
catering for people with the sort of problems that make them clients
of SSDs do not get involved in overt political activity and even
when they do their political impact is often small.   But the potential for political activity among such groups is often underestimated.

Although community workers have claimed for some time to be in
the business of helping people to put pressure on public institutions, the one institution that has for the most part escaped their

hostile attentions is the one that employs so many of them - the SSD. (11)   This remains true.   SSDs are among the biggest spenders of local authority departments.   Their services are used by a wide range of people.   Their powers, particularly the power, in effect, to have people 'put away', are of drastic importance in the lives of some of their clients.   Yet community workers in the departments have done little to assist public pressure for better services in this field or justice for particular individuals or groups that have to deal with them.

There are reasons for this neglect.   They include the fairly reasonable one that it is difficult to organise many client groups because of the isolation I have already mentioned.   But I think the major reasons are unacceptable.   They are that we are willing to help people attack other agencies, but are scared of helping them attack our own because repercussions are more likely and that we share the well-established contempt in our society for the mentally ill, the elderly and the handicapped, the ultimate cause of which is their restricted ability to contribute to the productive process for capital.   If that judgment seems harsh, I would remind you that the criticism is also self-criticism.   In any case, I think the evidence justifies what I have said at least as a generalisation.

WELFARE CUTS AND COMMUNITY WORKERS AS FIELDWORKERS AND TRADE UNIONISTS

The need to promote community action to secure a better deal for social services clients is heightened by the cuts that are being made in that field as a result of government policy.   And the subject of the cuts brings together again the two themes I have treated so far - SSDs as a base for community work and as an area for concern.   As people with good contacts with community groups that represent the users of services and as members of public sector unions, community workers (especially in SSDs where unionisation is more likely to be developed) can play a very important role in the struggle against the cuts.   But they can do so only if they are already active trade unionists.   And, while most community workers would probably be in favour of trade unions as a matter of principle and might even undertake union office out of some sense of duty, the extent of their commitment to the trade union movement is not always clear.

It is well known that social workers are more radical than community workers.   Social workers, through their work in the field, have a much clearer, more detailed, less romantic view of the cost extorted from millions of people by the way our society is organised.   More than any other group in society, they are placed, because of their jobs, directly face to face on a daily basis with the sheer bloody misery that there is around.   In their efforts to work for clients within the system they develop a far clearer picture of the way the state controls people and the power it can exert.   There is a stark contrast between, on the one hand, the ideals that brought most of them into the job and their ordinary human sympathies and, on the other hand, many of the things they have to do and the compromises they have to make.   In considering

this contrast most of them become acutely aware of the fact that
their labour is alienated, even if they do not use that kind of
language.   For all these reasons they often have a consciousness of
the depth and extent of the problems of society and of their own
position in society that community workers lack.   So many of our
activities are fun and so much of our work is left relatively uncontrolled because of our marginality in the local state that things do
not have the same impact on us as they do on social workers.

But, if social workers have a more radical consciousness, it is
to a large extent a negative one.   They are clearer on problems,
pessimistic about solutions.   To some extent this is because of the
overwhelming nature of many of their experiences in everyday work.
It is also a consequence of the fact that the subculture of social
work into which they are socialised on courses, in the supervision
process and by the very way their work is organised, encourages the
privatisation of problems, introspection, even irrational guilt.
There are hence many ideological and psychological obstacles to the
development of collective solutions among social workers to problems.   In the light of this it is impressive that social workers
have succeeded in developing their own collective action over the
last decade and have played a role out of all proportion to their
numbers in the radicalisation of NALGO.   The culminating point so
far in this process was the social workers' strike in 1978-9.   But
the struggle against the cuts could well begin a new climax.   Community workers have, on the whole, trailed along in the wake of all
this with a slightly bemused expression on their faces, sometimes
even suggesting that their work should be exempt from industrial
action because it is so special and good for people.   This suggests
a grotesque misunderstanding of their own position and represents a
missed opportunity.   In my own department active involvement in the
union has not only provided community workers with virtually their
only effective basis for co-operation with other staff and improvements in their own service conditions, but has also been crucial in
the links so far formed between the trade union movement in the city
and the community groups with which we work.

CONCLUSION: SHOULD COMMUNITY WORKERS BE IN SOCIAL SERVICES
DEPARTMENTS?

Is there, then, a case for some community workers, not only accept-
ing employment in SSDs, but also working within areas of activity
that particularly relate to those departments?   I think there is,
although it is what one might call a tactical case.   It is not
based on any assumption that the departments could become in the
foreseeable future an instrument for radical change.

In the first place, SSDs are likely for some time to offer a
considerable number of the employment opportunities in our field.
Even those who feel least comfortable with that fact have to reckon
with it, especially at a time of rising unemployment when jobs of
any kind are becoming more scarce.   The initial reason why many
community workers do work in SSDs is simply that that is where jobs
are to be found.

In the second place SSDs do have certain advantages as organisa-

tions for which to work.   Most of the literature on this subject
has dealt with the disadvantages and problems - and some of the
things I have said earlier in this chapter also point to potential
difficulties.   But, precisely because we have been so preoccupied
with these difficulties, it is worth looking at the other side of
the picture.   The area team model of fieldwork organisation in
SSDs, for example, has certain potential advantages for community
workers compared to the sort of structure likely to be found elsewhere in departments where fieldwork as we understand it is not
normal practice.   This is an issue that has had inadequate attention in the British literature on community work.   And, while the
imposition of social work forms of practice on community workers in
the departments has been a source of contention, it remains true
that the organisation of social work (in terms of teams, supervision
and recording) offers models of the organisation of fieldwork practice to community workers.   I do not mean that they are models that
ought necessarily to be followed.   But they are models that have
been produced over a period of time with a good deal of thought that
reflects practical experience.   They merit consideration, even if,
in the end, they are rejected or heavily modified by us to suit our
own needs.

In the third place, I do not share the distaste exhibited by some
community workers for those areas of community work that tie in most
closely with the personal social services.   It seems to me an advantage of working in SSDs that it brings people face to face with
some of the worst consequences of the way our society is organised.
To have one's attention focused on victims rather than causes is to
risk sentimentality.   But it is a necessary part of the picture.
Community workers, like social workers and other staff in the
departments, have particular knowledge to contribute to the socialist and labour movements.   I further believe that the sort of service delivery in which one is likely to become involved in SSDs is a
useful thing in itself.   It forms part of the pattern of services
needed by the most vulnerable groups in society.   Work on that type
of service delivery also allows effective contact with people who
would otherwise probably not come into contact with radical political thought on the problems they face.   It allows opportunities for
such people to learn from each other and begin to organise.   This,
together with the considerable difficulty that clients in SSDs have
in influencing the way the departments work, means that the location
of community workers within the departments offers particular opportunities for forms of community action that are unlikely to occur
spontaneously, though I would not want to exaggerate the importance
of those opportunities.

I suspect that many of those who would have reservations about
the case I have outlined above would have them less because they
disagreed with any particular points I have made, than because they
are afraid of the social work profession taking over community work.
For more than a decade British community workers have struggled
against the thesis that community work is 'the third method of
social work'.   We have been right to do so.   But, in resisting
that thesis, we have often sought to establish our own identity by
using methods (such as securing control over our own training) that
are typical of the professions in general.   That has fed in to the

covert professionalism that I would see as the dominant ideology in British community work.   And this has happened at precisely the time that professionalist ideology is under heavy attack within social work.   We now need to spend less time insisting on how different we are to social workers and more time examining what we have in common with them and other related occupational groups in the welfare state.   In fact, the histories of community work and social work are closely interwoven.   They are not as interwoven as many social workers think.   But the connection is there.   This is crucial not merely as a matter of history, but in relation to our present situation.

In the history of social work and in the lives of individual social workers the desire to help as an equal has been central. That desire may have become encumbered by the alienating processes of work for the state and diluted by cynicism.   But it is there. The ways in which it has been damaged threaten to damage the similar aspirations of community workers.   For better and for worse community work and social work are very similar phenomena.   We community workers need to have the humility to recognise that and act upon it. Only the enemy stands to gain if we do not.

NOTES

1   M. Loney, The British Community Development Projects: questioning the state, 'Community Development Journal', vol. 16, no. 1. R. Mitton and E. Morrison, 'A Community Project in Notting Dale', Allen Lane, 1972.   D. Thomas, 'Organising for Social Change', Allen & Unwin, 1976.   S. Jacobs, 'The Right to a Decent House', Routledge & Kegan Paul, 1976.

2   T. Smith, Community work: profession or social movement?, in P. Henderson, D. Jones and D.N. Thomas (eds), 'The Boundaries of Change in Community Work', Allen & Unwin, 1980.

3   London-Edinburgh Weekend Return Group, 'In and Against the State: Discussion Notes for Socialists', Pluto Press, 1981.

4   By 'community care' in this context I mean, of course, those aspects of community care in its broader sense that entail departmental co-operation with neighbourhood care schemes and other community groups engaged in voluntary service.

5   J. Gallacher and I. Robertson, Community workers in Scottish Social Work Departments, 'Community Development Journal', vol. 15, no. 2.

6   D. Thomas and R. Warburton, 'Community Workers in a Social Services Department', National Institute for Social Work and Personal Social Services Council, 1977.

7   See Harlesden Community Project, 'Community Work and Caring for Children', Owen Wells, 1979.

8   C. Brewer and J. Lait, 'Can Social Work Survive?', Temple Smith, 1980.

9   One of the facts that emerges from the Thomas and Warburton study (op. cit.) is the amount of naive mutual stereotyping that went on between community workers and social workers in the department studied.

10   See J. Lambert, B. Blackaby and C. Paris, 'Housing Policy and the State', Macmillan, 1978, chapter 3.

11 H. Specht, 'Community Development in the United Kingdom', Assoc-
    iation of Community Workers, 1975.   Specht's address to the
    1974 Annual Conference of ACW met with a deservedly hostile
    reception, but one or two of his observations on British commu-
    nity work were right on target, including the point being made
    here.

4 Whose side are we on? The damage done by neutralism

Elizabeth Filkin and Michael Naish

A lot has been written recently about community work practice which seeks to generalise the community worker's job, so that a very wide range of activities can be defined as community work. This has its value in that it reassures workers up and down Britain that they do indeed work as community workers. For example, in a recent collection of essays describing some interesting community work projects, the editors say, 'The most fundamental task for community workers is to bring people together and to help them create and maintain an organisation that will achieve their goals.' (1) This would open the definition of community work to a very wide variety of workers, regardless of where they work or what they are aiming at. Many people living in middle-class communities have said to us, 'Isn't community work just as appropriate with middle-class organisations and in middle-class neighbourhoods as it is in less well-off areas and with less well-off groups; we too have our problems?'

In this chapter we want to advance the notion that although bringing people together is an important skill for community workers to possess, and one which we need to practise continuously to improve, it is a long way from being the 'most fundamental task'. Moreover, where it becomes so, it leads at best to community work by luck and, at worst, to activities which community workers should, in our view, judge as harmful. Our own definition of what community work should be about is both sharper and narrower.

Much recent discussion has focused on skills in community work and there is no doubt that skills are important and should be identified and analysed. But no package of skills, however expertly practised, does anything more than describe mechanical performance. In our view the first task for the worker is to define the goals for the work in both broad and detailed fashion and to determine priorities for action. Once we are clear where we are going the skills can be wheeled out to help us get there more effectively.

In what follows, we do not wish to duplicate lists of skills but to focus on the goals for community work. In doing so we want to attack what has been called the 'neutral' (2) tradition. (We are talking, of course, about neutrality in general aims and about a general practice of fence-sitting. In specific daily situations it may well be appropriate for a worker to judge that in this particular situation it would be best to stay out of a particular argument because it would be unhelpful, irrelevant or harmful to become involved.)

We are not engaged in a mere disagreement about words; goals should be of central concern to practitioners. If we rely on skills alone to provide the definition of community work, there is every chance that those skills will be taken over in a range of activities and by a variety of professionals who will use them to achieve disparate ends. Community work then becomes an amorphous mass of functions. The means to achieve our goals or ends do matter. But the definition of those ends is the lifeblood of the work. Without it community work is amoral and hollow and community workers are people of straw. There is, we believe, a very real struggle going on for the possession of the soul of community work.

Clarity about our priorities is necessary not as grand sloganising but because community workers have daily to make choices about how they spend their time, and to decide which skills they use. Such judgments are not only to be exercised about which area or streets to work in, and which issues to pursue; but also about how to help groups define their own goals and when to enable a group to exclude a member or faction. Without clarity of goals community workers have no star to steer by and, in such circumstances, expediency, a quiet life, the ego trip, the management's views, the fashionable cause or job preservation - particularly the latter in present times - can be the determinant of community work practice.

Some scorn has been poured on those of us who see the maldistribution of resources in Britain as the target for community workers on the grounds that to have priorities is to be arrogant. Criticism is certainly justified when 'macro-community work' is used by some people as a stick to beat those whose concerns are small-scale local change and who do not see the links between small-scale change and fundamental shifts in the organisation of British society. To be concerned about such shifts should not lead a worker to do down small-scale effort or condescend to it. But community work is still of little value unless it aims to create a better world, albeit in a small way. The definition of that world is crucial and does more to guide practice than the most clearly presented textbooks describing a set of skills. This insistence on having a vision of a society towards which we are struggling can be misinterpreted as megalomaniac, or highly controlling, as naively idealistic, or impossibly vague. It could of course be all these if allied with bad practice; good community work practice should be none of these things.

If the nub of good practice is to have a definition of a better world at which to aim in a practical way then what - in a non-megalomaniac, non-controlling, non-naive, realistic and precise way - is its goal? We would say the main aim is resource - redistribution from the powerful to the weak, and this means 'providing help and support to people taking group action to secure more or better resources for the most needy neighbourhoods, or for people experiencing the most severe kinds of disadvantages.' (3) We now think, since the uproar in 1981, that the word oppressed is more accurate than the word needy. When community workers take this as their 'fundamental task' they then make judgments and choices, in those neighbourhoods, about the groups and individuals who share those aims. It is highly likely that much of their working time will be spent supporting the efforts of those groups and individuals.

Occasionally, even, choices have to be made to support some individuals in groups against others on issues such as redistribution, but
provided this is done in a straightforward way it is neither manipulative nor controlling.

While making her or his own position clear and helping groups to
define their own aims, the worker should not prescribe the small or
large aims of the groups she/he works with, nor the method that a
particular set of individuals will choose to achieve those aims.
To do so would mimic the methods of the powerful who seek to control
the weak.   For a worker to determine, directly or surreptitiously,
a group's aims or methods would merely confirm its powerlessness. (4)

It can be argued that many other individuals and institutions are
engaged in redistribution.   This is so.   Some administrators,
teachers, housing workers, trade union officials and members, councillors, tenants' association secretaries, and planners actively
pursue redistribution.   Community workers are defined not only by
these goals but by the amount of paid time they can allocate to it;
for them it's a full-time job which may often mean making alliances
with other workers when they are seeking to achieve redistribution.

This view of community work also requires the worker to make an
appraisal of the British class structure and to take serious note of
ways in which such a structure promotes, colludes with, and is per-
petuated by the neutral view of community work that has no concern
about goals and priorities.   Most resources are still distributed
in a grossly unequal fashion between classes in Britain.   A more
equal distribution of resources would bring enormous benefits to
people living in inner city areas, outer city estates or in rural
feudalism, or belonging to groups which society discriminates
against, such as women, black people, teenagers, gays or the poor.
If only two such resources - housing and education - were allocated
not, as present, by class, ability to pay or sex, but by less damaging and more egalitarian criteria, the life-chances of many people
and neighbourhoods would be transformed.   This point was consistently missed in most public comment on the 'riots' of the summer of
1981.   To achieve such allocation in the future requires, of
course, massive changes in the policies, practice and attitudes of
the ruling classes and their middle managers wherever they are to be
found in political parties, central government, local government or
the traditional voluntary organisations.   Community work can only
hope to achieve very limited change but the attempt is none the
worse for that.

Aiming at the redistribution of resources should also mean promoting collectivity because power is a resource and in a world dominated by hierarchical institutions it is distributed in stunning
imbalance between the strong and the weak.   Community workers
should seek to support collective action as opposed to individual
action and collective gain as opposed to individual gain as part of
the vision of a better world.   Working together as equals is a
necessary condition if the society is to be significantly altered
and not just one group of individuals with power substituted for
another.   Intimately related, also, to the 'fundamental task' of
attempting resource redistribution is the provision of direct service to groups who are powerless vis-à-vis other organisations and

institutions.   We do not try, here, to analyse the skills of neighbourhood work (5) but merely to stress it as a fundamental element
because it is often downgraded and regarded as of secondary importance by some writers and 'community workers': (6)

> There are workers who are so caught up in working with other paid
> workers or elected representatives, in attending policy and plan-
> ning meetings or conferences, in writing position papers, in
> liaising, in organising conferences, in political manoeuvering,
> in 'working at the macro-level', in research, in 'managing' other
> community workers, and in downplaying the strengths of local
> people, that they seem to have lost any sense of purpose for the
> work.   To ascribe supremacy to the support of neighbourhood
> groups and local people at least serves as some kind of check on
> these tendencies, and ensures that complex and problematic though
> it is to be able to know what local residents want and to cope
> with the conflicts that sometimes arise between different sets of
> wishes, those wishes are what should govern the activities of the
> community worker.

There are many fundamental conflicts of interest in community work -
between the interests of the poor and the interests of the affluent;
between racists and the people they harrass and oppress; between
tenants and landlords; between the unemployed or the homeless and
those who own or manage jobs or houses; and on the whole question
of how resources are distributed in an outrageously unequal society.
We believe that there has been a tradition of 'community work' that
chooses, wherever possible, to ignore these conflicts of interest,
to be embarrassed by any discussion of them and where they can no
longer be concealed, to try to smoothe them over blandly and to stay
above conflict by remaining 'objective' and striving to achieve a
'balance' of interests.   This is the neutral tradition.   We do not
advocate conflict for conflict's sake but we know that there is
another tradition of community work - much in evidence over the last
twenty years in local community action though not publicised in the
press (7) - that is infused day in and day out with an active concern about conflicting social interests and that is willing where
necessary to take sides.   The clearest account of work of this
kind, demonstrating conflicts in the housing field, is Jan
O'Malley's. (8)

In order to illustrate the difference between different traditions of community work, as it works out in daily practice, we have
selected examples from work with which we are personally familiar;
theory about practice that is not built on personal experience is
built on a weak foundation.   Many community workers could supply
other examples.

WORKING FOR THE REDISTRIBUTION OF RESOURCES

We have said above that we regard direct neighbourhood work as the
fundamental service to be provided by community workers, but that it
must be guided by the redistributive aim.   The worker has choices
to make about which groups to work with and which individuals to
support.   The neutral worker may not easily perceive which groups
to spend time with and which to avoid, and may not feel confident

enough to identify with, and be committed to, the relatively powerless in their struggle to achieve redistribution of whatever kind.
How can a neutral worker adequately support such demands, sometimes
expressed angrily - for instance by a group setting up its own nursery facilities and seeking a grant that will enable it to pay
decent salaries to its workers?   On such occasions neutral workers
fall short in their support and group members sense this.   The neutral worker then tends to spend less and less time with people who
can be written off as 'angry', 'radical' or 'militant' and more time
with quietist supporters of the status quo - which often means withdrawing from much direct neighbourhood work and associating mainly
with other workers in the neutral tradition, e.g. in some 'co-ordinating committees' or 'neighbourhood councils', (9) or else finding
some quiet untroublesome neighbourhood group to exploit.

Unless workers have a clear perspective on goals and priorities,
they may as individuals, or in teams, fail to get clear which local
groups require the most support.   Within the limited hours available in the working week, workers have to attempt such clarity.   In
a hard-pressed area, of course, there may be many more groups who
require community work assistance than there are resources available, but at least it should be possible to identify the broad categories of oppressed groups requiring support.   There are, for
instance:
(1)   groups who directly experience oppression/disadvantage;
(2)   groups who seek to provide support or improve services to
      oppressed groups;
(3)   groups pressing for better services or facilities in their own
      or other oppressed/disadvantaged neighbourhoods. (10)

Where there are, in the worker's judgment, oppressed neighbourhoods, or issues involving oppression and/or exploitation, but no
group in existence, then it should also be a priority to initiate
neighbourhood exploration or information-gathering to see if local
people want to take collective action.   By implication community
workers should not spend precious, limited time supporting other,
more privileged, groups - especially if the interests of the two
different categories (more and less privileged) are in conflict.
Unless such priorities are set, some work time may be influenced by
personal self-indulgence, and a team of neutral workers may be
spending most of their time with groups or individuals who are much
less in need of community work assistance.

Workers in the neutral tradition may not perceive clearly the
middle-class stranglehold on resources and that choices have to be
made - even in the 'voluntary sector' - between groups who need help
and those who don't: in the local authority approach to local
groups for example there are often degrees of acceptability.   The
relatively traditional groups - well known, with middle-class
management committees, staffed with professionals and often part of
a national association - are invited to send representatives to
council committees and are accorded recognition as 'voluntary organisations'.   But the phrase is a misnomer.   It is precisely some of
the least recognised groups who are most often entirely dependent on
their voluntary resources, whereas the established 'voluntary organisations' often have money to pay their workers.   The less respec-
table a group - by virtue of its membership or methods - the less

likely it may be to receive support and recognition.   It may take a
long time, for instance, before a local authority department can
accept that a tenants' association, or a group of single parents, or
a claimants' union, or a trade union, may be an organisation whose
contribution to meeting social needs is comparable with the contribution of the more recognised 'voluntary organisations'.

If community workers are not clear about the goal of resource-
redistribution and about ordering their work priorities accordingly,
then there are numerous muddles in the work.   Not only are they not
clear about who to spend time with;   there is also lack of clarity
about what they are achieving and how to evaluate what they are
doing.   Accountability gets muddied and workers show an inability
to be straight - with employers, for instance - about what they are
doing and why they are doing it.   They conceal any involvement with
'radical' groups or issues because of feeling guilty about association with them instead of openly avowing that such involvement is
central to the work.   With the employing authority (whether voluntary agency, central government or local authority department) it is
important to begin immediately on the task of job definition, for
instance getting clear with the employer that a worker will provide
support to local groups to help them achieve their own objectives.
Such a job definition may prove useful on occasions - particularly
in the early days - when senior management may object to activities
or groups they don't happen to like: (11)

For example, two workers were invited to attend an evening meeting protesting against rent rises (under the Conservative Government's Housing Finance Act, 1972) which was called by the Brent
Federation of Tenants and Residents Associations outside the Town
Hall.   At the meeting with the assistant director the conversa-
tion went:

  A.D.:   The public relations officer saw you there....
  Workers: Yes, the Brent Federation had asked us to be there
           and we decided to go.
  A.D.:   But you can't do that sort of thing in local govern-
           ment....
  Workers: It's our job which we agreed with you.... (Worker's
  Notes, 1972)

Whichever the employing agency, the difficult issues about what
is or isn't the job have to be faced.   In the example given, it
was important not to fall back on let-outs - for example, that
the workers were at the Town Hall out of working hours - but
instead to argue that what was done was integral to the job and
in the original agreement.

Community workers should actively seek opportunities to assist
resource-redistribution to the most oppressed groups and areas
whenever those opportunities arise.   In addition they may need
actively to seek out and create such opportunities.   This example
is from our own experience.   We have doubts about how effectively
workers in the neutral tradition seek such opportunities: (12)

Although the urgent needs of an area, for example of a Borough,
are often well known, especially to the residents of the neediest
neighbourhoods themselves, very little may happen over the years
to meet those needs.   Inaction has many causes, but particularly
occurs when the political party in power is supported by senior

officers who do not regard those urgent needs as the top priority.   Pressure for more resources in needier areas comes primarily from local groups or coalitions of groups.   But community
workers can try to assist the process with whatever supporting
information about social needs they can generate, for instance,
social-indicator research.   This activity may be particularly
important when a section of the local population does not have
sufficient political muscle of its own, for example, black youth.
    We started picking up the evidence of unemployment, homeless-
ness and disaffection amongst a number of black youths from 1974,
when a worker began working with such a group (the needs were
already well known by a number of black parents but no one had
been listening to them).   The urgency of the needs became even
more apparent as the pressures on us from those kids mounted,
when the residential side opened.   We kept on and on about the
needs of these youngsters which the services were not meeting.
They were kids who were sleeping rough, squatting, living at home
in very inadequate accommodation (e.g. sharing a room with a sib-
ling of the opposite sex), or going round dossing in a mate's
house.   They were out of work and needed very solid support and
effort to get over the hurdles of applying for jobs, and much
more than we had the time to give.
    We developed statistics and made proposals again and again -
for a night advisory service, for a dossing service staffed by
workers at night, for the creation by the council of bedsitter
accommodation in converted property and in purpose-built blocks
with provision for friendly landlady care, for the employment of
workers to help these kids, for play provision of all kinds.
    (Paper, project worker, 1977)
Workers may come under pressure from their employers to alter the
course of their work and be neutral, where direct and positive support to certain community groups is perceived as a threat to the
employers' interests.   Such pressure to subvert direct neighbourhood work is not often recorded but many community workers are
familiar with it: (13)
    There are many ways, other than reasoned discussion, in which
    attempts may be made by some managers to control, modify or
    divert the course of the work.   They range from anger, coolness,
    threats (direct or veiled), and blandishments, to dishonesty,
    cynicism and false affection.   Two examples - of veiled threat -
    come from workers' notes:
    (1) A.D.:   You are making yourselves very unpopular.
         Workers: With whom?   How?   (Silence)
         Workers: With whom?   We need to know because we should
                   sort it out with them.   What don't they like
                   about what we are doing?
         A.D.:   I can't tell you....
    (2) A.D.:   I don't want you to lose your jobs.
         Workers: Why should we lose our jobs?
         A.D.:   If people don't like what you do....
         Workers: Which people?
         A.D.:   I can't say.   What was said to me was said in
                   confidence.
Sometimes threats to job security are much more direct than in these

examples.   Workers in the neutral tradition find it hard, under
such threats, to maintain work that is disapproved by bosses;   or,
in anticipation of threats, they never attempt it.

Workers in the neutral tradition may be slow to perceive them and
even slower to counteract, when powerful conservative forces are
seeking to deny resource-redistribution.   It is possible occasionally to get direct glimpses of these forces at work and to observe
how a conservative manager may be resisting redistribution.   For
instance, a director of education commented as follows on social-
indicator research which showed clearly that the poorest areas had
far worse educational opportunities than the richer areas: (14)

> I am very doubtful about the usefulness of your research to the
> deliberations of the Youth and Community Service working party.
> When the evidence was presented the other evening, I had to agree
> that it was 'interesting', but it is only of use if there has
> been a policy decision that the resources of the Youth and Commu-
> nity Service have to be concentrated in areas of deprivation.
> Any report on the future of the Youth and Community Service which
> makes it clear to the ratepayers at large that there would be
> concentrated effort in part of the Borough, would lead to an
> immediate outcry to which the council members would be obliged to
> pay regard.   I do not say this just from conjecture but from
> experience.   We have tried in dealing with schools to improve
> the standards of those in the most deprived areas and to concen-
> trate the limited resources to their benefit.   This is a policy,
> which has, at fairly regular intervals, had to be reversed
> because of the pressure of groups in the more 'suburban' parts of
> the Borough to have their facilities made even better.   It has
> pained me personally sometimes to have to relinquish a project in
> a priority area so that something could be done elsewhere, but,
> in fact, we had no option.

We knew that the director had in fact had the option to report her
thinking to her Committee, in a Labour-controlled council, a number
of whose members were concerned to achieve redistribution of educational resources;   but she was anxious not to give them the evidence
which could justify their reducing the resources for the richer
areas.

The ways in which local community groups are done down by powerful resource-controllers are not always very apparent, and community
workers need to be quick to perceive when groups are attacked in
this way: (15)

> The deep cynicism of those in local government (professionals?)
> about the competence of ordinary folk was starkly revealed last
> year in a 'problem' West of Scotland housing scheme whose commu-
> nity efforts had attracted national attention and whose youths
> offered to save the District Council at least £20,000 a year (and
> incalculable savings from reduced vandalism and more responsible
> and skilled citizens) by taking over the management of a new
> sports centre.   It took more than a year of hard bargaining with
> a highly suspicious Council whose officers - whether deliberately
> or not - were very obstructive before this was achieved.

This had its echo in pronouncements about the Liverpool 8 riots in
1981 when consultation was bandied about as a new idea by government
ministers and senior local government officers.   Local groups (and

a flood of government reports and research studies) have been urging
this since the early 1960s.

Neutral workers have no conception of the ways in which such en-
trenched managers block change.   Indeed, they themselves may -
deliberately or not - hamper the activities of community groups by
being ignorant of their difficulties.   There may be little realisation that if voluntary effort is to be encouraged in areas where
people have few material resources, then the provision of such resources is a very important first step in enabling a group to
develop its work: (16)

> Many local groups in this area rely on the voluntary work of
> people who are living in overcrowded housing, who are paid low
> wages, who are maybe bringing up families and working many hours
> overtime.   Such groups need very basic kinds of help, like some-
> where to meet.   I remember one very well-paid professional work-
> ing in the area saying to me, 'But can't they meet in somebody's
> front room?'   He obviously didn't know anything about trying to
> do voluntary work from the base of a small flat with two small
> children around, not being able to afford a telephone, and not
> owning enough chairs to offer to your committee!   Very often the
> professionals' experience of 'voluntary work' is limited to know-
> ing the middle-class secretaries of established groups whose hus-
> bands earn comfortable salaries and whose free time at home is
> made even freer by the fact that they can afford (good luck to
> them) a cleaning lady.   Curiously, however, it's those groups
> which tend to get the greater amount of material support from
> local authorities.   (Project worker, research interview, 1977)

Neutrality in community work supports the myth of even-handed and
impartial distribution of resources that has for long been a main
thread running through social policy in Britain.   Thus schemes that
positively discriminate in favour of the poor are attacked because
they contravene some notion of 'fairness of allocation' and such
pressure builds up that even discriminatory programmes can be sub-
verted to the benefit of the relatively affluent: (17)

> The National Sports Council initiated a programme for funding
> sports projects in 'areas of special need'.   It took the local
> authority four years to respond to it.   The first project to be
> supported was the re-siting of a middle-class rifle club.   (Pro-
> ject worker, research interview, 1977)

But even when some marginal redistribution is achieved, the old
fears of the better off areas that they might lose out may surface
again and a number of officers in a local authority may identify
themselves with these fears: (18)

> People were continuously making remarks about the area of Harles-
> den getting everything.   People made remarks like 'If there are
> many more professional workers down there they'll out-number the
> population.'   There was resentment in the northern areas - that
> Harlesden was being over-generously treated.

> You'd talk to an area manager.   He'd say, 'We're going to put
> up this urban aid idea.'   Even if it was a potty idea.   One of
> the reasons we're going to put this up is that we deserve some-
> thing.   Harlesden gets everything.   And one of the arguments we
> shall put forward for doing this in Wembley is because Wembley
> hasn't had very much.   Harlesden's had it all.   Now even if it

was a bad idea Wembley would then get it because it was argued
that Harlesden had too much....
    There was the empire-building thing.   One area manager wanted
to be seen to have control of as much as the other area manager.
(Headquarters worker, research interview, 1977)
One of the ways in which conservative forces deal with pressures
for change is to seek to absorb them, for instance by suggesting
that a new group, pressing for more resources for handicapped children, should be merged with a moribund 'larger' group that had for
long sought not to rock the boat: (19)
    A student with the local social services area team had undertaken
a survey of parents of mentally handicapped children in Harlesden
to find out whether they felt the need for some kind of holiday
centre to which they could take their children during the school
holidays.   After the completion of the survey the student left
and the area manager, having no resources to continue any work,
discussed the next moves with the Harlesden Community Project
workers.   A student, just starting a six months' placement, then
took on the job of gradually meeting all the parents who took
part and feeding back the results of the survey.   As she kept
going back to see people and do jobs for individuals, over the
ensuing months, some of the parents talked about meeting
together.   They knew about a borough-wide organisation, the
Brent Society for Mentally Handicapped Children, but they wanted
their own local support group.   The student introduced some
parents to each other;   others knew each other already.   Gradually a first meeting was set up at our offices at which parents
agreed with each other to meet weekly and to call themselves the
Harlesden Parents Special Group.   All this time the student kept
telling a local social worker, who had a special interest in mentally handicapped children and contact with the Brent Society,
about what she was doing, but also suggested that if the worker
or the Brent Society wanted to know about the new group they
could contact its secretary directly.
    At this time two community workers (one of whom supervised the
student) were invited to a social services area advisory group to
explain their work.   At the meeting a member of the Brent Society was present and he raised the issue of the new group.   He was
angry that the social services department had not told him about
'their' project.   We explained that this was not our project.
He said that the parents should join the Brent Society.   We said
that, as far as we knew, the parents had discussed this point and
decided to form their own group.   He said again that they should
not do this but join his group.   We suggested that he should
contact the new group directly himself and gave him the name and
address of the secretary.
    The local group continued in its work and the community
workers continued to provide whatever support they wanted.
In the neutral tradition of merely 'bringing people together', and
of working with existing and well-established organisations, however
moribund, the workers might well have gone along with the pressure
to merge.
We have had space only for a few illustrations of the different
ways in which community workers work with and perceive oppressed

people.   When these methods and perceptions are neutral the effects are damaging to those people.   Community workers who do the job in the way we define it will always have to deal with the criticism that they are 'being political'.   Any activity concerned with the allocation of resources is by definition political - whether it is about altering society or is concerned to maintain things as they are.   This is, of course, as true of the work of the most neutral, passive local government officer or committee member of a voluntary organisation as it is of anyone engaged in party politics.   Community workers who are attempting to achieve a better world are in a vulnerable position.   They can be sacked when they work for allocations of resources of which the powerful do not approve. (20)   Community workers need to have the nerve to stick to the job as it should be done.

NOTES

1   Paul Henderson, David Jones and David Thomas (eds), 'The Boundaries of Change in Community Work', Allen & Unwin, 1980, p. 1.
2   See Jan O'Malley, 'The Politics of Community Action', Spokesman, 1977, p. 172:   '..."the neutral" community worker has such a low opinion of working-class organisational ability and political sophistication that they encourage the people they work with to pitch their expectations of achievement very low.'
3   See our discussion of this in 'Community Work and Caring for Children: A Community Project in an Inner City Local Authority', by a group of workers from the Harlesden Community Project, 1971-6, Owen Wells, 1979, chapter 8.
4   Those who give allegiance to the redistributive aim sometimes fall into this trap of failing to work also for redistribution of power beginning with their own power.   Jan O'Malley (op. cit.) gives examples of manipulative radical community work. On how men fall into that trap in relation to women, see S. Rowbotham, L. Segal and H. Wainwright, 'Beyond the Fragments', Merlin Press, 1979.
5   See Harlesden Community Project, op. cit., chapter 8.
6   Ibid., p. 121.
7   Short accounts are written up regularly in 'Community Action', PO Box 665, London SW1X 8DZ.
8   O'Malley, op. cit.   See also the various reports of the Home Office Community Development Projects.
9   On how neutral community work of this kind may be promoted by local government see Cynthia Cockburn, 'The Local State', Pluto Press, 1977, chapters 4 and 5.
10   For a detailed list of such groups, see Harlesden Community Project, op. cit., pp. 133-4.
11   Ibid., p. 123.
12   Ibid., p. 177.
13   Ibid., pp. 200-1.
14   Ibid., p. 181.
15   Ronald Young, Community Development - its political and administrative challenge, 'Social Work Today', vol. 8, no. 18, 8 February 1977, p. 8, footnote 20.

16   Harlesden Community Project, op. cit., p. 211.
17   Ibid., p. 213.
18   Ibid., p. 213.
19   Ibid., p. 126.
20   For example, Wandsworth Borough Council sacked community workers
     when the party in power changed at a local election in 1978.
     In 1979, Islington Borough Council similarly refused to continue
     funding some community work projects.

5 Bringing socialism home: Theory and practice for a radical community action

Mike Fleetwood and John Lambert

Housing provided the focus for much of the community action which has been so marked a feature of urban neighbourhoods since the 1960s. There is hardly a town of any size anywhere that has not produced some action group or another; the number of individuals involved must run into hundreds of thousands. Despite the short-lived nature of many campaigns and organisations, not all were failures. Schemes, plans and policies were delayed or amended, councils did think again, and the legitimacy of owner/tenant/resident participation was advanced.

Yet no lasting structures appear to have survived and all that protest and activity could not shift the seemingly inevitable decline in housing standards and provision. Housing has taken the lion's share of cuts; production and repair and maintenance of council houses have been ground down; rents have been raised. Waiting lists and homelessness have grown. And all this without any sustained or coherent popular protest. On the contrary the policy measure in recent years with the most potential for popular mobilisation (certainly in terms of votes at local elections) appears to have been the sale of council houses at large discounts - a policy which benefits the better off, limits opportunities for those unable to buy, and in the medium- to long term will add to the financial burdens of local authorities.

None of this suggests that the prospects for a radical practice for effective community action on housing are at all promising at the moment. But there are, we believe, important lessons to be learned from the recent past; debates and arguments continue and there are clues and signs that work in progress is radical and worthwhile.

Trying to sustain a socialist commitment and an engagement in community action in the 1970s was like walking in shoes soled with banana skins: the weight of orthodox socialist theory shot a leg sliding one way whilst the experience and evolving practice of community action sent the other leg in the opposite direction. Spending most of the time doing the splits is not the best way of intervening in class struggle. And if what felt like a few tentative steps towards firm land were made, it proved to be a rug which Thatcherism pulled from under us. But the company with us on the floor seems to have grown - just how we pick ourselves up is unclear.

What we want to argue here is that the upsurge in community

action needs to be seen as a symptom of malaise in the British
socialist and labour movements.   Community action reveals a poverty
in socialist practice.   But without a socialist practice community
action has been short-lived, it posed no alternatives, it became a
means for co-option, it collapsed into the maw of the repressive
tolerance of the British state.   Orthodox socialist analysis
scorned non-workplace struggles.   Community action was left isolated.   But if theory exhorted activists to link up with trade
unions and trades councils in the muscle of the labour movement -
where, then, was the muscle, where the movement?   So now, since the
very existence at the moment of a labour movement can be seriously
doubted, we want to argue that socialists have a lot to learn from
community action about how movement may again characterise their
political efforts.   Our business must be in William Morris's words
'the making of socialists, i.e. convincing people that socialism is
good for them and is possible ... therefore I say make socialists.'

Housing is a good place to start - not an easy one but good
because, especially in the public sector, there are many thousands
who have experienced a kind of socialism in practice: and this is
an experience that socialist practitioners must come to terms with.
Housing issues can help us see the way forward and the pitfalls.
Given the huge encroachment of the state into every sphere of life -
more than ever before people do now live in the shadow of the state
- dangers and diversions will abound.   For example, there is a particular temptation for socialists, seeing sales to tenants proceed-
ing apace, to rush to defend the public sector as an essentially
socialist tenure.   Yet there is precious little in its history, its
production and management that smacks of socialism.   Socialists
must beware of defending the institutions of state capitalism in the
name of socialism.

In what follows we will try to do three things: account for the
damaging return to isolation and distance between socialism and community action to which we have referred, review some of the features
of community housing action which brought it into conflict with the
labour movement; and outline, in the light of some recent theoretical and practical developments, the elements of an appropriate radical practice.   It will be apparent that our conclusions are tentative and are offered as a contribution to debate and dialogue within
the labour movement about where to go from here.

THEORETICAL ISOLATION

The dominant perspective among socialists this century has been that
the real class struggles capable of challenging the capitalist
system occur at the point of production.   It is here that the contradictions inherent in capitalism are most visible, here that
workers, initially through trade unions, can organise to resist exploitation.   The task of a socialist labour movement is to raise
trade union consciousness to the realisation of an alternative economic and social system.   Struggles away from the workplace are of
secondary importance or (worse) dangerous diversions from the central task.   Alongside this analysis has developed a style and
method of intervention which stresses party organisation, where the

discipline and rigour needed to combat exploitation were located in
party organisation.

As theoretical debate has developed, it has tended to focus more
on organisational forms and tactics to achieve the overthrow of
capitalism rather than with processes to involve the mass of working
people in political activity.   A series of parties claiming to be
the authentic vanguard to lead the mass has been developed and these
parties have become more concerned with moving from conflict to conflict in search of recruits to the party, than with recruits for
socialism.   These organisations increasingly adopted a style that
comes across as bullying, authoritarian, inflexible and intolerant.
It is the 'correct line' which must be defended - those who disagree
are put down and put off.   The Labour Party, dismissed by the
smaller revolutionary factions as irretrievably reformist, also
developed a highly bureaucratic form designed, it seems, to lock the
already committed into organisational debate but ready for occasion-
al local and national elections when the task was to 'get out the
vote';   this vote was presumed to remain static and loyal, a few as
members, but more as non-participating 'natural' supporters of
Labour's cause.

These theoretical and organisational tendencies were not such as
to generate instant identification between community action and the
parties of the labour movement.   For many involved in community
action, the theoretically grounded dismissal of community struggles
by the party activists confirmed the irrelevance of the parties;
for others, it was simply that where Labour councils were in power
they were the opposition to be challenged.

For those in orthodox left politics, community action was
sporadic, its organisations were many and varied, populism and conservatism seemed rife, and it did not lead to any permanent structures which might constitute real change.   Spontaneity, said Lenin,
collapses spontaneously.   Community action seemed to confirm this;
so the conventional left response was 'we told you so!'   But we
would argue that, since community action was denied any legitimacy
as class struggle, and lacked an input from the socialist movement,
it was deprived by the left of the body of ideas and substance that
it required to situate it within a socialist framework.

The space between community action and socialism has not remained
unfilled.   An opportunistic 'community politics' prospered briefly
for bourgeois radicals in the Liberal Party.   A community work profession concerned itself with establishing ways of working collectively to tackle immediate problems.   Starting from people's experience, it brought few preconceptions but a concern for techniques.
Such techniques could be applied to progressive social processes;
they could be a basis for opposing the controlling power of the
state.   But divorced from socialism, denied legitimacy by the
labour movement, such work has tended to be small-scale, cautious,
uncoordinated and individualistic.   Again 'we told you so' has been
the conventional verdict of the left.

The non-involvement, absence of dialogue was especially damaging
for those seeking to maintain a socialist commitment within community action.   But the confusion experienced by many who have been
radicalised by their involvement in community action has to be
understood not as a personal inability to reconcile socialist theory

and practice but as a difficulty stemming from the poverty of practice in British socialism and the latter's failure to discuss the
features of class struggle in the community-based activities of the
1960s and 1970s.

SOCIALISM AND WORKING-CLASS EXPERIENCE

The theories and forms of socialism which arose at the beginning of
this century could present themselves as a radical alternative to
the old tried, known and failed models of capitalism.   Those
theories and practices did not have to reckon with the suspicion and
hostility that exists today about socialist practice and organisation.   For whether 'real' socialists like it or not, many different
things have been done this century in the name of socialism and it
is this contemporary experience which socialists need to consider
carefully;   it is an experience moreover which underlies the form
and content of community action.   That has involved, characteris-
tically, residents of run-down neighbourhoods or on neglected housing estates demanding an improvement in their social conditions.
As often as not this has found sections of the local working class
in conflict with Labour-controlled councils over policies shaped
nationally by Labour governments.   Council housing - experienced by
many tenants as poor quality housing, inadequately maintained, in a
form that is a stark contrast to the private house and garden of
their 'dreams', incompetently managed at ever-rising cost with no
parallel rise in standards - is seen as the 'socialist' solution to
the housing crisis.   Community action groups on council estates
often have good reason to complain about the standard of service
provided by Direct Labour Organisations.   In an area like South
Wales with its huge dependency on nationalised industries and its
highly developed trade unionism, people involved in community action
know that these 'socialist' solutions haven't brought them the
better life.   They read their papers, watch their televisions, they
learn about what is happening in the 'Socialist' countries of East-
ern Europe.   They find little reason to be impressed with socialism, but plenty of reasons to be sceptical.   Contemporary socialist
practice and theory has to confront that reality.
     Community workers on housing issues have a special need to appre-
ciate the way housing policies have developed during this century.
Yet despite a marked preoccupation with housing problems, a distinctive socialist contribution has been lacking.   It is as if, for
socialists, Engels said it all in 'The Housing Question'. (1)   The
1919 Housing Act, which first provided funds for building public
housing, needs to be seen not as the triumph of a socialist alternative but the state's solution to capitalism's persistent problem.
What should seem remarkable to present socialists about Bevan's
post- Second World War efforts is their rare, exceptional and short-
lived quality.   His much-vaunted house building machine to produce
sufficient, good quality, classless estates depended upon private
capital and a private construction industry and at the drop of a
government, it was switched to produce all over Britain the most
appalling new slums in which so many working-class families find
themselves trapped to the present day.   It was a 'socialist'

housing minister (Crossman) who in the 1960s sanctioned the production of high-rise flat blocks in the public sector.   It was Labour-
controlled local councils who took credit for the far-reaching comprehensive redevelopment schemes in central and inner areas of
cities - processes which swept away working-class communities and
which promoted a style of housing management that was bureaucratic,
authoritarian and paternalistic.   If any government can claim
credit for halting large-scale demolition - the aim of much community action in the early 1970s - it is the Tory government.   And it
was the public expenditure cuts required as part of the deal between
a Labour government and the International Monetary Fund which exacerbated conditions on council estates where major design defects
generated vain demands for high levels of maintenance expenditure.

This brief catalogue is not included simply to knock the Labour
Party and government, but to emphasise how community action arose
under conditions which were experienced, whether present-day socialists like it or not, as a form of socialism in practice.   It is
going to take more than a new generation of labour activists armed
with more radical policy proposals to erase this experience of
'socialism' in the corrupt, self-perpetuating, self-congratulatory
paternalism of 'old fashioned' Labour politics.

It is no wonder there has been a decline of working-class politics, since these processes have distanced electorates from their
representatives.   But such experiences have not produced a generation of the politically naive thirsting for rational political
debate, ready for a socialist vanguard to fuse their consciousness
to a higher plane.   Their experience not in the workplace but in
the home and the neighbourhood have made 'politics' and 'socialism'
dirty words.   Community action articulated that protest full of
scepticism and self-interest though much of it was.   If a radical
practice is to develop, this is an experience that cannot be
ignored.

THE THEORETICAL DEVELOPMENTS OF THE 1970s

But if the orthodox and conventional analyses and organisations
meant suspicion and hostility between community action and the left,
the social processes also entailed a search for some common ground.
For the moment we need to examine the strategies and practice emerging in the late 1970s, from the difficult experience of socialists
in community action, drawing on the revival in academic Marxism
especially in its treatment of the state and the urban crisis.   The
first important developments occurred within the Home Office Community Development Projects (CDPs), some of whose workers and researchers developed an historical and materialist analysis side by
side with efforts at local intervention.   Their vital contribution
was to establish the fact that the urban crisis was the inescapable
result of market forces.   After the CDPs, there was no going back
to scapegoating the deprived nor to seeing the government or state
as bystanders helplessly witnessing industrial change and decline.
Through the CDP work came the most eloquent analyses of the limitations of council housing and policies for improvement. (2)   Yet the
CDP reports could only exhort activists to find the implications for
practice for themselves.

Parallel to this work came valuable theoretical developments in the field of reproduction of the labour force and of the consumption process as part of production. (3)   But these too provided cold comfort for community action.   The all-determining shadow of the state, central and local, seemed to provide no room;   community was a terrain belonging to capital.   The old orthodoxy of reliance on workplace struggles (albeit in the new territory of the public sector) was reasserted.   Only from the European neo-Marxists was the message different. (4)   Their analysis recognised the novel significance of state-provided facilities consumed collectively rather than individually in the extended reproduction of labour (i.e. health, education, transport, leisure services etc.), which contained scope for new alliances going beyond mere protest groups to become urban social movements for real change.   Yet here too initial enthusiasms among British activists and academics did not last, for these European Marxists emphasised that the role of a party was crucial in moving beyond a protest group into an urban social movement which would link the diverse elements with a shared interest - the social base - into a social force.   The Communist parties of France and Italy, and in other countries, could claim such a role: but in Britain the factionalised revolutionary parties held no credibility and the Labour Party was irredeemably reformist. Again the advice seemed to be for socialists in Britain to devote all their efforts to the traditional sphere of the workplace.

But such a prescription is not wholly consistent with the analysis.   The new Marxism and its sophisticated analysis of the modern state makes it no longer possible to refer crudely to the needs of capitalism nor to the working class but to recognise conflicting interests and fractions within capital and layers and fragments of a working class.   The state apparatus is not a smooth, effectively controlling machine masterminded by lackeys of capitalism.   Policies are inconsistent and contradictory reflecting the crisis-torn and competitive nature of capitalist economies.   Moreover a century of capitalism advancing through monopolistic and state capitalistic forms has divided and subdivided subordinate classes.   Contemporary Marxists are similarly concerned to stress the artificiality of divisions between production and consumption.   Consistent with all this, but contained within the current analysis of the state, class struggle is to occur between various kinds of groups in a variety of spheres without any necessary primacy being attached to the workplace (where a rising proportion are state employees) nor secondariness to non-workplace.   So increasingly the theoretical and practice work in the 1970s, whilst breaking up old orthodoxies, could not by its nature be rapidly or simply synthesised into a rapprochement between community action and socialists.

But in the theory and practice debates of the 1970s perhaps the most difficult question to resolve was the one concerning the importance attached to the party in traditional socialist theory.   Were socialists to work with groups as a recruiting agent for the Labour Party?   We have already suggested the problems that follow from taking that path.   Or was it to be the nursery for the revolutionary left, whereby activists would be taken away from their areas of competence to become sellers of newspapers and supporters of industrial struggles they knew nothing about?   Or was there to be a series of independent parties embracing a potentially reactionary populism?

There were, however, other models to follow. The women's movement had sought to develop as an autonomous, politically conscious movement. It too had faced the problem of existing political parties but recognised that rational debate and organisational loyalty were not a hopeful basis for an alternative society. Nor do people want to listen when, instead of dialogue, all that they get is a repeat of the same argument more loudly and stridently. But those who sought in community action a separate politics for the parties of the labour movement were misunderstood by the left and community action became labelled as a refuge for anarchists and libertarians and the anti-party elements: students of 1968 who never grew up.

But there was after 1975 a material basis for a new kind of politically conscious movement separate from established party. Until then the primary focus of community action was the old working-class communities under sentence of death by demolition. Experience had pointed out the extreme difficulties in establishing links between such groups or building federations, since their concern was to maintain something intangible, localised, unique - that was the point of their essentially defensive campaigns. The severe public expenditure cuts miraculously saved such areas - demolition, clearance and rebuilding was too expensive (except where commercial property development could replace housing). Now these areas were to be rehabilitated and local authorities started organising various forms of participation to oil the bureaucratic wheels of improvement grant machinery. Council estates became a new focus for community action. They increasingly suffered, as the cuts bit deeper, from scant maintenance and repairs; cheap design features surfaced in a recent generation of council buildings, and whole estates became soaked in condensation and irreversible damp. On others elaborate, but very expensive central heating systems, a proud feature of the Parker Morris standards introduced in the late 1960s, proved disastrous for tenants who increasingly faced the choice of freezing or starving or running up huge arrears. There had of course been some council tenant protests in response to the 1972 Housing Finance Act and there was in places a skeletal system of tenants' associations. But it was only after 1975 that militant campaigns, occupations, pickets and marches were organised. Community action here seemed to be on surer ground, it was more clearly a class issue than in the more varied inner-city areas. The extent and depth of grievances was more marked - a feeling of being second-class citizens was rife. No wonder the Tories wanted to make owner-occupiers out of them. Here it should have been possible to link groups together in a common cause and find a better fit between socialist theory and community action practice. It became feasible to conceive of a broad tenants' movement using a socialist strategy, linked to a form of local organising concerned with short-term objectives to remedy local grievances. It seemed for a while that local pressures and national action might produce radical policy changes which recognised the rights of council tenants, the scandalous state of much public sector housing and the waste of a housing system based on private profit.

But such moves have not been able to compensate for the other

consequences of the decline of socialism and the sweeping success of
Thatcherism with its wholly different set of remedies for the public
sector.   The cold wind of monetarism has been as damaging to community action as to workplace struggles.   As rents rise and services
decline, the appetite for struggle is lessened as the prospects of
success recede.   The response of councils in the face of tenants'
pressure is to wring hands and pass the buck to central government,
and to offer more participation and involvement and improved tenant
liaison, even welcoming tenants' associations, knowing resources are
not there.

DEVELOPING A STRATEGY

A great deal of this analysis remains valid, however, and provides
the context for the search for a radical practice at contemporary
times.   First let us try to sketch the essentials of a strategy involved in building a tenants' movement.   This sketch is not simply
a negative reaction to the absence of any appropriate party, but is
based on a number of features of contemporary reality which stand in
the way of any process of making socialists.   In the first place it
is based in the belief that the socialist parties have not in the
past nor are likely to develop the capacity (whatever their rhetoric) to involve the grass roots.   Secondly, it relates to the profound alienation from socialist politics we sense in those sections
of the working class who are council tenants on the worst estates:
it is an alienation due to highly bureaucratic forms of state institutions through which welfare, broadly defined, is administered.
What is needed is a form of practice which can remedy this.   A
long-term process of political education which starts with everyday
issues about rents, repairs, estate management, allocation of tenancies etc. seems like a feasible and legitimate way of beginning to
develop new experiences and understanding.   Such a strategy requires a lot of groundwork, of rooted, consistent, undogmatic work
which contrasts with the manner and style and reputation of existing
parties on the left.
     Only if this groundwork is successful will the issue of party
arise on the agenda.   It can of course be greatly influenced if
parties themselves adapt, or if in power, seek to break from the
past and respect the need for a tenants' movement without working to
control it.
     A number of other aspects would seem consistent with this bare-
bones of a strategy.   One is that a region is the appropriate area
for activity.   This follows from the great variation in the inten-
sity of local problems and in willingness to participate, which can
be overcome when groups meet, exchange experiences and help each
other in their activities.   This overcomes the conventional
approach of patch-based work beloved of local authorities and likely
to find increasing favour among hard-pressed housing officials.
Patch-based work limits the scope of action, gives workers and residents a narrow sense of 'their' sphere and a narrowing definition of
collective possibilities.   By taking a large geographical area it
is possible to make links with groups who share a militant perspective.

This militancy is also seen as being a vital component of building a movement.   Militancy is a profound experience for people who
have been cowed by authorities all their lives.   Community workers
will be familiar with the syndrome in community organisations whereby, quite rapidly, a group's demands can become a basis for entreat-
ing the authorities to help them in their hour of need - so the
sense of dependency gets reinforced.   Alternative socialist practice must avoid this.   Participation in a militant style seems a
safer bet than mild forms of deferential organising if one's aim is
to replace fatalism and alienation with confidence and self-esteem.
Socialists, in our experience, hardly seem to believe that the fear
and fatalism existing in sections of the working class are important.   For that fear to be overcome - fear often of Labour councillors, it should be remembered - a lot of time is needed to discover
that from militant action can arise the sense of solidarity and
safety needed to combat it.

A further advantage of linking and helping between groups over a
wide geographical area is that it becomes possible for people to be
engaged in struggle and militant action over a protracted period,
over a succession of campaigns, thus avoiding the spasmodic and
back-tracking character of industrial struggles.   And it is with
continuity that the weight of experience enables political lessons
to become clear.

So space and time are of the essence of such a strategy to build
a movement of tenants.   It is commonplace in the literature of community organising to stress that, whereas middle-class organisations
quickly coalesce around personalities and issues, working-class participation depends on mutual respect and trust; people need to feel
comfortable with an organisation before they will commit themselves
to it.   Yet community workers often find themselves stuck with the
articulate and experienced few who are familiar with standard organisational forms, and fail to reach the cautious and reticent many.
Time and patience are essential if a form of organisation based on
trust and respect is to be created.   But only with such grounding
will it be possible for new and often frightening values and opportunities to be explored.   And only with such a grounding can
socialists get into a position to learn about theory and practice
from working-class people themselves.   With such a grounding it
does become possible to involve tenants in fruitful meetings and
more educational sessions in contact with other tenants.

There are other practice implications in such an approach.
There is the need to avoid being put into leadership roles but to
develop a habit of self-effacement.   It means refusing to cut
corners and assume control in order to get things done but to rely
on the appropriateness and abilities of 'ordinary tenants'.   Sometimes moments of leadership to overcome a crisis or for a specific
task will be required.   But the essential role for the worker is a
backseat one, an expression of solidarity and support without domination, being available for advice and opinion.   But it goes with
an insistence that tenants are the organisers and controllers of
their organisations.

Perhaps it is necessary to stress how, especially in large urban
areas, council housing has assisted the fragmentation and subdivi-
sion of the working class.   It may no longer be sensible to

continue using the term 'working class' if it entails a belief that
a working-class organisation or party can be fashioned.   Any movement based on organisation of council tenants will comprise many
highly stigmatised groups whose sense of being second-class citizens
living in second-class housing is most marked.   The scale of
depression, marital breakdown and pill-popping is so widespread on
some estates that, like the bad housing itself, it is almost taken
for granted.   But socialism cannot ignore this;   nor can it rely on
strategies and practices which only come naturally to those who have
been spared such experiences.   Yet socialism can't be taken like a
pill.   If it is to prove a solution for such groups of tenants then
an appropriate practice must be developed.   Militancy can become
another expression of desperation: the important thing to develop
is confidence which, like understanding, needs time to develop.   It
involves the emotions;   these too can be so smashed by growing up a
'failure' or 'second class' that co-operative work is enormously
difficult, and personal troubles constantly interpose themselves
when public issues are being tackled.   Again the experience of the
women's movement and the importance if attaches to personal politics
appears to be of crucial significance for tenants' movements.

Such matters are of intense practical importance when it comes to
determining how a tenants' group should be organised for of course
the basic elements of any tenants' movement are its constituent
groups.   But whether groups need chairpersons, secretaries, formal
constitutions and the like are difficult questions.   Such forms can
recreate in miniature the bureaucracies from which tenants are es-
caping: without them a tyranny of structurelessness can occur (as
the women's movement discovered). (5)   Often when pressure of time
forces people to adopt conventional procedures it will be found that
discussion is stifled and decisions arrived at have to be reversed
when later a 'real' business meeting occurs outside of formal procedures.

There is a risk that formal procedures and conventional constitutional concerns can be imposed, which promises a busy time for conventional tenants' associations helped by bureaucratic community
workers with a brief to involve tenants more closely in management.
And no doubt these will provide comfort and satisfaction to paternalistic councillors that progress is being achieved.

Socialist practice is something else;   a process which starts and
grows with the experience of people in struggle.   It is a long-term
process aimed at constructing a form of political education amongst
a small group of tenants who would then go out and link up with
others.   It is a practice that involves developing techniques,
organisational forms and relationships which recognise the personal
barriers (constructed by capitalist society) to a class consciousness.   It will require all sorts of diverse efforts to be attempted;   it will entail people to do extraordinary things, to dress up,
sing songs, perform antics in council chambers, to travel unprece-
dented distances to enable people to discover that there is a world
elsewhere and there is a form of politics different from the tired
routines or solemn sloganising of their experience.   It won't, of
course, all work, or work out neatly, or develop a trajectory of un-
interrupted progress.   Such a practice can achieve some notable
victories which (before the cuts) got some estates transformed.   It

hasn't had a huge impact on the electoral politics of any region, but that is hardly the point.

CONCLUSION

Such is the strategy and such are the practices and difficulties entailed in neighbourhood-based work on housing issues.   It is work in progress.   Such a practice contains an assumption that socialist work in the community is a viable enterprise, and tries to be consistent with our understanding of the new hegemonic character of the contemporary capitalist state and the need to oppose it.

We are not of course saying that the only way of making socialists is along these lines: the need, of course, is for myriad forms of socialist activities in all sorts of milieux.   What we want to challenge is the orthodoxy which attaches primacy to workplace struggles and which limits socialist practice to a party political sphere or style.   Trade unions and trades councils seem to pose as many problems for radical practice as do council estates; each needs its own sort of activity.

Community action and its trials and errors contain lessons for socialists.   Some drew the lesson that the essential task was to work to make Labour parties and Labour councillors more democratic, accountable (and therefore, socialist): others concluded that it was work in other parties that needed doing.   Our point is not that such responses were wrong but that they have led to a neglect of an important sphere.   It has allowed a managerial kind of community work to develop and in places has delivered up territory for the right-wing and potentially reactionary populist parties to exploit. That is a serious neglect with serious consequences.

What we have tried to suggest here is the basis for a debate among socialist radicals about the content of a distinctly socialist practice.   The 1970s were not remarkable for this kind of debate; our hope is that the 1980s will be seen as the decade for such argument and for a radical community work practice to emerge.

NOTES

1 F. Engels, The Housing Question, (1887) in K. Marx and F. Engels, 'Selected Works', Foreign Languages Publishing House, Moscow, 1962.
2 See particularly, 'The Poverty of the improvement Programme', revised edn, Community Development Project Political Economy Collective, 1977; and 'Whatever Happened to Council Housing?', Community Development Project Information and Intelligence Unit, 1976.
3 See particularly, Cynthia Cockburn, 'The Local State', Pluto Press, 1977.
4 Notably that of Manuel Castells.   See his 'City, Class and Power', Macmillan, 1978.
5 See Jo Freeman, 'The Politics of Women's Liberation', Longman, 1978.

6 Feminist perspectives and practice

Gill Dixon, Chris Johnson, Sue Leigh and
Nicky Turnbull

INTRODUCTION

Who we are and our perspectives

The women writing this paper are community workers in the north-east
of England.   As socialists and feminists we believe that the dominant power relations within our society are based in capitalism and
in patriarchy and because of this most of the women we work with are
doubly oppressed.   As community work is about challenging power
structures so people can have more power and control over their own
lives it is necessary to understand and challenge both of these.
To challenge patriarchy alone is to ignore both the enormous oppression capitalism places on us all – men and women – and the fact that
patriarchy is useful to capitalism.   To challenge only capitalism
is to ignore the fact that patriarchy pre-existed capitalism and
will not automatically go away with the advent of a socialist
society. (1)
   Although feminists, we are not separatists, neither do we claim
to speak for all feminists.   There is no one feminist viewpoint,
any more than there is one socialist viewpoint.   We believe that
women suffer oppression as a result of being women and that it is
good for women to organise on their own – partly because sometimes
we need to be away from men to develop our own confidence, ways of
thinking and working, and partly because sometimes it is more useful
to us and more fun.   We also believe that feminist insights are of
value to men as well as to women, that it is worth trying to influence men, and that our ways of working can benefit oppressed men as
well as oppressed women.   Much has been written about the class
position of women and their role in social reproduction, of the way
men and women are socialised into roles and of the way power is per-
petuated through structures. (2)   What seems to be lacking is working how this theoretical understanding can inform and influence our
practice.

The language of and concepts in the paper

We are writing for people practising community work.   We are also
writing for a male, as well as a female audience.   Many radical men
reading the chapter will, we believe, subscribe to the theory;   they

acknowledge the oppression of women that takes place at all levels of society, but this does not always alter their practice and this is a book primarily about practice.   Hence we have spelled out some things that are self-evident to women.

We may be accused of using language and concepts that would not be intelligible to ordinary working-class women.   This may be true but we would argue that they are unlikely to buy a book of this type at this price.   We are, in addition, struggling with a language that is man-made. (3)

We begin our chapter with a brief look at women in the north-east and at the relationship between the women's liberation movement and community work, then go on to look with a feminist perspective at some areas of community work.

WOMEN AND CAPITALISM IN THE NORTH-EAST

The ideas put forward in this paper have come mainly from our col-lective experience of working in the north-east of England.   Tyne-side, Wearside and Teesside have been dominated by the growth and decline of heavy industry (coal mining, ship building, heavy engineering).   The reports of the Benwell CDP have shown clearly how capital and the ruling class control the region and dominate the lives of the men and women living there. (4)   The dominance of capital and its interests and the oppression it exerts on men and women, are both so clearly seen here that it is impossible to ignore them either in our analysis of the oppression of women or in the issues we tackle as community workers.

Women in the north-east are strong in many ways.   They have an amazing ability to cope with poverty, bad housing and hardship and to be resourceful and imaginative.   Yet as a group they suffer enormous cultural oppression from male institutions such as the working men's clubs, and from cultural norms, such as having to be in to cook the man's tea.   If men serve capital in the north-east how much more do women serve men.   None of this may be unique to the north-east but by comparison with the experience of our sisters who work in London, it seems more extreme here.   Feminism and its ideas seem to have had little impact on working-class women.   Job opportunities are poor and there is little choice offered to a teen-age girl contemplating the future.   With few jobs, and even fewer well-paid interesting ones and with housing largely provided in nuclear family units, the option of marriage and children may well look the most interesting prospect going.

THE WOMEN'S LIBERATION MOVEMENT AND COMMUNITY WORK

Undoubtedly the women's movement has been an important force in the lives of many women community workers and has influenced the way we think about community work.   Women's groups do not assume there is a single correct way that can be learned and preached at people, but start from the point of personal experience.   We start with a per-son's own specific experience of oppression because that experience is valuable in itself and is most easy to identify with.   The

women's liberation movement (WLM) has taught us to see that process
and goal are inseparable.   We cannot achieve real liberating change
in the dominant power relations in a society by working in an
oppressive manner;   by doing so we will only replace one elite by
another.   Because the WLM is essentially a movement of women
struggling together, it helps us see our own oppression.   We are
not outside 'enablers' helping the 'deprived' community.   Although
we accept that we experience oppression to a differing extent, and
in some respects in different ways, yet there are things we have in
common and these have influenced the issues we take up;   for
example, women community workers' interest in health is linked to
the abuse we have all received at the hands of the health service.
On the other hand we recognise that most women community workers
have the advantage of reasonable earning power and the freedom of
choice that brings, whilst many of the women we work with are
trapped in an unenviable domestic situation with low income and poor
housing.
    As well as influencing us as workers, the WLM has given rise to a
whole range of projects like women's centres, refuges and rape
crisis centres, and both the projects themselves and their structures and ways of working offer lessons to community work.
    On a theoretical level women's analyses of specific aspects of
their oppression have shown clearly the links between it and the
interests of capitalism. (5)   Our responsibility for child-bearing
and child-rearing, for family life and caring for male workers,
gives us a special role in relation to capitalism so that questioning our oppression ultimately questions capitalism itself.   Yet
despite the theory and despite initiatives like refuges, the women's
movement has largely affected middle-class women and our forms of
expressing (writing, politics, drama) are often elitist and our
language alienating.   Add to this the bra-burning image we get from
the media and it is not surprising that most working-class women
feel we are nothing to do with them and their lives.
    Nevertheless community work needs the influence of the women's
movement and feminist politics because developments within it, however necessary in themselves and however radical in intention, have
reinforced the low status of women.

WAYS OF ORGANISING: THE DEBATE ABOUT STRUCTURE

As feminists we are aware of the oppression certain structures can
entail.   We can see every day that women are virtually excluded
from every major institution of power in society.   The models of
organisation given by these powerful institutions have, however,
been absorbed quite uncritically into the practice of community
organisations;   so much so that community work is often as oppressive and exclusive as the power structure it seeks to challenge.
Many women working together have sought to create relationships
which try to help every individual to maximise her contribution
rather than impose the will of the few onto the many through the
centralisation of knowledge.   But in rejecting traditional hierarchical forms of organisation we are left with the question of what
to put in their place.   No group is structureless and in the

absence of formal structure, informal structures will develop which
can be even more exclusive as there is no way of challenging
them. (6)   The answer is not simply to abandon structure but to try
and create structures which enable everyone to participate.   In
community work we are often constrained in our practice by external
pressure and demands (from funding bodies, management committees,
local people) which make it difficult to experiment and take risks
in our work.   Various groups within the women's movement have had
more freedom to experiment and we can learn from their experiences.

The Cleveland Women's Centre, for example, went through just such
a period of experimentation.   It is only in retrospect that we can
see that the particular struggles and difficulties may have a more
general relevance.   The women founding the centre fell into an
acceptance of what they understood were feminist perspectives: no
patriarchal or hierarchical structures, no small clique pulling the
strings, everything to be open, collective and democratic.   But
despite achieving great successes, it soon became clear that the
centre was not operating wholly successfully.   Women came to meetings, listened passively and went away feeling alienated;   a small
number took the majority of the work and responsibility.   They had
good open meetings but a tiny handful of women met separately as a
steering group, so that the smaller group felt unappreciated and
abused and the larger group felt excluded.   Decision-making was not
clear - who made what decisions and who carried them through.   Differences of opinion on issues connected with the centre were felt as
personal disagreements because there was no structure through which
to express dissatisfaction.

These symptoms only gradually became apparent.   They began to
realise that it was a mistake to equate structure with hierarchy.
Without a formal structure all that happened was the emergence of an
informal structure based on personal relationships.   Outsiders felt
cheated because although they experienced an 'in group' the dominant
myth was that no such thing existed.   Better to assert who is who,
what they do and how one can fit into this structure rather than to
deny its existence, thereby denying right of entry.   Eventually
they adopted a constitution which tried to express their feminist
ideals.   For example, the question of elections was left open as
many people felt that this procedure intimidated women;   in the
first year the co-ordinating group was agreed by discussion and consensus.

From our experiences no one right way of doing things has emerged.   The Cleveland group chose to have a rotating chair and found
this structure successful, whilst Newcastle Inner City Forum (a
group concerned with inner city policy) found this structure unsatisfactory as it left the secretary to the group (whose paid job it
was to service it) with all the power and responsibility.

Another example of an attempt to share knowledge and power
amongst those involved comes from a housing co-operative.   Representatives of this and other co-ops form the management committee of
a secondary housing co-operative, a body that employs workers with
specialist technical skills to help co-ops buy, improve and manage
their own properties.   Committee meetings often have long agendas,
with complex information on money and various negotiations being
presented.   It is hard for members to keep up with and understand

all the changing information and therefore hard for them effectively
to control the workers and the direction of the organisation.   This
is inevitably a problem when some people work five days a week in an
organisation and others come to monthly meetings.   At the same time
the members of the co-op do not want to build up an elite within
their own group, of those who sit on management committees.   They
are trying to overcome this by having each representative serve on
the committee for a year but staggering the changeover by six
months;   thus each new representative serves alongside someone who
knows what's going on and has the confidence to question things she
or he does not understand.

In work with one
tenants' association hardly anyone came to meetings, yet dozens of
As well as looking at ways of making meetings work better we need
to be aware of structures outside meetings.   In work with one
tenants' association hardly anyone came to meetings, yet dozens of
tenants and their children would turn out regularly for lobbies of
Housing Committee meetings.   They lived in old terraced streets and
the informal network of people chatting on their doorsteps seemed to
work;   people got the information they wanted without, on the whole,
going to meetings.   These informal structures may seem undemocratic
in that there is no formal representation but in terms of participation they often involve more people than do formal associations.
Obviously there are problems.   It is difficult to challenge power
within these systems, and responsibility often falls on the shoul-
ders of one or two key people;   but community workers should, perhaps, direct their thinking to ways of making these structures work
better rather than try and impose other, more formalised, structures
on people.   The debate on structure raises many questions which we
have not really begun to answer. (7)   Traditional forms of organisation are formal and intimidating;   the emphasis is on getting
through the business.   This leaves many people unable to contribute
and often results in them feeling their presence is worthless so
they leave the group.   We seem trapped between two pressures;   the
pressure of time, the need to get through the business without which
the group will not achieve its purpose and the pressure of needing
the involvement of a lot of people.   Our campaigns need good organisation but they also need mass support.   We have to find a way of
reconciling these pressures because people will not give their time
to things that do not produce satisfactory results;   but neither
will they stay involved if they feel alienated and unneeded.

In the past, radical community work has tended to ignore the
'process' part of community work, to see it as non-political,
partly, perhaps, because early community work theorists, such as
Dr Batten, who were concerned with 'process', attempted to present
community work as apolitical.   Feminist analysis shows clearly that
process is political, and needs urgent consideration if our campaigns are to achieve their aims.

ISSUES AND PRIORITIES

The majority of community work is carried on with women - a fact
which is recognised by many community workers, though without its
implication being greatly considered.   Currently, fashionable
trends in community work define radical practice as being that which

is related to the 'hard' issues of the factory floor, i.e. work with trade unions, trades councils and on unemployment.   Next down in this hierarchy comes housing, then the 'soft' issues such as play, childcare and the health services.   These assumptions about impor- tance are reflected in much current community work literature.

We believe however that the 'soft' issues are of equal importance and that such categorisation should be rejected by men as well as women.   To accept such categorisation is dangerous because it obscures the links between our oppression as workers and our oppres- sion as consumers.   In particular it obscures the role of the state as provider of services to capitalism as well as to consumers. (8) Again it is important not just to see all these links in theory but to begin to develop them in practice.   We are not arguing against work on employment and housing;   these are obviously vitally neces- sary.   But, in working in the community, we find women in particu- lar often expressing interest in other issues, such as children's play and nursery facilities.   Yet a vociferous community work lobby has not developed on these issues.   Is this because with the pres- ent division of labour they are seen primarily as the responsibility of women, and women do not have a powerful political voice in our society?   Certainly, in ignoring them we are contributing to a sit- uation where many women are stuck in a life style over which they have little choice or control, and we mask the real extent of unem- ployment and cuts in service.

Without good nursery provision women who wish to work will never be able to take full advantage of job opportunities and be able to compete equally with men in the labour market, having rather to rely on poorly paid, low status, part-time work.   Nor will services for the elderly, the sick, or the disabled ever be adequate so long as women are at home to fill the gaps in state provision.   Governments talk of taking caring back to the community;   they never say that 'community' means 'women' - that women are to be unpaid carers for people whom society prefers to forget about.

We have argued that radical practice is not only about the issues we work on but also the way we work.   Our work with women can be a liberating experience or can subtly reinforce their role in society. For example, our work around health care can be concerned with more service provision or it can also be about what sort of service we want and by whom it is controlled.   As the authors of 'In and Against the State' (9) argued, one of the reasons people do not fight more strongly against cuts in services is that they were never 'their' services in the first place.

What follows is a discussion of different issues and the impact on these of a specifically feminist perspective.

Health

Of all community work issues, health is the one which has developed in a way most clearly linked to the women's movement.   The seeds of this lie in the struggle for adequate maternity, contraceptive and abortion services, i.e. the services through which women exercise control over their physical reproduction.   The reasons why this struggle should have evolved as the particular focus of the women's

health movement are easily understood: in contrast to all other
health service consumers, most women approaching these particular
services are not, by any definition, sick, and they are therefore in
a favourable position to evaluate (from a political perspective) the
services they receive. (10)   Women's role as carers has also confronted them with the inadequacies of health provision.

The majority of community health work at a neighbourhood level is
carried out with groups of women, and much of it begins specifically
with women's health issues: notably menopause groups; campaigns
for well women clinics; and less obvious, perhaps, groups concerned
with diet, keep fit, and the over-prescribing of tranquillisers.
At one level, these are areas of work in which neighbourhood-based
community workers can, and increasingly do, develop work very effectively.   But at another, broader, level, there are some fundamental
questions to be asked about the way in which the NHS treats women,
and their ability to influence it.   In line with other state services, health services are almost completely controlled by men, even
though the NHS itself is one of the largest employers of women.   It
is in the positions of power and influence over resources that men
dominate, as doctors, consultants, teachers and administrators. (11)
It is here that battles for well women clinics, or changes in the
pattern of antenatal care, for example, have to be fought, often
with people inherently unsympathetic to women's particular needs,
and hostile to anything which threatens to undermine their traditional, strong hold over medical services.

At the same time, the whole orientation of the NHS is away from
the community and towards the expensive high technology of curative,
hospital services.   Ninety per cent of health service queries are
dealt with at the primary care (i.e. community) level, where they
receive less than five per cent of Area Health Authority
budgets. (12)   Decisions over these resources are made largely in
accordance with the wishes and influence of hospital consultants,
often to meet their clinical and professional ambitions.

A striking example of the kind of power exercised through the NHS
lies in the field of mental health.   Women are major consumers of
drugs, such as Valium and Librium, and hence they are an important
source of profit to the drug companies.   Such drugs are prescribed
by GPs frequently as a matter of course, to alleviate the stress and
anxiety caused by the social and economic conditions under which
women live: poor housing, low incomes, isolation, having 'two'
jobs.   The response of the NHS to these problems is to act as an
agent of social control: to keep women functioning so that they can
continue to bring up their families, whilst suppressing any tendency
to question, or rebel.   We are not suggesting that GPs consciously
make these decisions, but without any wider debate about the context
in which such decisions are taken, this is the net effect.

Even radical opinion has a fair way to go in understanding how
policies affect women's health specifically.   The Black Report,
'Inequalities in Health', shows that the difference in life expec-
tancy between social classes has actually widened since 1948, despite thirty years of the NHS, but it does not focus on the position
of women.   Current debates on the links between unemployment and
health tend to highlight almost exclusively male unemployment, without having regard either to female job loss, or to the additional

stresses imposed on women whose menfolk lose their occupations and incomes.

In addressing health as an issue in our work, therefore, we cannot do so without regard for the wider context.   Self-help alternatives at neighbourhood level are valuable and essential starting points, as are campaigns to keep hospitals open, or to pro- mote new services.   But we must also question the global decisions over resources and policy being taken by those who control the health service;   and ultimately ask in whose interests the NHS is actually run.

Employment

Although crucially important as an issue, this is too often seen in terms of male employment.   This perpetuates assumptions about the nature of women's employment (the 'pin-money' concept) and means that in employment struggles women are often see not in their own right but as support for men.

At a seminar in January 1981, Maureen Williams cited an example of this when she described the response of local women to the strike of Dunlop workers in Speke. (14)   Instead of setting up a 'wives'' support group, as requested by the men, they established a Dunlop Women's Action Group, comprising women workers, mothers, wives and local residents and focusing on issues as they affected women.   The interests of women as workers and women as family members were seen to be indistinguishable;   but this is a rarity.   Fights to keep factories open are often so crucial for the whole community and so little time is available to organise a campaign, that women's issues are felt to be diversions and women themselves acquiesce in such demarcation.

The trade union movement itself is male-dominated and community workers, struggling to gain credibility with trade unions, find it difficult to raise women's issues.   Yet in a time of economic depression and high unemployment women suffer triply - as the people who have to feed and clothe a family on an insufficient income;   as an easily expendable, unseen part of the workforce and as the prime users of services that are being severely cut back. Women also have an important perspective on the employment issue in addition to that normally seen by male workers.   It is women who are the majority of home-workers, the part-time workers, the non- unionised workers, and it is women who, on the whole, suffer the worst of low pay.   Furthermore, women's lack of involvement in unions isn't because they are uninterested or apathetic (some of them may be, but so are many men) but because unions are geared to full-time male employment preferably located in one workplace. They cannot cope generally with female employment where the paid job is only one of a woman's jobs, with part-time work, or with occupa- tions like home helps where the workers (nearly all women) are dis- persed across a city.

Community work around employment often focuses on the factory floor, which reinforces the separation of work and community.   But working with women on employment often arises directly from work in the community.   The Kennington Cleaners Co-op in South London, for

example, arose from a mother and toddler group; and in Newcastle
the Hardwork Cleaners Co-op set itself up partly as a response by a
group of women living in one area to the exploitation they experienced as employees of commercial cleaners.   Co-ops are not the
answer to unemployment, but in a situation where women have little
opportunity to do more than low-paid, low-status work, co-ops offer
them an element of control over their wages and working conditions
which they would never otherwise experience.

Women's employment is also inseparable from the issue of childcare, and ultimately this will impinge on men's working patterns
too, if sharing paid work and family responsibilities become the
norm.   But this will not happen without a radical change of attitudes; and it is as much for men community workers as for women to
challenge the assumptions and practices of the groups they work with
and to support them in looking for alternatives.

Housing

Traditionally, community work has concentrated often on campaigns
connected with council housing.   We fight for more and better
public housing, but how often do we question the basic design of
housing, nearly all of which, public or private, is built to accommodate the nuclear family?   There is no room for the extended
family (indeed there are so few five-bedroomed council houses that
it is difficult even to accommodate all the large nuclear families);
no room for groups of people living together;   no concept of living
units where some space is communal and some private;   nothing in
fact except traditional family houses, unless perhaps you are in a
'special needs' group and somehow not 'normal'.

This type of housing isolates women from each other - indeed from
anyone else other than their partners and their children.   It
leaves women seeing their difficulties as personal failures with
little opportunity to meet others and to see their oppression as
something shared and imposed on them.   The design of new estates
often separates us from each other more than did the old terraced
housing.   It also tends to separate housing from other facilities,
such as shops, thus lessening our chance of contact with each other
outside the home and contributing further to our isolation.

In simple terms, council housing policy is conceived in terms of
being 'a roof over your head' and fails to recognise that facilitating social interaction is as essential a component of housing design
as the house itself.   Councils seem to be adept at placing people
in need in socially isolated situations, such as rehousing women
from refuges into dismal blocks on the edge of towns.   Again, by
giving people an increased element of control over their lives, co-
ops can rescue this situation, for some.   In Newcastle, a single
parent's co-operative is in the process of establishing shared
childcare as well as communal facilities such as a freezer and bulk
buying.   But this is an isolated example;   the experience of this
kind of alternative needs to be incorporated into council and governmental thinking.

Play

Play is far and away the commonest community work activity, but
paraodxically, in the community hierarchy of issues, it is also the
least regarded.   As feminists, we should not accept this low status
as a fact of life, but question its validity and seek to reinterpret
some of the priorities on which such status is based.

   The key fact about play as a community work issue is that it is,
almost without exception, something which is perceived by women as a
principal need.   This should not surprise us.   For women, particularly single parents living in highly inadequate urban environments,
the lack of appropriate play facilities is an unending source of
stress as they struggle to cope equally with the demands of their
kids when at home, and anxiety about them when they are out.   The
need for a secure play environment can take precedence over the need
for improved housing conditions; we should not underestimate
mothers' abilities to determine their own priorities in the light of
such circumstances.

   In addition, play is also usually something about which 'something can be done'.   It is probably the easiest area over which to
secure positive action from the local authority.   In downgrading
play as an issue, we are in fact denying women this power to achieve
change and to achieve it according to their realistic perceptions of
what their situation is.   Neither they nor we can transform the
power over production, the power relationships between men and
women, or the nature and control of services overnight.   What we
can do is to recognise that the informal, mutual support groupings
of women concerned with issues such as play have a vital role in
developing their confidence and consciousness that changes for the
better can be achieved.

   At a slightly different level, the experience of youth workers in
developing 'Working with Girls' conferences can reveal opportunities
to challenge prejudices and attitudes.   Although organising such an
event in Sunderland provoked unexpected responses (both hostile and
supportive), it has enabled the idea of positive discrimination for
girls in play and youth provision to be raised in an area where play
is frequently equated with 'kickabout areas' and five-a-side football.

WORKING WITH MALE COLLEAGUES

Women in employment generally suffer indirect discrimination because
of their family commitments.   We are not as easily able to attend
union meetings after work; if our children are sick, it is usually
the mother who stays at home to nurse them; many women have a gap
in their employment record for the years they have spent having
children.   These problems are common to women in all fields of employment and they are just as real for women in community work.   An
additional problem for women in community work is that commitment
and credibility are often measured by visible presence.   Our male
colleagues do not seem to be aware of the pressures placed on us by
partners not involved in our work (or even those partners who are!),
and by the demands of our children; they cannot understand that we

have difficulties in coping with four office evening meetings per
week on top of a full week's work.   Our home commitments are often
belittled by male colleagues, and this has led in some cases to a
downward spiral where, ultimately, all of our work is belittled.
Few - if any - women workers have a full-time housekeeper to cook,
clean and look after the children, yet many men only work incredibly
long hours because they have this service.

One of the things the women's movement has taught us is that personal politics are important.   We cannot divorce the way we work
with our colleagues from the way we work in the community.   Indeed,
it is as we recognise and confront our problems as women workers
that our perception of women's issues generally will be sharpened
and our ability to raise these issues in other areas of our work
will be strengthened.   Our experience has been that many male community workers are very good at preaching socialist principles at
their colleagues;   they're right behind campaigns supporting decent
play and childcare facilities and all those really 'important'
things - as soon as we've got unilateral nuclear disarmament/a
socialist government/troops out of Northern Ireland.   They often
fail to realise the intimidating and intolerant way in which they
present themselves to us.   If we are intimidated, how much more
will the intolerance be felt by the 'ordinary' people in the communities we are there to work with?

We must take our feminist ideas about structures and the sharing
of tasks through into our working situations.   However difficult it
may be in theory, and seemingly impossible as it often is in practice, we must not collude in male dominance.   As colleagues in the
workplace, we can be guilty of this in many ways;   we may passively
allow ourselves to become the ones responsible for the 'domestic
life' of our project, perhaps by ensuring adequate stocks of coffee,
toilet paper or stationery, or by making our workplace cleaner or
more comfortable.   By assuming such responsibilities without question, we are perpetuating the system we challenge in other areas of
our work and our lives.   If we are to combat sexism in the community, then it is important for us to be seen to be taking roles different from those expected of 'the stereotyped woman'.   Indeed, we
should not be blind to the fact that by our presence (as women community workers) we are already, even if unknowingly, challenging
some of those stereotypes.

Just as importantly, we must not collude as workers in the community.   We should question situations in which, in a tenants' organisation, for example, a man acts as chairperson or spokesperson when
the majority of the people in the group are women.   We must support
women to be as much a recognisable part of the group as they are the
unseen workers in the background.

In male-dominated groups there is often a concentration on the
product, the immediate tangible goal, to the exclusion of the process.   To work in this way will not in the end achieve real change
in power relationships - yet there is a balance to be struck.
Experiences of success (in terms of definite concrete goals) are
important to the groups we work with both in their own right and as
a way of building up people's confidence.   Looking at the ways in
which we have developed confidence is important.   If community work
is about people gaining confidence and taking power then we need to

think about the lessons we ourselves have learned and the ways in
which they might be applicable to community work practice.   Also we
must look at the ways we use confidence once we've gained it; if we
use it to put others down in order to get our point of view carried,
it is not much of a gain.   The women's movement has taught us that
it is all right to say 'I don't know'.   This is not an excuse for
incompetence, but a recognition that we cannot always know the
answers.   In saying we don't know, we permit others to do the same.
Male-dominated groups of committed workers often don't accept this.
To participate you have to be competent and confident; to question
is to have your commitment questioned by others.   We know that (in
theory at least) in the women's movement we can have room to explore
ideas and feelings and to be insecure, and this is something we must
pass on to our male colleagues.

Being involved in community action can lead to women seeing themselves differently; it can create tensions in the home as women
think about and challenge the role they have always accepted.   This
can lead to a delicate situation - on the one hand we are working to
help women to see themselves as people in their own right, and not
'just' as wives and mothers, whilst on the other hand we must not
devalue these roles that many women have no choice about adopting.
Nor must we devalue those who choose not to extend their activities
into those fields.   Feminism, like community work, is about examining the options available, making further options available if none
of the existing ones answer the needs, and finally allowing individuals to make the choice they want.   By devaluing housework and
motherhood, either consciously or subconsciously, we are belittling
these options.   We must be aware that, if there is a breakdown of
the family that can be attributed to involvement in community
action, we may be called upon to support the family through that
crisis, and in responding to that call we must handle it sensitive-
ly.   Helping women in our communities to develop their own support
is one way to challenge, but not destroy, women's views of themselves.

In conclusion, we believe that we must all be aware of the limitations we bring to bear on our work simply by being who we are.
We must constantly re-evaluate our practice and the way in which we
interpret issues; it is no good preaching a vague sympathy with
feminism and the women's movement whilst perpetuating the dominance
of male issues in the work we undertake and the way it is pursued.
Most of us would accept that we are 'community workers' because we
seek to challenge the processes and decisions that affect our lives
and the lives of those around us and we wish to see a more just and
egalitarian society.   But this will never be achieved unless there
is a more effective consciousness of the existing inequalities
between male and female, black and white, and the ways in which they
experience oppression.   Challenging us for our 'passivity' will
achieve little.   Our male colleagues must become more prepared to
listen than to talk and to follow rather than to lead.   Then, perhaps, we will begin to see a truly feminist influence on community
work, beyond the limited horizons of so-called 'women's issues'.

The authors of this chapter would like to thank Wear Women and the
Lambeth Women Community Workers' Group for access to their material;
women at the ACW Women and Community Workers Conferences in Liverpool and Sheffield for letting us draw on their discussions;
Marjorie Mayo for reading the chapter and making helpful comments;
and Blanche Callan, Carol Glass and Evelyn Rae for typing our innum-
erable drafts.

NOTES

1 See, for example, F. Engels, 'The Origin of the Family, Private
   Property and the State', Lawrence & Wishart, 1972.
2 See, for example, Mary Farmer, 'The Family', Longman, 1970.
3 Dale Spender, 'Man Made Language', Routledge & Kegan Paul, 1980.
4 See, for example, 'The Making of a Ruling Class', Benwell Community Project Final Report Series 6, Benwell Community Project,
   Newcastle upon Tyne, 1978.
5 J. Cowley et al., 'Community or Class Struggle?', Stage One,
   1977.
6 See J. Freeman, 'The Tyranny of Structurelessness', 1970 (mimeo-
   graph).
7 See, however, S. Rowbotham, L. Segal and H. Wainwright, 'Beyond
   the Fragments', Pluto Press, 1981.
8 See Cynthia Cockburn, 'The Local State', Pluto Press, 1977,
   pp. 52-61.
9 London-Edinburgh Weekend Return Group, 'In and Against the
   State', Pluto Press, 1981, pp. 52-61.
10 These issues are explored more fully in the chapter on Women,
   Medicine and Social Control: the case of the NHS, in Lesley
   Doyal, 'The Political Economy of Health', Pluto Press, 1979.
11 To cite some examples: the national average for women practising as GPs is 15 per cent and they are usually to be found in
   part-time posts. Newcastle Area Health Authority has twenty-
   four members; five are women, only one of whom is a professional nominee. At senior consultancy level, the ratio is nineteen
   men to one woman. Surprisingly, men figure in greater propor-
   tions in traditionally 'female' sectors; the nursing staff is
   divided equally between men and women, and men hold three of the
   top eleven nursing posts.
12 Of course, more is spent on primary health services via GPs,
   dentists, etc. but these figures are never published.
13 'Inequalities in Health': Report of a Research Working Party
   chaired by Sir Douglas Black, Department of Health and Social
   Security, London, 1980.
14 'Women in Community Work', day seminar at the Institute of Extension Studies in Liverpool, 17 January 1981. See ACW Talking
   Point, no. 25, May 1981, Association of Community Workers,
   London.

Part II Issues and strategies

7 Community work and the elderly
Chris Jones, Tony Novak and Chris Phillipson

This chapter will present a critique of community work attitudes
towards the elderly.   We shall both review the present crisis in
the welfare state and its implications for older people, and explore
a range of possibilities for the practice of community work with the
elderly.

COMMUNITY WORK AND THE ELDERLY

Despite the increased proportion of older people in the population,
community workers have had but limited involvement with the
elderly. (1)   The work of Task Force and Newcastle-upon-Tyne's
Search Project are obvious exceptions to this trend;   in general,
however, older people have received little attention in the growth
of community work literature and practice.   Four main factors have
inhibited this area of work.   Firstly, activities with older people
figure only fleetingly in the various contexts which provide the
historical base to community work (e.g. social work and community
development).   Moreover, some of the early activities depart only
marginally from a broader voluntary tradition of regarding the
elderly as objects of good deeds. (2)
   Secondly, there has been little understanding amongst activists
about the role of the state in defining the way in which ageing is
viewed.   The association of old age with 'deterioration' and
'dependency' has been enshrined within the organisation of state
services and facilities.   Unfortunately, these definitions have
often been adopted quite uncritically by workers, who see the
elderly as incapable of the kind of involvement characteristic of
other age and/or social groups.
   Thirdly, it needs to be remembered that more than two-thirds of
people over 75 are women, many of whom will be physically disabled.
Studies on women and community work are relatively few.   Those
which do exist often make no reference at all to one of the most
significant groups within the female population . (3)
   Finally, there are a number of factors associated with growing
old (particularly in a capitalist society) which raise an important
challenge for community workers.   Problems of physical disability
combined with low income and poor housing are prevalent amongst the
elderly population.   Older people may also experience more general
environmental problems because they frequently reside in inner-city

areas, and experience wholesale economic and social decline.
Material factors such as these may have an important influence on
political behaviour. Poor health, for example, combined with low
income, may make it difficult for older people to attend meetings
regularly. Moreover, with only a minority of older people living
in households with a car, the availability and cost of public transport may be crucial in affecting a person's level of community involvement. The influence of these factors will be reinforced by
cultural stereotypes of ageing. Older people, for example, are
often presented as apathetic and indifferent to social and political
issues: voting only 'according to habit'. Worse still, there is,
it is often argued, an inherent conservatism accompanying old age,
with people beyond 60 or 65 becoming disinterested in the world
beyond their home and family. We would argue that stereotypes such
as these should be challenged by community workers. Moreover, they
should resist views which see the elderly as a distinct and separate
group from the wider population. Many of the difficulties facing
older people - problems of poverty, poor housing or social isolation
- are similar to those faced by other groups in society. Before
considering the range of initiatives which community workers can
develop, the effect of current state policies towards the elderly
will be reviewed.

STATE POLICIES AND THE ELDERLY (4)

If we were to ask a group of people to identify the least well off
section of society, there is a good chance that they would identify
the elderly. There is no shortage of evidence to support this
view. Around 2 million old people live at or below the poverty
line. Nearly 20 per cent of pensioners get supplementary benefits
and at least 600,000 pensioners do not claim the benefits to which
they are entitled. The elderly are not a homogeneous group, and it
would be a mistake to assume that the experience of poverty in old
age is common to all, or that old age in itself is a 'cause' of
poverty. The crucial factor affecting the experience of growing
old in Britain is that of class, and it is class which, as in working life, determines both the quality of life and the quantity of
resources which the individual receives. In this section we focus
our attention on the experience of the working-class old.
   The past ten years have seen a steady deterioration in the living
standards and conditions of the working class as a whole and the
elderly working class in particular. The state pension has never
been adequate for a comfortable and easy life in old age; still
less will it be so as government policy shifts its emphasis and resources in favour of private occupational pension schemes. For a
largely upper middle-class clientele, private nursing homes, clinics
and hospitals and private pension and insurance schemes flourish.
   Government policy actively encourages this growth, to the detri-
ment of the state welfare system and with the effect of creating
further divisions within the population. Yet for many millions of
older people state benefits provide the only source of income, and
leave very little margin for manoeuvre beyond a basic subsistence.
In the past ten years the steady increase in the prices of basic

necessities - of fuel, housing costs and food - have further reduced
this margin. Many thousands of older people now spend their
winters confined to one room, afraid to heat the rest of the house,
afraid often to spend what is necessary to maintain their health.

Cuts in public expenditure have increased the problems faced by
older people. Surveys by the Personal Social Services Council
(itself a victim of government cuts) (5) and by New Society (6)
reveal the extent to which services such as meals-on-wheels and home
helps have been a favourite target for economies. Many authorities
report the closure of residential homes, and the abandonment of
plans for building new ones; reductions in staffing levels are also
increasingly common. Expenditure has been curtailed in areas which
directly affect the quality of life in residential homes. Westminster Council saved a pitiful £1,000 by discontinuing the sweets
and tobacco issue in its old people's homes. Other authorities
report ending the provision of a subsidised hairdressing service or
of newspapers.

Surveys by the Confederation of Health Service Employees
(COHSE) (7) and by researchers such as Tom Snow, (8) have revealed
the deterioration in health services for older people. On the
question of staffing in hospitals, COHSE pointed out that: (9)

> Understaffing in hospitals leaves a burden for staff that can
> become intolerable. Nurses are exhausted. Elderly people are
> left sitting about wet. One COHSE branch secretary said 'The
> nurses are so distressed by the state of the patients that they
> are pressing for industrial action.'

The shift in state expenditure away from the welfare services
towards areas such as defence and law and order has produced a keen
debate within the pensioners' movement and amongst community work
organisations. As a consequence, we are finding the emergence of
more militant forms of community organising.

POLITICAL ORGANISATION AND THE ELDERLY (10)

In Britain, a pensioners' movement started in the inter-war depression, with the founding of the National Federation of Old Age Pensioners Associations (NFOAPA). After the war (in 1953) there was
also founded the London Joint Committee of Pensioners and Trade
Unions. In the early 1970s, dissent within the NFOAPA led to the
formation of the British Pensioners and Trade Union Action Association (BPTUAA) - a group which has been active in forming links
between pensioners and the labour movement. As well as organising
national campaigns to improve the state retirement pension, deteriorating public services have provoked militant action at a local
level, as this report from Camden illustrates:

> In March we organised a successful Unity Day attended by hundreds
> of pensioners. There has been a lot of militant action in
> Camden, Kentish Town, Highgate and Hampstead. Elderly people,
> previously isolated, have joined up with one of our local groups.
> In the past year we have held regular meetings with represen-
> tatives from Camden Social Services Committee and our banner has
> been seen and our voices of protest heard in the streets and
> market places. (Camden Branch, BPTUAA)

There have been important initiatives by a limited number of community work groups. The Task Force organisation, for example, has developed twelve local centres in the London area. These offices co-ordinate a range of activities which include: work with volunteers; welfare advice and advocacy; support for pensioner action groups; liaison work with other community organisations. There is, in addition, a central office which is active in national campaigns affecting the elderly, as well as providing research and administrative support for local centres. (11)

Newcastle-upon-Tyne's Search Project was formed in 1974, to examine the take-up of benefits amongst elderly people in the inner-city area of Benwell. The project's objectives are: (12)

(1)   to experiment in new ways of advertising and spreading welfare rights for the elderly.

(2)   to develop among the elderly and those working with them a consciousness of 'welfare benefits' as 'rights' and not as 'charity'.

(3)   to prove that through such developments the material comfort of many elderly people can be markedly improved.

Search's main activities have been the running of an advice shop providing help on pensioner rights and entitlements; the production of a newsletter; guides on leisure facilities and fuel problems; research on old age; and, as with Task Force, involvement in national and regional campaigns. (13)

Britain is not alone in the development of a more radical approach to issues affecting elderly people. For example, in the case of the United States we find the rise of the Gray Panthers' movement. Founded in 1970, this organisation had by 1979 reached a membership approaching 15,000. Although originally formed to campaign against mandatory retirement, the Gray Panthers' movement eventually led a more general campaign against all forms of age-based discrimination. In a statement of principles, the group argued that: (14)

> Like racism and sexism, ageism is a destructive force that permeates our social institutions. In all our efforts to help solve societal problems, our primary goal will be to attack any manifestation of ageism, as well as racism and sexism.

The group went on to describe the need to link together both the old and the young in the campaign against ageism: (15)

> We are a group of people - old and young - drawn together by deeply felt common concerns for human liberation and social change. The old and young live outside the mainstream of society. Ageism - discrimination against persons on the basis of chronological age - deprives both groups of power and influence.

Conventions organised by the group have explored alternatives to compulsory retirement; new approaches to the health crisis; women and ageing; consciousness-raising; new politics and life styles. The Gray Panthers have also conducted campaigns on issues such as the rights of patients in nursing homes; fraud against the elderly; and regulation and reform of private pension systems.

It is uncertain whether the rapid growth of the movement will be maintained in the decade of the 1980s - in conditions perhaps less favourable than the community-orientated politics of the previous

decade.   None the less, the development of such a movement indi-
cates the capacity of older people to initiate campaigns challenging
basic assumptions about their rights and needs.

Whilst these examples from Britain and America are undoubtedly
encouraging, we should be wary of exaggerating their significance.
The elderly face formidable obstacles to mounting political and
pressure group campaigns.   Organisations composed of elderly people
may - because of illness and death - face a high turnover in their
membership.   For this reason alone, support from a community worker
may be crucial if the organisation is to exist over time.   Community workers also have a vital role to play in broadening the range
of activities in which the elderly are engaged.

COMMUNITY WORK AND THE VERY ELDERLY

There are now 2.5 million people in Britain aged over 75.   By the
year 2011, the number aged 85 and over will have increased by 62 per
cent and about 80 per cent will need help to live in their own
homes.   This is a demographic change of profound importance, one
which poses many new challenges for the community worker.   We know
from surveys (16) and reviews of the literature (17) that considerable strains are placed upon carers (women in particular) in the
tasks connected with looking after the physically and/or mentally
infirm elderly.   This is a responsibility which women (especially
those who are single) may perform in great social isolation and with
only limited support from statutory services.   Community workers
can play an important role in encouraging links amongst such women
and in helping them to campaign for better community support and
improved financial resources.   There is also a case for linking
groups at different stages of the life-cycle.   For example, campaigns against day nursery closures on the one hand, and old
people's homes on the other, tend to be conducted separately and by
different groups.   However, the combined effect of such closures is
the same, namely to increase the burden upon women and to perpetuate
their position within the sexual division of labour. (18)

It is also important to remember that old people's homes and
geriatric hospitals are themselves inside communities.   This is an
aspect often ignored by many community workers.   There has been a
tendency to reject involvement in 'total institutions' and to view
them either as unnecessary (to wither away, presumably, in a future
and better society), or the responsibility of other professional
groups (e.g. social workers).   We would argue, however, that these
institutions will not conveniently disappear.   Community workers
can raise distinctive questions about democratic organisation
inside old people's homes as well as considering broader issues
about the relationship of homes and hospitals to other community
groups and organisations.   Some educationalists, for example, have
developed outreach work, taking drama, art, and local history projects inside homes and hospitals. (19)   There is also, we would
suggest, an outreach role for the community worker, particularly in
developing new forms of organisation in the day-to-day running of
homes.

BROADENING THE BASE OF COMMUNITY ACTIVITIES

Many community workers find themselves active in areas with an
ageing population on the one hand, but with a sizeable group of
younger people on the other.   As we suggested at the beginning of
this paper, community work has tended to see work with the elderly
as having limited appeal, with older people rarely participating in
the more innovative projects mounted within communities.   For
example, Community Arts projects - silk screen printing, photog-
raphy, community newspapers, film clubs - rely heavily on the young.
If the elderly are considered, it is usually in the context of traditional items such as bingo and coach outings.   We believe that
community work should start to develop a more imaginative range of
projects involving older people.   How can the arts, for example, be
used to express the images and feelings which people have about
ageing?   What are the resources inside communities which can assist
retired or widowed people in forming new contacts and activities?
What sort of links can be formed across generations in social and
political campaigns within communities?   These are issues in which
community workers can play a vital mediating role, relating older
people to a broader network of relationships and activities than
they might previously have experienced.

DIFFERENCES WITHIN THE ELDERLY POPULATION

Finally, it will be important for community workers to move beyond
generalised notions of 'old age' or 'the elderly' and to isolate
distinctive groupings within this population.   Two examples may be
used to illustrate this theme.   First, there are major problems
faced by older people in inner-city areas.   In Inner London, for
example, an elderly person officially considered to be isolated is
only marginally more than half as likely to receive meals-on-wheels
than his or her counterpart in England as a whole, and his or her
chance of getting a home help is little better. (20)   Moreover,
life in the inner city can pose social and psychological problems
for the elderly. (21)   We would argue for a strategy which provides
survival skills for those growing old in the inner city.   Knowledge
of housing and welfare rights is vital.   It is also important to
develop skills to cope with problems arising from the early stages
of retirement and widowhood, the losses and anxieties attributed to
these periods having more profound consequences in communities where
alternative forms of support are less easy to find.
     Second, there is increasing concern for the position of elders in
ethnic minorities. (22)   This group may be particularly disadvantaged in respect of welfare and financial rights in retirement.
Research in Lewisham found that 25 per cent of elderly people
belonging to ethnic communities were receiving less than their full
entitlement to welfare benefits; an equal percentage lacked awareness about bus passes, meals-on-wheels and home care. (23)   A
survey of ethnic elders in Birmingham found that lack of knowledge
about services was particularly marked among Asian minorities.   The
survey report suggested that this was particularly apparent amongst
those who had migrated to Britain as elders, some of whom 'may never

have used certain services (for example, dental treatment), do not know where to obtain them or believe that expensive charges for services are levied.' (24)

Because of limited information about numbers and circumstances, community workers may need to organise their own surveys about the needs of the elderly in minority groups.   They will also have to consider the specific interaction between institutionalised racism and ageism: how is growing old perceived within specific racial groups?   Are negative stereotypes of ageing exacerbated by hostile racial stereotypes?   What changes will need to be made to voluntary and social services to respond to the growing number of ethnic minority elders?   The survey report from Birmingham lists the following amongst its recommendations: 'specialised day centres which take account of major ethnic and religious differences'; (25)   in-service training for staff in residential homes about the needs and cultural backgrounds of ethnic elders;   improvements in the quality of information about social and health services;   and provision of Asian and West Indian food in hospital catering and in the meals-on-wheels service.

CONCLUSION: COMMUNITY WORK AND THE PROCESS OF REDEFINING OLD AGE

In the preceding section we identified a number of specific tasks for community workers.   Community work also has a broader role in exploring the basis of a new social identity for old age.   We noted earlier in this paper that the state has traditionally defined old age as a form of dependency.   This definition is now being challenged by sections of the elderly population.   Community workers in their activities with groups of older people can assist the development of alternative perspectives on ageing and retirement.   A start to this process, albeit in a localised way, will have repercussions for national campaigns to improve both the social status and the financial position of older people.   In the present economic crisis and in a context of mass unemployment, attitudes towards retirement are being radically redefined.   Mass redundancies and early retirements are stimulating debates about the meaning of retirement and old age.   Community workers can assist this debate by encouraging groups of older people to examine both the way in which resources are distributed and dominant ideologies about growing old.   In addition, they must experiment with new methods and organisations in their work with the elderly.   We need new ways of reaching the thousands of elderly people who fail to claim the benefits to which they are entitled;   we need to experiment with new, non-institutionalised living arrangements for those living alone;   to encourage democratic forms of organisation in community day centres, social clubs and homes and hospitals;   and to encourage a broadening in the range of leisure, educational and cultural activities in which the elderly are involved.   These are issues which have been neglected by community workers who have - with exceptions - accepted dominant stereotypes of ageing.   We would urge that these be rejected and that community workers become involved in social and political campaigns which are currently being developed by older people.

NOTES

1 For a review of the background to the increase in the number of elderly people, see A. Tinker, 'The Elderly in Modern Society', Longman, 1980.
2 See G. Goetschius, 'Working with Community Groups', Routledge & Kegan Paul, 1969.
3 See, for example, M. Mayo (ed.), 'Women in the Community', Routledge & Kegan Paul, 1977.
4 For a more general analysis of the state and social policy see C. Jones and T. Novak, The State and Social Policy, in P. Corrigan (ed.), 'Capitalism, State Formation and Marxist Theory', Quartet Books, 1980.
5 Personal Social Services Council, 'Reductions in Local Authority Expenditure on the Personal Social Services', PSSC, 1980.
6 S. Weir and R. Simpson, Are the Local Authority Social Services Being Bled Dry?, 'New Society', 10 July 1980.
7 Confederation of Health Service Employees, 'In Defence of the Old', COHSE, 1981.
8 T. Snow, 'Services for Old Age: A Growing Crisis in London', Age Concern, 1981.
9 COHSE, ibid., p. 20.
10 This section draws on material from C. Phillipson, 'Capitalism and the Construction of Old Age', Macmillan, forthcoming.
11 For a valuable review of Task Force's work with pensioner groups, see Buckingham et al., 'Beyond Tea, Bingo and Condescension: the Work of Task Force with Community Groups of Pensioners', Stoke-on-Trent, Beth Johnson Foundation, 1979.
12 Newcastle Search Project, 'Welfare Rights for the Elderly', mimeo, no date.
13 Newcastle Search Project, Annual Report 1980/81.
14 Gray Panthers, Statement of Principles, in B. Hess, 'Growing Old in America', Transaction Books, 1976, p. 462.
15 Ibid., p. 463.
16 Equal Opportunities Commission, 'The Experience of Caring for Elderly and Handicapped Dependents: A Survey Report', EOC, 1980.
17 C. Phillipson, Women in Later Life: Patterns of Control and Subordination, in B. Hutter and G. Williams, 'Controlling Women: The Normal and the Deviant', Croom Helm, 1981.
18 This argument is developed further in Phillipson, ibid.
19 F. Glendenning (ed.), 'Outreach Education and the Elders: Theory and Practice', Stoke-on-Trent, Beth Johnson Foundation, 1980.
20 See T. Snow, op. cit. An isolated elderly person is defined as one whose relatives are not normally in close enough contact to be available for basic personal and household needs.
21 C. Phillipson, Boredom in Benwell, 'New Age', Winter 1980, pp. 29-32.
22 F. Glendenning (ed.), 'The Elders in Ethnic Minorities', Stoke-on-Trent, Beth Johnson Foundation, 1979.
23 C. Kippax, 'A Step into the Unknown', Lewisham Age Concern, 1978.
24 All Faiths for One Race, 'Elders of the Minority Ethnic Groups', Birmingham AFFOR, 1981, p. 41.
25 Ibid., p. 39.

8 Policies for community care in the context of mass unemployment

Martin Loney

Involving the community - using volunteers - getting people to
help people - is not a 'cheap alternative'. Volunteers
are never going to replace professional workers. But as everyone in the caring profession knows, demand is always going to
outstrip provision.... For instance, not only is it kinder to let
elderly people remain in their own homes with neighbourhood support, it costs far less than residential care. (Linda Chalker,
1978) (1)

Compulsion could remove the stigma of being unwanted and useless,
which is too often the hallmark of present government voluntary
schemes. (Sir Hugh Fraser, 1981) (2)

Of course, we have been misrepresented, even roundly abused.
Our approach is betrayed as trying to get welfare on the cheap;
as an affront to social workers and social service departments;
as an attempt to replace skilled professional people with well-
meaning or even non-existent volunteers; or in the imposition of
insupportable burdens on hardpressed families. (Patrick Jenkin,
1981) (3)

Successive governments have urged the virtues of community care and
the do-it-yourself ethic is by no means the prerogative of the Conservative Party. David Ennals, Secretary of State for Social Services in the last Labour government, argued in 1976: (4)

The thought that the responsibility for an elderly person is not
theirs - that 'mum' is not theirs but is the Social Service
Department's - that's not right.... We need more self-help.

In the same year former Liberal leader Jo Grimond offered his own
blueprint for a caring society: (5)

It will be necessary for individuals to do more for themselves.
... The first step (is) to reduce non-productive bureaucracies -
and ... the number of social workers and the resources which they
use.

This all-party commitment to encouraging the helpless to help themselves is, in part, a reflection of a growing concern over the
rising costs of state welfare provision. Expenditure on social
services has risen rapidly and continuously this century, from 4.2
per cent of GNP in 1910, to 12.7 per cent in 1931, 16.1 per cent in
1951, 17.6 per cent in 1961 and 28.8 per cent in 1975. (6) The
scale of this last increase gave a particular urgency to the

question of containing costs.   The level of public sector spending
was now thought to threaten the prosperity of the economy as a
whole.   In the 1976 economic crisis the issue of public spending
was to the fore and in his 'Letter of Intent' to the IMF, the Chan-
cellor of the Exchequer, Denis Healey, committed the government to a
continued reduction in public spending: (7)

> An essential element of the Government's strategy will be a con-
> tinued and substantial reduction over the next few years in the
> share of resources required for the public sector.

The 1975 and 1976 public expenditure White Papers announced substantial cuts in the proposed rates of growth in social services
spending, while the introduction of cash limits encouraged further
savings by local authorities.   Attempts to reduce expenditure on
the personal social services took place against a background of
unmet need.   Townsend has noted the consistent failure to bring
services up to the levels laid down in DHSS guidelines: (8)

> Day care places in 1978-79 had reached only 77 per cent, 54 per
> cent and 18 per cent of the official targets set respectively for
> the elderly, the mentally handicapped and the mentally ill;   the
> number of home helps had risen to 52 per cent and of meals per
> week to 59 per cent of targets for people of 65 years of age and
> older.

Demographic forecasts indicate that the number of over-75s will increase by a fifth before the end of the century and that the number
of over-85s will double, but this has not resulted either in a cor-
responding increase in residential accommodation or in community-
based services.

The accession of a Conservative government, and the demand by
Heseltine that local authorities reduce their 1981 expenditure to
5.6 per cent below the level of 1978-9, resulted in further cutbacks
in both community-based services such as meals-on-wheels, day
centres for the elderly, home helps, nursery schemes and pre-school
playgroups and in residential provision for all groups: children,
the elderly, the physically and mentally handicapped.   Under a
smokescreen of 'community care' platitudes, government policies were
simultaneously undermining residential provision whilst decreasing
the capacity of the community-based services to provide alternative
support.

Denied appropriate housing, the elderly are compelled to seek
help from relatives or are forced into residential care or hospitals.   Alternatively they are simply left to survive as best they
can.   The periodic discovery of an old person who has died, unnoticed for several days, in conditions of primeval squalor provides
a graphic illustration of what happens to those who slip through the
welfare state's ever more inadequate net.

Wheatley has drawn attention to the stress experienced by the
relatives of the mentally infirm elderly, some 75 per cent of whom
are cared for by their own families. (9)   Westland, a former
Director of Social Services, has noted that, against an estimated
3 million handicapped people: (10)

> We know only one million of these in our local authority records;
> and we know they are often not receiving all the services they
> require.   So even if the services continued at their present
> level, they are in many ways inadequate and are not yet reaching
> the majority of those who would be eligible to receive them.

The care of the mentally handicapped, whether in the hospital or the community is particularly unsatisfactory.   Indeed as TV programmes document, with depressing regularity, treatment appears to be informed as much by the principles of Bedlam as by more contemporary thinking.   There is strong evidence that 'normalisation' programmes which place the mentally handicapped in small community-based homes result in dramatic improvements in the capabilities of the handicapped. (11)   In the long term, such treatment may be no more expensive than the maintenance of large hospitals in which many of the mentally handicapped are currently incarcerated.   In the short term, local authorities are either unwilling or unable to provide adequate community facilities leaving many with no choice but hospitalisation.   Within the NHS the power of medical and union vested interests, and the traditional neglect of this sector of care, combine to block innovation.

In practice the burden of community care falls unequally on the families of those in need: (12)

An examination of the reality of community care, in a situation where there is minimal input of statutory resources, reveals that the provision of primary caring falls not upon 'the community' but upon identifiable groups and individuals, in a way which is not necessarily equitable.   Indeed, this can be best expressed in terms of a double equation - that in practice community care equals care by the family, and in practice care by the family equals care by women.

Part of the rhetoric behind community care is a call for more effective voluntary sector involvement in meeting needs and for active links between statutory services and the community.   This is the motivation behind Social Services Secretary Patrick Jenkin's support for the patch system in social work.   The problem for Jenkin is that while the patch system may constitute an ideological vindication of Tory philosophy it can also lead into precisely that identification of the existence of a vast amount of unmet need which the government seeks to deny.   This contradiction became clear at the press conference called to launch the National Council of Voluntary Organisation's publication on patch systems. (13)   Jenkin made it clear that care in the community meant care by the community rather than by more vigorous provision of welfare services. (14) Jenkin subsequently further clarified his support for the patch system because it recognised 'the role of social workers as primarily working to create and stimulate the community to look after its own'. (15)   At the same press conference, Jennifer Joslin, a contributor to the book, attacked Islington Council's decision to centralise its social work operations.   The decision, Joslin claimed, reflected councillors' concerns about the high level of demand for services, identified by the patch system.   In short the patch system encouraged by cost-cutting Tories may, like other initiatives, prove to be a two-edged sword.   Much will depend upon the ability of social workers and community workers to use it to build alliances with local community groups, with a view to ensuring not only that clients are involved in the determination of policy and practice in the social services but also that unmet need is adequately identified and forcefully represented.

It is worth recalling that the objectives of the Community

Development Projects, set up in 1969, also included encouraging
self-reliance.   The use of community action, by local project
teams, was seen as a means of 'reaching a minority of the population
suffering from multi-deprivation and of enabling them to function
more autonomously'. (16)   The Labour Social Services Minister,
Richard Crossman, bluntly stated the objective, which was to see how
'a community can pull itself up by its own boot straps'. (17)   The
outcome of the Community Development Projects was, of course, a
radical criticism of existing government policies and a call for
measures to redistribute wealth and to control private enterprise. (18)

ORGANISING THE VOLUNTEERS

Margaret Thatcher has argued that 'the volunteer movement is at the
heart of all our social welfare provision.' (19)   The statutory
services, according to the new Tory philosophy, as expounded by the
prime minister, should primarily have a back-up role: (20)
    I'm very encouraged by the way in which local authorities,
    Directors of Social Services, the social work profession and the
    specialist press are increasingly determined to shift the empha-
    sis of statutory provision so that it becomes an enabling ser-
    vice, the statutory provision enabling the volunteers to do their
    jobs more effectively.
    In fact the government's relations with the voluntary sector have
been increasingly fraught - in spite of the instinctive conservatism
of much of the sector's leadership.   The increase in VAT to 15 per
cent, the steady decline in local authority support for voluntary
organisations - caused by central government cutbacks - the growing
demand for services from those affected by the economic slump, the
encouragement to health authorities to engage in public fund-raising, in direct competition with the voluntary sector, and the failure of the government to offer any response to the voluntary
sector's increasingly vigorous lobbying have led to a new bitterness
in relationships.   The National Council of Voluntary Organisations,
with its customary caution, noted the government's failure to put
resources behind its speeches: (21)
    Yet there is still a tinge of rhetoric in these words rather than
    hard evidence that government intends to back up its statements
    with real investment in the pluralist future which a strong vol-
    untary sector implies.... There is no doubt that many local
    authorities have made ... substantial cuts in financial aid to
    local voluntary organisations.
    Less cautiously the normally sedate Royal Association for Dis-
ability and Rehabilitation sought leave to sue the Secretary of
State for Social Services for failing to ensure that local authorities fulfilled their responsibilities to the disabled.   The particular case concerned a married couple from Wiltshire who, because
of the wife's handicap, had previously received council support so
that they could take a holiday.   Wiltshire County Council had cut
back its financial support and in defence suggested that voluntary
organisations should have provided an alternative scheme.
    In a situation where reductions in grants to the voluntary sector

were being actively considered it was inevitable that more radical
groups would be particularly vulnerable targets.   The Conservative
Council in the London Borough of Wandsworth, which has achieved a
singular reputation for mean-mindedness and vindictiveness, was one
of the first to point the way forward. (22)

Traditionally the voluntary sector has been under conservative
leadership but as government seeks to restructure the welfare state
that leadership will experience increasing pressure to adopt a more
aggressive response in defence of both client and organisational
interests.

VOLUNTEERING THE UNEMPLOYED

With the government's community care policy visibly no more than a
cloak to disguise the increasing hardship caused by public sector
cutbacks and with a voluntary sector actually gathering the courage
to attack a Conservative government, the intervention of the Commission on Youth and the Needs of the Nation could hardly have been
more timely.   Funded by the multinational Carnegie Foundation and
the National Westminster Bank the Commission, soon to announce
itself as Youth Call, began to canvas support for a scheme of
national social service for the young.

Youth Call brought together a diverse range of people, including
Alec Dickson, founder of Voluntary Service Overseas and Community
Service Volunteers, and Lady Pike, the Tory head of the WRVS.
Political backing included left-wing Labour MP Michael Meacher, and
Tory MP Anthony Steen.   (Steen founded Task Force and then subsequently sought its closure when staff refused to accept a reorgani-
sed management structure which, staff argued, was intended to cur-
tail militant advocacy of client interests over welfare rights and
other issues affecting the elderly.)   Steen is an enthusiastic
supporter of another aspect of contemporary Thatcherism - the
hiving-off of public services to private entrepreneurs; he envisages
the privatisation of a range of activities from social work services
to garbage collection and has argued in the latter context: (23)

A private contractor has no need to maintain a permanent workforce, he is less at the mercy of union demands and has the
experience to do the job more effectively.

In the same article Steen noted with enthusiasm: 'MacDonald's, the
American hamburger chain, provides school lunches in one American
state.'   In 1980 Bill Utting, the Chief Social Work Adviser to the
DHSS, made a visit to the United States to study provisions for the
purchase by government of personal social services from the private
sector.   He was concerned to explore alternative methods of social
service delivery 'that might result in greater efficiency and, in
particular, economy'. (24)

Initially Youth Call advocated a voluntary scheme of national
social service but it was clear that just as there would be rewards
for those who participated so there would be sanctions against those
who didn't: (25)

Employers will also need to be made to accept that to give pref-
erence, in a competitive labour market, to those who have completed a period of community service will be in their own long-
term interests.

Colombatto, in a paper which seeks to provide academic credibility
for the proposal, has put this point more succinctly: (26)

> An effort could be made in order to create a situation where you
> may not have particular direct material advantages by having been
> in the NWSS (Nationwide Social Service), but where there is a lot
> to lose by *not* having been in the NWSS.

None the less Youth Call argued: 'Promoting community service work
as a requirement for all young people would be to risk alienating
them.' (27)

By the time Youth Call launched itself publicly however the position of its chairman was that the arguments between a compulsory and
a voluntary scheme were 'evenly balanced'. (28)   By this time the
bandwagon was gathering speed and support for a compulsory scheme of
national service had been advocated by Sir Hugh Fraser, a Conservative MP, in 'The Times'.   Fraser's proposal was free of some of the
humanistic wrappings of the Youth Call scheme: (29)

> The cost of rehabilitating housing, sewers, railways and indus-
> trial dereliction would run to thousands of millions of pounds
> and at going rates for unionised labour are unlikely ever to be
> swiftly or effectively undertaken by any government elected by
> tax payers.   Yet undertaken these tasks must be.... Purposeful
> national service must ask youth for sacrifice.

Why a society which can afford to spend billions of pounds on
defence and a government which can return £4,500 million to upper-
income tax payers within months of being elected cannot afford to
repair the nation's sewers at union rates of pay, or look after its
elderly without conscripting its youth, is unclear as is the argument that youth service might cement national unity: (30)

> At a time when we hear a great deal about 'two nations' and
> 'divisiveness' it can be hoped that the impact of this shared
> endeavour will help to minimise divisions in the longer term.

The idea that the conflicts caused by class and racial inequality
will disappear as the graduates of Eton and the local comprehensive
decorate the old folks' home is delightful, but somebody should perhaps ask whether a greater familiarity with the gross inequalities
of conditions which exist in Britain is not more likely to increase
the resentment of those who will be leaving the scheme, not for
Oxbridge and the City, but for the dole queue.   No doubt in
Fraser's scheme the latter will be confined to sewer renovation
while the Old Etonians run holiday schemes for deprived children.

Sir Hugh quickly followed his article with a motion in the House
of Commons specifically calling for a scheme of 'under-compensated
publicly useful service'.   Indeed Fraser proposed to pay his hapless conscripts the princely sum of £10 per week.   Fraser's notion
attracted a significant amount of support from Tory MPs as well as
some Liberal and Social Democratic backing.   In the meantime an
'Observer' poll found strong backing for a non-military national
service scheme with over 50 per cent thinking it should be compulsory. (31)

The proposal for a national youth service scheme appeared to
offer the prospect of resolving two major problems at once in that
it would provide a cheap fillip to public and social services and
also find some resolution to the dramatic and continuing growth in
youth unemployment.   Youth Call listed some examples of the contribution which young people might make: (32)

An inner-city council housing estate

Despite the considerable efforts of local authorities and voluntary
organisations to improve the quality of life on large housing
estates a number of challenges remain to make life better.   Young
people could make an important contribution in the following areas:
Surveying needs;
Helping old people with shopping;
Environmental improvements;
Cleaning graffiti;
Organising holiday play schemes;
Assisting residents' community associations.

Ancilliaries in social service departments

Experience already suggests that young people can play a useful role
in helping in various social service establishments, for example:
Devising activities for old people in residential homes;
Helping with personal care of individuals, e.g. bathing;
Helping with games in residential schools;
Working with additional instructors in day centres for the handi-
    capped;
Aiding home helpers to extend the range of domiciliary services.

Youth Call has argued that this will not be at the expense of permanent jobs: (33)
    The availability of large numbers of young people should not be
    used however as an excuse to cut back permanent jobs.   Rather
    the skills and contributions of young people must be channelled
    to improve the quality of services, and to undertake those addi-
    tional activities which society will never get round to doing by
    more conventional means.
    The fear of charges that the scheme is a means of exploiting
cheap labour is undoubtedly the Achilles heel of the campaign, since
it would generate union opposition and effectively prevent the
scheme operating in large parts of the public sector.   Ralph
Dahrendorf, the Director of the London School of Economics, was
sensitive to this issue in introducing the Colombatto report, referred to earlier: (34)
    The objective of a social service, voluntary or general, is not
    to provide cheap labour which competes with those in employment.
    Perhaps Mr Colombatto has not made this altogether clear.
This is an understatement.   Colombatto envisages allocating his
conscripts to such tasks as live-in duties in residential homes,
building renovation, and hospital duties - including gardening,
night watch, portering and general maintenance.   How this can fail
to displace permanent staff, even in Britain's inadequately staffed
NHS, is unclear.   Colombatto in fact envisages local authorities
spending £350 for an NWSS placement in residential care by providing
free meals.   He makes no allowances for accommodation which is also
to be provided, but it is clear that in the present climate of
public sector cutbacks such expenditures will displace existing
spending and not be additional to it.   This must have clear

consequences for the size of the authority's permanent establishment.   Even the Director of the London School of Economics will
find it difficult to explain away the impact on the labour force of
injecting upwards of three-quarters of a million conscripts into the
British economy.

The Youth Opportunities Programme was set up with parallel assur-
ances that there would be no displacement of permanent jobs yet
the Manpower Services Commission, somewhat belatedly, has acknowledged that between one in three and one in four of the places
created has been at the expense of regular employment.   In effect
young people would be paid £15 per week (the Youth Call figure), to
do work which would otherwise either remain undone or have to be
paid for at a considerably higher rate.   Local authorities and private welfare establishments will not be slow to recognise the commercial advantages in the scheme and it is idle to suppose that the
number, for example, of home helps employed will not be reduced as a
consequence or that there will not be a decline in pressure on local
authorities to provide regular services if communities are inundated
with conscripts.

YOUTH UNEMPLOYMENT

The rise in youth unemployment has been dramatic.   In July 1974
there were 80,000 under-twenties unemployed, and by July 1980,
532,000.   The Youth Opportunities Programme was established to deal
with rising youth unemployment.   When the programme was launched,
the MSC's Director of Special Programmes, Geoffrey Holland, claimed
that only 10 per cent of programme graduates would find themselves
'reunemployed'. (36)   In fact even in the early days this figure
was nowhere near achieved and as youth unemployment has risen the
number of graduates finding employment has fallen dramatically.   In
some areas less than 30 per cent of programme graduates find work.
When YOP started in 1978-9 it was dealing with one in eight young
people.   In 1979-80 it was assisting one in six, in 1980-1 it was
one in four and it is expected that in 1981-2 it will have to assist
one in two young people. (37)   As the number of young people using
YOP has risen so the relative advantage, previously gained by programme graduates over other members of the young unemployed, has
disappeared.   Faced with an ever-increasing number of unemployed
school leavers YOP has found it more and more difficult to provide
placements.   The 1981-2 target had to be moved up from 440,000
places to 550,000 places, yet in many parts of the country the MSC
was already experiencing difficulty in finding sufficient sponsors
for the scheme.   This was in spite of the fact that controls over
'sponsors' who accepted trainees were very lax and that private
nursing homes, for example, had been allowed twelve months community
service YOP placements, placements supposedly intended for non-
profit-orientated activities.   In the face of YOP's increasing
administrative difficulties and mounting criticism of the programme's effectiveness there has inevitably been a search for alternatives.

YOP has served some useful functions - at least from the point of
view of government.   It has systematically kept a significant

number of young people out of the unemployment statistics, it suggested through a nationwide advertising campaign that the cause of
youth unemployment was the lack of skills and work experience of
young people, rather than the organisation of the economy and government policies, and it has allayed fears about the social order
implications of youth unemployment.   The MSC had specifically
warned in YOP advertisements of the dangers of 'a growing number of
young people who feel discarded by the "system"'. (38)   The MSC job
creation programmes were clear evidence that government 'cared'.

Mounting pressure on YOP and the continued growth of youth unemployment prompted the Thatcher government to make proposals for a
revamped youth training scheme to be launched in September 1983, a
time when a new government might be in office.   The new scheme
would provide each unemployed 16-year-old school leaver with a one
year 'traineeship' with an allowance of approximately £15 per week.
The low level of payment would undoubtedly provoke widespread resistance to the scheme but under the proposal those who refuse will be
denied supplementary benefit.   There is no evidence that the
traineeships will be any more coherently organised than existing YOP
schemes.   The decision to allocate further resources to the MSC, to
purchase educational services, rather than granting money direct to
local authorities to provide courses, reflects the concern of central government to control the content of the educational package.
In short what was proposed was the extension of enforced dependency
for most young people together with a training package which would
emphasise conformity, the acquisition of basic 'social skills',
literacy and numeracy and leave trainees open to continued exploitation as cheap labour.

For those fortunate enough to find work the government introduced
incentives to employers to keep wages low.   Under the Young Workers
Scheme, launched in January 1981, employers received £15 per week
for each employee under the age of 18 who earned less than £40 per
week.

Behind the proposals to revitalise YOP or to launch a nationwide
youth service scheme lie fears of the social order effects of increasing youth unemployment, summarised by Tory MP Nicholas
Scott: (39)

> If we do not take the necessary action we shall be sowing the
> dragon's teeth of social unrest in the future.   The National
> Front, the Socialist Workers Party and their allies are recruit-
> ing young people.   An immensely dangerous problem could emerge
> on our streets if we do not take early action.

MATCHING UNEMPLOYED RESOURCES TO COMMUNITY NEED?

It is clear that the existence of unemployed workers, drawing benefits without providing anything in return, challenges the very roots
of the Conservative conscience.   In July 1980 the Minister of State
for Employment, Lord Gowrie, indiscreetly suggested that unemployed
workers who refused to do voluntary work might have their benefits
withdrawn.   This produced a storm of protest and James Prior, the
Secretary of State for Employment, quickly distanced himself from
the proposal. (40)   The government did however develop other
schemes to encourage voluntary work by the unemployed.

The Community Enterprise Programme, which replaced the Special
Temporary Employment Programme (STEP), specifically offered funds to
voluntary organisations to recruit 'fulltime temporary employees to
open up opportunities to the unemployed for part-time voluntary work
in the local community'. (41)   The government then moved to change
the regulations governing receipt of unemployment benefit and supplementary benefit to encourage claimants to do voluntary work.
Patrick Jenkin recommended that the earnings limit for unemployment
benefit be raised from 75p to £2 per day and that the restrictions
on the kinds of work which could be undertaken be relaxed.   Under
the new regulations the unemployed should be deemed to be available
for work 'whilst they are performing duties in an emergency as members of an organisation set up to provide help in such circumstances;   attending a work camp involving residence away from home;   or
providing services which prevent them from being instantly available, so long as they can attend for employment or interview if
given at least twenty-four hours notice.'   The changes were specifically designed to 'ease the rule so as to make it easier for unemployed people to engage in socially useful activities'. (42)
STEP and the current Community Enterprise Programme constitute
more elaborate and expensive attempts to harness the energies of the
unemployed into community service.   In the designated areas, in
which STEP operated, there was a rapid blurring of the distinction
between the roles of STEP workers recruited to local social service
projects and the role of the regular employees.   Indeed the most
significant difference was that STEP workers were paid less (a maximum of £83 per week) and had no job security.   An obvious consequence of this was that social services which might otherwise have
been delivered by permanent staff at union rates of pay were increasingly provided by low-paid and insecure substitutes.
These attempts to harness the services of the unemployed were
further developed by the Home Office Voluntary Service Unit which
financed a scheme in Cleveland to encourage those who had been tem-
porarily employed on MSC-funded social services projects to continue
as volunteers when their temporary employment ceased. (43)

CONCLUSION

It is unlikely that a compulsory youth service scheme will be introduced.   More probably, other measures will be taken to remove 16-
to 18-year-olds from the labour market along the lines proposed by
the Thatcher government and the MSC. (44)   What is significant
about the proposals is that they reflect a growing tendency to seek
to utilise the unemployed in cost-cutting social service strategies.
They also reflect an opportunistic, if misplaced, concern to simultaneously cater for the social education of the young and fill the
growing gap between service need and service provision - a marriage
of convenience which has been tried and found wanting before. (45)
Community workers are necessarily centrally involved in these
issues whether through direct MSC funding to run YOP schemes,
through the use of CEP funding, or simply by virtue of the central
position they occupy in any community care strategy.   This does not
mean that community workers need necessarily be compromised by the

dubious political intentions or specious promises which currently
characterise community care strategies and job creation programmes.
The content of a particular YOP scheme and the kind of social education received by participants can be crucially affected by the attitudes and practices of those who are running the programme.   Clearly
this may involve some conflict with the MSC, which has already shown
that behind the mask of benevolent paternalism lies a firm intention
to prevent any rebellious behaviour amongst its trainees.   (This
was clearly evident, for instance, in the MSC's response to projects
whose trainees took part in the 1981 summer campaigns to unionise
trainees and increase the trainees' travel allowance.   A number of
projects were closely scrutinised and it was made clear to project
administrators that their futures could be jeopardised if trainees
were not more tightly controlled.)   None the less the MSC must take
some care not to antagonise too large a constituency.   Union participation, for example, is crucial to the success of YOP.   The
Commission can also be relied on to shy away from too public a controversy which might explode the propagandistic claims which it has
made for YOP.

In the community care field the prospect that the strategy may
backfire, as greater levels of unmet need are identified and communities are mobilised to participate, has already been discussed.
Clearly community workers can help to articulate the redistributive
demands which must underlie any meaningful attempt to combat deprivation.   It is worth recalling too that there is an authentic radical tradition which relies on self-help and co-operative provision
rather than on some variant of municipal socialism.   There are
strong progressive arguments for creating more popular participation
in social service delivery and for giving clients a greater role in
control over services.   Similarly self-help is not an issue which
should be meekly surrendered to the definitions of the new right.
It is a principle which finds full support in libertarian socialist
traditions as well as more contemporary critiques of professional
dominance and the cultivation of client incapacity.   Illich is
perhaps the best known exponent of this view. (46)

Strategies which seek a more active involvement of the voluntary
sector, and the community, necessarily raise questions about professional prerogatives and can open up decision-making to a wider range
of pressures.   Centralised and hierarchical structures provide some
protection to those who shelter within but, in seeking to engage the
community, politicians and administrators may find that the terms of
co-operation are not open to bureaucratic or political dictat.

As with other government initiatives a rapid extension of youth
employment initiatives is a two-edged sword.   Government programmes
seek to deflect attention from the severity of the underlying
changes in the economy and their labour market implications.   They
seek to substitute for the disciplines of labour and the crucial
role that work plays in a transition from adolescence to adulthood,
a series of ever-more elaborate make-work and training programmes.
Such programmes cannot conceal the reality of long-term youth unemployment from those who are its victims.   Nor, in the absence of
any prospect of those rewards which adulthood traditionally offered,
financial independence and the support and comradeship of workmates,
can the programmes provide a satisfactory alternative route to adult

status.   The effect of these programmes on their participants may
well be both to increase their anger and to provide a forum for
mobilisation.   Community workers involved in these programmes have
a key role to play in the social and political education of the
young participants and in assisting their attempts to form their own
organisations to demand real work and real wages.

NOTES

1 L. Chalker et al., 'We are Richer Than we Think', Conservative
   Central Office, 1978.
2 Sir Hugh Fraser, The acceptable new face of National Service,
   'The Times', 8 May 1981.
3 P. Jenkin, Trumpet volunteers, 'Guardian', 21 January 1981.
4 G. Stewart, The politics of community care, 'Community Care',
   23 August 1978.
5 Ibid.
6 I. Gough, 'The Political Economy of the Welfare State', Macmillan, 1979, p. 77.
7 N. Bosanquet, Labour and public expenditure: an overall view, in
   N. Bosanquet and P. Townsend, 'Labour and Equality', Heinemann,
   1980, p. 31.
8 P. Townsend, Imprisoned in a casualty model of welfare,
   'Community Care', 3 September 1981.
9 V. Wheatley, Relative stress, 'Community Care', 28 August 1980.
10 P. Westland, Protecting the disabled, 'Municipal Review', July
   1980, p. 86.
11 C. Drinkwater, Life on the outside with mentally handicapped,
   'New Society', 23 October 1980; and A. Shearer, No place like
   home, 'Guardian', 10 June 1981.
12 J. Finch and G. Groves, Community care and the family: a case
   for equal opportunities?, 'Journal of Social Policy', vol. 9,
   part 4, October 1980, p. 494.
13 R. Hadley and M. McGrath (eds), 'Going Local: Neighbourhood
   Social Services', Bedford Square Press, 1980.
14 Jenkin: Stay out of politics, 'Community Care', 19 February
   1981.
15 First line of defence the community, says Jenkin, 'Community
   Care', 9 July 1981.
16 M. Loney, Community action and anti-poverty strategies: some
   transatlantic comparisons, 'Community Development Journal',
   vol. 15, no. 2, 1980, p. 92.
17 R. Crossman, 'The Diaries of a Cabinet Minister, vol. 3',
   Hamish Hamilton/Cape, 1977, p. 126.
18 CDP, 'Gilding the Ghetto' and 'The Costs of Industrial Change',
   1977.
19 M. Rose, Volunteers fume over Tories' token support, 'Community
   Care', 5 February 1981.
20 Prime Minister's speech at the WRVS National Conference, Monday
   19 January 1981, Prime Minister's Press Office.
21 NCVO Annual Report, 1979-80, p. 6, 1980.
22 D. Paul, Anatomy of Wandsworth, 'Voluntary Action', Spring 1980.
23 A. Steen, Getting service for the rates we pay, 'The Times',
   13 February 1980.

24 B. Utting, 'Purchase of Personal Social Services by Government
    Agencies in the USA', Report to the United States German
    Marshall Fund, DHSS, 1980.
25 'Commission on Youth and the Needs of the Nation', Youth Call,
    initial paper, London, 1981.
26 E. Colombatto, 'Nationwide Social Service; a Proposal for the
    1980s', Centre for Labour Economics, London School of Economics,
    1980, p. 60, emphasis in original.
27 'Commission on Youth and the Needs of the Nation', op. cit.
28 N. Stacey, Why we need a National Youth Service, 'Community
    Care', 14 May 1981.
29 The acceptable new face of National Service, op. cit.
30 Ibid.
31 'Observer', 26 April 1981.
32 'A Debate on Youth and Service to the Community', Youth Call,
    London, 1981, p. 9.
33 Ibid.
34 E. Colombatto, op. cit., p. ii.
35 Hansard, 7 April 1981, Column 825.
36 'Observer', 2 April 1978.
37 Hansard, 7 April 1981, Column 858.
38 M. Loney, The politics of job creation, in G. Craig, M. Mayo
    and N. Sharman, 'Jobs and Community Action', Routledge & Kegan
    Paul, 1979.
39 Hansard, 7 April 1981, Column 850.
40 'The Times', 14 July 1980.
41 MSC, press notice, 21 November 1980.
42 Social Security Advisory Committee, 'Unemployment Benefit',
    3 June 1981.
43 VSU sponsors Scheme, 'Community Care', 30 July 1981.
44 'A new training initiative: a programme for action', Cmnd 8455,
    HMSO 1981; 'A new training initiative: an agenda for action',
    MSC, 1981.
45 See C. Allinson, 'Young Volunteers?', Community Projects
    Foundation, 1978.
46 I. Illich et al., 'Disabling Professions', Marion Boyars, 1977,
    p. 16.

9 Race, politics and campaign activity: A comparative study in Liverpool and Wolverhampton

Gideon Ben-Tovim, John Gabriel, Ian Law and Kathleen Stredder

INTRODUCTION

Since the mid-1960s there has been an increase in activity by anti-racist, community and racial minority groups whose collective aims have been the elimination of racism, discrimination and disadvantage; the equalisation of opportunities between racial minorities and the indigenous white majority; and meeting the culturally specific needs of racial minority groups. The nature of involvement by these organisations has related to the type of political intervention pursued, and the specific reform, initiative or response (or lack of them) which has resulted. It has also been influenced by the position of the organisation within the state and its relationship with the formal institutions of the state.

A common basis for the development of these activities has been the campaign. This term suggests the identification of specific objectives, and their realisation by means of particular tactical judgments. A campaign embraces a range of organisations whose specific objectives might be distinct but whose interests at some level would be served by the realisation of common campaign objectives.

The focus of this article will be a consideration of the nature and role of local race-related activity in both policy and community development. Our analysis is based on and illustrated through case studies in Liverpool and Wolverhampton. The first, in Liverpool, centres on the promotion of equal opportunity through a campaign to persuade the local authority to draw up and implement an equal opportunity policy for employment and careers as well as in service provision, e.g. education and housing. The second, in Wolverhampton, focuses on the attempts by a number of organisations to make local youth policy more accountable to the needs of racial minorities.

The objectives and nature of both campaigns distinguish them, in the field of race relations, from two other forms of activity which we have referred to elsewhere; (1) those concerned exclusively with oppositionist forms of anti-racist activity, and those aimed at securing a specific resource-based initiative. The significance of the two campaigns lies in their capacity to achieve the goals of anti-racist and resource-based activities and to mobilise a range of local organisations. In this sense we have referred to such campaigns, and their reforms, as structural. (2) We would consequently link this type of campaign and reform to a notion of intermediary reform, which may not secure social transformation but which, through its implementation, facilitates the means by which such transformation might be achieved in the future.

The conclusions point to the potential role of community and grassroots pressure in local policy development; a role which has been ignored in some analyses of local and central policy initiatives.   It is also our intention to assess the impact of campaigns on certain aspects of community development.   The latter, which can be seen as a potential by-product of the types of political intervention considered here, can, in the long term, be as important for race struggles as the realisation of the campaign objectives.

THE CAMPAIGN FOR EQUAL OPPORTUNITY IN LIVERPOOL

Liverpool City Council passed a resolution to adopt an equal opportunity policy in December 1980.   The council acknowledged that the aim of the policy was to ensure, in its provision of services and as an employer, equality of opportunity for all persons, regardless of race, colour, ethnic or national origins. (3)   At the same time the council also agreed to establish a Liaison Committee, to be made up of twelve councillors and twelve representatives from local minority organisations.   Formally linked to the Policy and Finance Committee, the Liaison Committee was established to oversee the implementation of the equal opportunity policy.

Although the adoption of the equal opportunity policy marked the result of almost two years of sustained and co-ordinated campaigning by an alliance of sixteen local organisations, there exists a history of efforts to achieve equality of opportunity for racial minority groups in Liverpool.   As far back as 1951 a group of Labour councillors called for higher levels of black employment by the city council.   The Colonial People's Defence Association (CPDA) openly protested against the role of employers and trade unions in perpetuating racial discrimination and lobbied local councillors on this issue. (4)   Although opposition from trade union representatives forced this issue to be dropped within the council, the trades council did establish a sub-committee which promised after discussions with the CPDA that pressure would be put on the city council to accept black labour.   Evidence of action taken after this meeting is, however, lacking.

The mid-1970s witnessed the re-emergence of the equal opportunity principle as an issue in local politics.   The demands for positive action, articulated on this occasion by the Merseyside Community Relations Committee (MCRC) along with South Liverpool Personnel and the Race Relations Board, were rejected by the council.   As a result of further lobbying and a Labour Party resolution, a request was made by the council for a report from the Personnel Committee on the development of positive race policies.   The matter was dropped once more, however, on the advice of the Personnel Director who thought the report to be unnecessary and the issue, in any event, too controversial.

Although the MCRC continued to raise the issue of equal opportunity throughout the 1970s, it was the emergence of two particular organisations which transformed the local political context.   In

1979, the Liverpool Black Organisation (LBO) was formed to represent the interests of the locally born black community.   During the period prior to the adoption of the equal opportunity policy, the LBO was intensively involved in a range of race-related activities which included anti-racist demonstrations, marches and petitions, as well as social and cultural events.   The Merseyside Anti-Racist Alliance (MARA), a broad-based organisation with political, trade union and church support, was set up in 1978.   In addition to campaigning with the LBO, MARA had also been responsible for the introduction of a weekly programme on local radio for the black community and a fortnightly column on race issues in a Liverpool newspaper. Together MARA and the LBO, through the extent of their activities, popularised local anti-racist sentiments and created the opportunity for the black community to have a legitimate political voice.   At the same time, as a result of the involvement of a wide range of groups and organisations, including the Labour Party, they developed the basis for a broad anti-racist movement which was increasingly concerned with local policy issues.

While grassroots political momentum was building up, two official local committees were established which provided valuable experience for the development of the campaign strategy.   On both the Race Relations Working Party and the Ethnic Minorities Liaison Committee, representatives of ethnic and community organisations sat with local councillors and administrators and had an opportunity to gauge the predominant official attitudes towards the issues of race and racial discrimination.   They also were able to gain some knowledge of the success of (and the conditions for the success of) race-related initiatives which had already been set up locally.   For example, the Ethnic Minorities Liaison Committee was a formal Committee accountable to the Housing Committee, and specifically contributing to the development of housing policy by acting as a forum for housing issues related to ethnic groups.   The Race Relations Working Party (a sub-group of a Liverpool Inner City Partnership Working Party), on the other hand, had no clear brief and remained largely impotent because of its vague relationship to the local authority.   As a result it met on only three occasions before becoming defunct.

It was in the context of these committees and through other official contacts that the arguments against an equal opportunity policy were put by council officials and councillors of all three parties. First they opposed the policy on the grounds that it was unnecessary because the council did not discriminate.   Furthermore they argued that adopting such a policy could make race relations worse by seeming to favour preferential treatment for blacks.   Opposition was also premised on the belief that blacks did not have problems different from those of the rest of the working-class inner-city residents.   Finally they argued that the lack of support from the trade unions made the implementation of an equal opportunity policy impossible.

These arguments defined the context of the campaign.   For example, in response to the political and administrative concern over the lack of union support, the campaign undertook activities to convince the trades council and later the trade unions of the significance of an equal opportunity policy.   They did this not only to undermine the basis of official opposition but also to ensure that

the policy could be effectively implemented if the campaign were
successful.

The support of the trades council was not easily won.   Initially
members of the LBO and MARA, who were also members of the trades
council, reconvened the internal sub-committee on race relations.
This sub-committee then organised a survey of black workers on the
Liverpool City Council to demonstrate that there was substantial
evidence that black employees were under-represented.   This evidence was used to urge the trades council to recognise the need for
immediate positive action and to reconsider their position.   Eventually the trades council agreed to press the city council for an
equal opportunity policy.   This led to discussions on race and
equal opportunity in the branches of associated unions, which resulted in further union support and discussion and positive action in
local Labour Party branches.   Crucial gains for the campaign were
the winning of support from the local Joint Shop Stewards Committee
and from NALGO, numerically the most significant local authority
union.

Another example of campaign work designed to strengthen the growing support amongst the political parties and trade unions was
undertaken by the research group based at Liverpool University.   An
original aim of this group, made up of university staff and students, was to contribute to the development of local race policy,
and as an initial task the group set about producing an area profile, to document existing patterns of racial disadvantage with
regard to the access of racial minority groups to housing, health
services, educational opportunities, employment, etc. (5)   This
evidence was used throughout the campaign period.   It substantiated
the demands for an equal opportunity policy, in the final letter of
application which went forward from the MCRC to Liverpool's chief
executive, and it also provided a basis for a series of interventions made by the local campaigning groups.

One such intervention involved the Race Relations Sub-committee
of the Parliamentary Home Affairs Committee.   During its visit to
Liverpool in 1980, to collect evidence on the extent of racial discrimination in the city, the university research group had the
opportunity to present the contents of the area profile to MPs and
Home Office officials.   When the research document was accepted by
the committee, as important evidence, the local press began to pub-
licise it.   This, in turn, resulted in a 'Newsweek' television programme on black Liverpool which also argued the case for the need
for an equal opportunity policy.

The role of research in the campaign then was a central one.   In
the first place, it provided sound evidence of the need for an equal
opportunity policy to a variety of local organisations with different political outlooks.   It was also instrumental in gaining wider
support as a result of media coverage, particularly through the submission to the House of Commons sub-committee.   Without this research it seems probable that the campaign would have been limited
to more common forms of protest, demonstration and confrontation and
that less pressure would have been exerted on the local authority.

In Liverpool equal opportunity for racial minority groups had
been an important issue for thirty years before it was realised in
the form of a local policy.   It wasn't until a strong movement of

anti-racist and locally born blacks was established that the racial
discrimination experienced by the local black community was given
extensive publicity and accorded political priority.   The development of the campaign was linked to the identification and location
of opposition and support within local institutions and organisations.   Where opposition existed, as in the political parties and
trade union movement, the campaign had to take account of prevailing
ideas about race and racial discrimination as well as the role of
each organisation in local political life.

Even in the final stages, the campaign was organised so that
maximum co-ordination would result in a constant stream of pressure
on politicians and administrators.   Copies of the equal opportunity
submission were sent to each councillor in advance of the relevant
council meeting, discussions were held with key officials, and dele-
gations were sent to the leaders of the three parties.   At the
meeting itself, a substantial turn-out of the black community confirmed the significance attached to the issue and exerted additional
pressure on those present to agree to the policy's adoption.

The strength of Liverpool's campaign lay in the breadth of its
organisational support and the prevention, in certain quarters, of
active opposition to the principle.   The knowledge of institutional
structures and forces of opposition that were gained over time provided an invaluable base on which a campaign strategy could be developed.   The campaign's weakness lay in the absence of any integral
connection between community forces on the one hand and a local
institutional power base on the other.   Without this connection,
community pressure from campaign organisations is required subsequent as well as prior to the adoption of the policy in order to
ensure its effective implementation.   The necessity for such
follow-up activity would seem to place considerable pressure on a
movement made up of such a variety of organisations each with their
own very specific, sometimes quite distinct objectives.

THE CAMPAIGN FOR YOUTH PROVISION IN WOLVERHAMPTON

Proposals for Wolverhampton Borough Council to radically restructure
its youth service were approved in principle by the controlling
Labour group and by the Further Education Sub-committee in the
spring of 1981.   The proposed changes included the setting up of a
free-standing Youth Committee (separate from the Education Committee) with its own department (separate from the Education Department), a revised philosophy of youth provision broadened to take
account of not only the recreational and leisure requirements of
youth, but also their housing, welfare, employment and legal needs;
and an independent, funded and widely representative Youth Development Council (constituted to advise the Youth Committee and any
other service department whose remit includes youth).   Although
these policies are not overtly concerned with issues of race, they
include detailed changes which are designed to increase the role of
racial minority groups in the youth service and to ensure that youth
provision in Wolverhampton is multiracial.

Youth provision for racial minority groups, although neither as
clearly delineated nor as long-established an issue as equal oppor-

tunity in Liverpool, had been a focus of local interest for many
years.   The report of the Wolverhampton Council for Community Relations (WCCR) noted 'the lack of adequate provision for black youth
in the town', and in 1975-6 WCCR initiated a series of culturally
specific YOP and STEP schemes, to cater especially for the young
black unemployed.   The changeover of the Crypt (a centre with youth
facilities located in the town's main Methodist Church) and several
other local voluntary youth clubs, from a white to black clientele
in the mid-1970s evidenced the concern of local white voluntary
agencies for youth provision for the minority groups.   At about the
same time, the Afro-Caribbean and Asian communities were also extending their own church- and organisation-based youth activities to
include summer camps, summer schools and supplementary schooling
(e.g. typing, black studies, mother-tongue teaching, and basic
skills of literacy and numeracy).   In most cases this provision was
felt to be inadequate or absent from existing statutory educational
and youth services available to young black people.

Within this general context of locally organised voluntary action
to meet youth needs, and protestations about the absence of facilities, there were a number of events which precipitated local political interest in race-related matters.   Perhaps most important was
the ongoing conflict between the national Commission for Racial
Equality (CRE) and the WCCR over the appointment of the Senior Community Relations Officer.   To prevent the CRE from withdrawing its
funding, a local trust was set up in 1979 to oversee the administration of WCCR.   The membership of the trust included appointees from
the WCCR executive, from the CRE, and six local councillors, including the Leader of the Council.   The effect of the involvement of
these councillors was to produce in them a greater interest in race
issues.

Pressure from the black grassroots coincided with this development.   In 1979, the closure of the sole day centre for youth at the
YMCA, in a largely black-populated area, resulted in accusations by
black youth against the local authority.   Not long after, a unilateral decision to stage a sit-in at the town hall was taken by a
local Rastafarian group, who had been evicted from their premises by
the local authority.   This action required the response of politicians, and in this way young blacks achieved bargaining power with
them.   The incident was also further evidence that the interests of
racial minority groups were not being represented.

Another initiative which caused a great deal of local controversy, but which simultaneously brought youth to the attention of local
politicians, was the Afro-Caribbean Cultural Centre.   In 1979,
funds from the Inner Area Programme were allocated to the development of the centre, for the express purpose of creating recreational
and educational provision which would be organised and managed by
members of the local Afro-Caribbean community.   A majority of one
vote secured the council's commitment to this development, while the
vociferous objection from the indigenous white population was witnessed in the local newspaper's letter columns and front page news
items, as well as by a march against it mounted by the local branch
of the National Front in April 1981.   The counter-demonstration,
organised by the local Anti-Racist Committee, however, illustrated
the strength of support for the initiative, and assisted in the
alignment of various community, political and anti-racist groups.

In early 1981, when local grassroots and community organisations were still at the stage of making demands and articulating problems about youth provision, a leading Labour councillor, chairman of the Further Education Sub-committee, set up a branch committee under the wing of that sub-committee to consider a recommendation from a local report which called for 'a re-definition of the role of youth and community workers and the special needs of ethnic minorities.' (6) The brief of the branch committee was more open than this, and so when local black activists, community and voluntary workers were invited to meet with councillors and youth service administrators, it was inevitable that a range of local issues pertaining to both race and youth would be explored.

It was in the context of the branch committee that local organisations and individuals began to translate the needs and problems of racial minority groups into policies. The involvement of staff from the youth service and councillors from the Education Committee provided the other members of the committee, normally excluded from the process of official discussion and decision-making, with their first formal access to statutory bodies. This, in effect, encouraged aspects of local youth policy to be discussed.

The formation of the branch committee provided a further possibility. It created a forum for what had been up to then an unco-ordinated group of local organisations with a common interest in youth provision for racial minorities. It thus provided the potential for alliances to be forged and a broad-based campaign to develop. That potential has yet to be realised due to the infrequency of branch committee meetings, a certain factionalism, which has on occasions divided some of the participating organisations, and the lack of any other continuous independent context outside the branch committee for differences to be resolved and a co-ordinated strategy to be developed. The campaign has thus focused principally on an axis forged between the Council for Community Relations and the Wolverhampton South West Constituency Labour Party Race Relations Policy Group on the one hand and certain key members of the local Labour group on the other.

Opposition by youth officers and workers to a youth service responsive to the effects of racism and racial disadvantage was similar to the views expressed in Liverpool against the equal opportunity policy. Any sort of response was regarded as tantamount to reverse discrimination (and therefore unacceptable); as unnecessary because the problems and needs of black and white youth are the same; and as impractical because favourable treatment of one group might cause the others to make demands.

These were arguments which those who represented racial minority groups on the branch committee answered through extensive discussion and through the presentation of working papers. Two particular lines of argument were adopted for this purpose. The black radicals sitting on the committee emphasised the experience of racism and racial discrimination by young black people and related this where possible to practical situations within youth clubs and schools. Others used policy-related issues to confront the opposition. For instance, one paper outlined the policy and provision of inner London's youth service, (7) and was used to illustrate initiatives in a number of London boroughs which had been premised on the existence of racism and racial disadvantage.

The branch committee acted not only as a forum for the confrontation and exchange of ideas, but also as a channel which local organisations could use for bringing forward new evidence and making
policy recommendations. A local group particularly involved in
this respect was the Youth and Community Panel of WCCR (including
both voluntary members and staff). In the year preceding the
establishment of the branch committee, the panel had begun to make
contact with local black youth groups. These included the evicted
Rastafarians and the YMCA management board, as well as football
clubs and unattached youth groups, especially girls' groups. These
contacts had revealed evidence of racial discrimination in the use
of local facilities and a dearth of provision in the predominantly
black areas of town. At the time the branch committee was con-
vened, the panel was in the process of organising a conference on
local youth provision. The preparation for this conference had
also revealed an absence of black youth leaders and workers employed
by the local authority and a lack of take-up of youth provision by
significant sub-groups, including Asian girls. This range of evidence was used to argue for a youth service which provided for
racial minority groups.

The Labour Party Race Relations Policy Group, formed in 1980, had
begun its own work in the area of youth policy and provision. The
group had decided to produce discussion papers on those aspects of
local provision affecting youth, including education and housing,
and to formulate policy documents. These were to be processed by
the party machinery and eventually adopted in some form as local
party policy. Through the branch committee, however, the policy
group had an additional outlet for its work and this further increased the weight of pressure on the Education Committee from local
community groups. Because the membership of the policy group included local councillors and Asian and Afro-Caribbean leaders, the
work that was done in the context of the group built up a unanimity
of purpose amongst a very wide range of organisations, many of whom
were not active on the branch committee but whose support in the
campaign was extremely important. The policy recommendations of
this group were also important for securing and strengthening the
Labour group's commitment to a positive development of local youth
provision.

After a series of branch committee meetings, proposals were
introduced outlining an internal reorganisation of services for
youth. These were developed in response to the very wide range of
problems identified with local youth policy and thus to facilitate
those changes considered to be most significant and far-reaching.
For example, to ensure more adequate, across-the-board services for
young people, it was recommended that service departments of the
local authority provide a co-ordinated service for youth through a
separate Youth Department. The proposals also attempted to counter
the specific effects of racism and racial disadvantage.

The future success of these campaign efforts will depend on a
number of factors; the strength of officer opposition to the proposals, the extent to which the somewhat tenuous alliances can be
strengthened and co-ordinated and the continuing political will
within the Labour group. The latter, above all, has been crucial
in permitting legitimate community access to local authority members

and officers, and in exerting political pressure on the Education
Department.

CONCLUSIONS: REFORMS AND COMMUNITY DEVELOPMENT

We referred above to the structural objectives of both the equal
opportunity and youth campaigns and to the notion of intermediary
reforms.   The potential of both the Liverpool and Wolverhampton
campaigns and the reforms which have and could result lies in the
scope they afford for further initiatives and the nature of their
impact on local political and community development.

These reforms do not of themselves actually guarantee more radical or progressive initiatives, but they do have the potential for
further advances in several respects.   Firstly there is the official acknowledgment of racial discrimination and disadvantage with
its implications for the provision of local authority services as
well as employment practices.   The formulation of an equal opportunity policy in Liverpool, linked to the establishment of a liaison
committee, is analogous in this sense to the formation of the branch
committee, and the proposal for a more representative (in racial
minority terms) Youth Committee and Youth Development Council in
Wolverhampton.

The initiatives provide bases for further reforms which would
otherwise have been pre-empted in the context of a continuing refu-
sal to acknowledge racial discrimination and disadvantage as problems.   In the second place, the Race Relations Liaison Committee in
Liverpool and the proposed Youth Committee in Wolverhampton provide
structural mechanisms for the realisation of local political and
community demands.   The formation of such bodies will not necessarily satisfy those demands, and much will depend on the designated
powers conferred on them as well as the continuing involvement and
support of local organisations.   What they can provide is one
important condition for further advance, namely institutionalised
access to decision-taking bodies within the political apparatus of
the local state.

The effects of both campaigns should not be confined to the
reforms which result, but must include a consideration of their
impact on community and political development.   In Liverpool the
forging of alliances across numerous organisations is a crucial
aspect of this development.   However short-lived that collective
unity proves to be, the potential for its re-emergence can only be
stronger as a result of the equal opportunity campaign.

In contrast to Liverpool, attempts to reform the Youth Service in
Wolverhampton have been up to now much less characteristic of a campaign as we defined it.   The role of alliances and the presence of
a co-ordinating strategy were much less in evidence than in Liverpool.   Developments to date have been, above all, the result of a
political commitment to reform within the leadership of the local
Labour group.   Local organisations, including community workers,
representatives of teachers, and representatives from black youth
organisations, were permitted a forum through the branch committee
to strengthen the political case for reform presented to the officers of the Education Department by the controlling Labour group.

The second important channel for local race organisations has been through the Labour Party policy group on race relations with its direct access to the Labour group.

In so far as this political commitment is sustained, particularly in the face of officer opposition, the likelihood of success may be greater than Liverpool's campaign with its broad base but its tenuous links with any power base within the council.

Whatever the outcomes of both sets of initiatives, the lines of division between community organisations and formal political institutions of the local state will have been redrawn as a result of these campaigns. The starting points and the collective assumptions held by all parties involved will have moved in the light of the experience gained by pursuing these initiatives.

Evidence from both campaigns underlines the potential role that groups or agencies can play in campaign development. The use made by MARA and the MCRC of the profile of racial disadvantage in Liverpool is one example of an input which research can make. This profile, and the report on inner London's youth service used in Wolverhampton, were not produced in a vacuum. They constituted an integral part of the development of the two campaigns. Evidence from both Liverpool and Wolverhampton reveals the significance of an organic relationship between research and political intervention and one which stands in marked contrast to predominant forms of race-related research.

Although any reform can only begin to scratch the surface of institutional discriminatory practices, the campaigns considered here have at the very least restated those political boundaries within which the aims of racial equality and justice can be pursued. The potential created by these campaigns depends on many factors including the sustained pursuit of campaign objectives after the initial reforms have been conceded. There is thus no possibility of predicting any future development on the basis of this evidence. What can be claimed, however, is that such campaigns have established a series of conditions which make advance more likely. The reforms thus provide the potential for establishing new conditions for further, more radical reforms, both in terms of the resultant structural changes and the politicising effects of the two campaigns on the local communities.

NOTES

1 G. Ben-Tovim, J. Gabriel, I. Law and K. Stredder, A Political Analysis of Race in the 1980s, in C. Husband (ed.), 'Race in Britain', Hutchinson, 1981.
2 Ibid.
3 It is important to note that the idea of equal opportunity is officially encouraged in the 1976 Race Relations Act. The emphasis of the act on the promotion of equal opportunity and the elimination of unlawful discrimination in the field of employment, and especially Section 71 of the act which refers to a local authority's general statutory duty to 'make appropriate arrangements' to ensure the promotion of equal opportunity and the elimination of discrimination 'in respect of ... [its] ...

functions', have created a source of government pressure on
local authorities to review their policies and practices.   In
both the equal opportunity campaign in Liverpool and the youth
campaign in Wolverhampton, the Race Relations Act was used to
challenge official positions and to underline campaign goals
demanding further positive action.

4   Colonial People's Defence Association, 'Report of Activity',
1951-2, pp. 10-11.
5   See 'Racial Disadvantage in Liverpool: an Area Profile', 1980,
unpublished evidence, submitted to the Parliamentary Home
Affairs Committee, Race Relations Sub-committee.
6   See Report of the Working Party of the Youth Development Council
(Wolverhampton Borough Education Committee) on 'Pay and Conditions in the Youth and Community Service', 28 January 1981.
7   J. Gabriel and K. Stredder, 'The Youth Service and Provision for
Racial Minorities: the Case of ILEA', unpublished, 1981.

10　The temporary tenants' campaign

Coventry Workshop

THE POSITION OF TEMPORARY TENANTS

Tenants with rent arrears, homeless families, redundant workers, separated parents, all had one thing in common in Coventry in 1978 - they were likely to be thrown into the city's worst housing if they approached the council for help.   Coventry City Council used Part 3 of the 1948 National Assistance Act to punish these people by making them the tenants of houses that nobody wanted any more - houses that were shortly to be demolished to make way for new housing estates, new or widened roads, or were just empty waiting for the local authority to make up its mind what it was going to do with them. These houses were in the most appalling condition: roofs leaked, damp penetrated, windows fell out, plumbing didn't work, mould thrived, and the electrical installations were lethal.

This is the story of how Coventry's temporary 'Part 3' tenants organised to change the council's policy to expose this inhuman treatment of the most vulnerable section of the community. It is a story of the courage of a group of people overcoming the stigma of the 'problem families' label and how they gained the support of the tenants' and trade union movements in their campaign to be treated like any other council tenants.

Since it was set up in 1976 the Housing Sub-committee of Coventry Trades Council had been concerned about the plight of people living in 'Part 3' housing. The issue was first raised during the campaign to save a city centre street, Starley Road, from demolition to make way for a shopping, car parking and road widening scheme. The street had been threatened for some years, with many of the houses falling into disrepair. Some were empty and semi-derelict, many had been bought up by the council pending redevelopment and were used as temporary and 'Part 3' accommodation. Despite these pressures and the almost daily fires in the street, the tenants were determined to stay near the city centre and their work. Coventry Workshop and the trades council gave the tenants of Starley Road a lot of support and helped them not only to save the road, but to establish a tenants' co-operative that has now completed a most imaginative programme of improvement. The trades council and Coventry Workshop learnt at first hand of the plight and conditions in which the so-called 'Part 3' tenants were living.

Tenants who attended meetings of the Housing Sub-committee were bringing horrific stories of the conditions in which some of their

members were living; the common factor was that they were all tenants of short-life housing.   For example:
    in Smith Street, a seven-year-old boy was preparing for bed when
    he fell through the rotten floor of his bedroom onto a pot of
    potatoes boiling on the stove in the kitchen below;
    in Foleshill Road, a twelve-year-old girl could lie on her bed
    and watch the flowers in the garden grow, not through the window
    like everyone else, but through the cracks in the house wall;
    again in Foleshill Road, a family of four children and two adults
    were forced to live in just two rooms on the ground floor of
    their house, because all three of their bedrooms were made un-
    usable by leaking roofs and penetrating damp.
    These conditions occurred throughout the entire city, and so were
not the responsibility of a particular tenants' association; however, the sub-committee had as one of its terms of reference, to
generalise from individual campaigns issues of city-wide importance.
    Although there is a considerable history of community action in
Coventry there has been no city-wide organisation of tenants' associations since before the last war.   The Trades Council Housing Sub-
committee has always seen as one of its functions the provision of a
brdging structure that would not only join tenants and trade unionists in collective campaigns but would provide the framework for
city-wide activity amongst tenants and their organisations.   It was
therefore quite consistent for the sub-committee to set about trying
to establish an organisation of these temporary tenants throughout
the city.   With the help of Coventry Workshop, and a list of 'Part
3' houses provided by one of the Coventry MPs who had also been concerned about this problem in his constituency, the sub-committee
attempted to define the state of the houses and the circumstances of
the tenants by carrying out a one hundred per cent survey of the 130
or so such tenancies.
    The role of the trades council and the workshop in being able to
recruit a force of some forty tenants, trade unionists, and housing
activists to carry out the survey was crucial.   Tenants' organisations are often overstretched and rarely have the personnel to carry
out surveys within their own areas, let alone throughout the city.
    Care was taken in briefing the interviewers, recognising that
people in temporary accommodation had little experience of trades
councils, tenants' organisations and collective action in general.
It would be difficult for these people to understand that the survey
was not being carried out by the council, but by sympathetic organisations concerned to do something with them about their conditions.
Interviews were carried out in a similar way, by means of a standard
survey form.
    The survey was carried out over a two-week period in November
1978; interviews were held in 92 of the 'Part 3' houses and revealed that the 92 houses were home for some 446 people of whom 274
were children.   Of the houses, 44 per cent had no bathroom, 47 per
cent had outside toilets and 78 per cent were damp throughout.   Ill
health affected 70 per cent of the residents.   All of the tenants
were in temporary accommodation through homelessness caused by a
variety of reasons: 40 per cent had left their matrimonial home due
to violence, 25 per cent had been evicted from their homes due to
rent arrears, in both the private and public sectors, 8 per cent

because their homes had been repossessed by building societies and 5 per cent because their homes were overcrowded.   Contrary to the belief held by the city council and the views expressed in the Coventry Evening Telegraph, only 2 per cent of temporary tenants purposely withheld their rent, and in at least one case this was done as a personal protest at the state of repair of the house. All of the tenants interviewed said that they were made to feel like second-class citizens by the Homes and Property Services Department - temporary tenants have different colour rent books, they are not full tenants with the associated rights but merely licensees of the local authority, and there was some evidence to show that repairs to 'Part 3' houses were treated as low priority.

Perhaps the most remarkable revelation was that temporary tenancies were anything but temporary.   The greater proportion of tenants had been in these houses for anything from three to twelve years.

As a result of the survey, and the contacts the interviewers made with the tenants, the trades council was able to call a meeting of temporary tenants, firstly to pass on the results of the survey, and secondly to see whether they wanted to form their own autonomous organisation.   Sixty or so tenants turned up and were genuinely surprised to learn that there were so many people with the same set of problems.   This was clearly a source of some support as was the assistance they received from tenants' and residents' organisations that had sent along representatives to help get the organisation off the ground.

The chairperson of the Gulson Action Committee, one of these organisations, said:

My committee fully supports the setting up of an organisation to represent temporary tenants.   We have many such tenants in our area and will continue to represent them, but it will be a step in the right direction of removing the label of 'problem families'.   There are no 'problem families', but there are very few families that don't have problems.

After its first few teetering meetings chaired by members of the trades council, Coventry Temporary Tenants' Association was finally officially constituted by the election of officers and a committee.

The issue of temporary tenancies became a hot political issue in the period running up to the council elections in May 1979.   At the time the organisation was set up, the Conservatives were in power and were enthusiastically pursuing and defending this punitive policy (originally established by the previous Labour administration).

In an attempt to get public opinion on his side, the chairperson of the city council's Housing Committee held a seminar to discuss policy.   However, the whole thing blew up in his face.   The bishop and two of Coventry's MPs openly condemned the policy with the following statement from the bishop receiving prominent attention in the local press.

At a seminar at the Council House, the Bishop called for the (temporary) tenants to be housed elsewhere.   'I wake up at night and agonise for some of the children I see in this kind of housing' the Bishop said.   'And when I look at the future and think of children growing up in these circumstances I wonder whether we

are not extenuating (sic) these social problems.'   (Coventry
Evening Telegraph, 17 November 1978)
    At the same seminar the opposition spokesperson on housing, Coun-
cillor David Cairns, cited the case of a woman who lived with her
three children in one of the properties.

> The top floor could not be used, there was no hot water, no bath-
> room, no inside toilet, the electrics were dangerous, the tiles
> were off the roof and the ceilings were sagging.   The woman was
> expecting another child but she lost it.   She herself had suf-
> fered from pleurisy three times.   (Coventry Evening Telegraph,
> 17 November 1978)

    A disappointed chairperson of housing, Councillor Sawdon,
declared that the seminar had not been as constructive as he had
hoped; he did not favour rehousing temporary tenants on other council estates which he thought would be a politically unacceptable
move.   His solution was to set up a working party to discuss the
problem and its resolution.   Needless to say there was no suggestion that this working party should have any temporary tenants on
it.

THE CAMPAIGN OPENS

The Temporary Tenants' Association was not going to wait around and
see what this working party came up with; they decided that they
would have to mount a campaign to get the policy removed, to improve
the conditions of their members, and to counter the widely held
belief that they were all wantonly withholding their rent.   They
also saw that it was going to be important to offer an advocacy service to their members as well as to homeless and potentially homeless people.
    The association very quickly came to the conclusion that it was
going to have to use every device at its command to achieve its
aims, possibly including the use of the law.   As an opening salvo
in the battle the association gave notice of its intention in the
following petition to the December 1978 council meeting:

> THIS PETITION GIVES NOTICE TO COVENTRY CITY COUNCIL UNDER
> SECTION 99 OF THE PUBLIC HEALTH ACT 1936, FROM THE COVENTRY
> TEMPORARY TENANTS' ASSOCIATION.

We, the undersigned tenants of council-owned temporary accommodation, consider that many of our houses constitute a statutory
nuisance as defined by section 92 of the Public Health Act 1936.
This is obvious from the various forms of structural damage, lack
of basic amenities and especially damp, which puts our own and
our children's health at risk.   We call on Coventry City Council
to do repairs, as a matter of extreme urgency, and to provide
basic amenities in those houses which lack inside toilets, baths
and hot water.
    And so opened a long and protracted campaign of petitions, occu-
pations of the Housing Department, court cases and picketing.
Councillor Sawdon, Tory chairperson of housing, was the target of
much of this activity.   Demonstrations were held outside his place
of work, his committee meetings were disrupted, he was taken to
court and eventually he ended up issuing injunctions against

officers of the association.   (He even had a song made up about
him, sung lustily to the tune of 'Daisy Daisy':
    Sawdon, Sawdon give us your answer do,
    We're not fooling, we can see through you.
    Injunctions you can issue,
    We'll use them for bum-tissue.
    And you'd look sweet, upon the seat,
    of a typical Part 3 loo.)
The Conservative ruling group, however, did little to repair the
homes of temporary tenants, refused to take part in a tour of some
of the houses, and stuck rigidly to its policy.   The association
had no alternative but to continue with the threatened court action.
They initially issued summonses on three properties under section 99
of the 1936 Public Health Act.   It is well known that the law is a
slow and cumbersome device for tenants' associations to use;   it requires a good deal of resources, and the necessary use of professionals can mean that an association becomes distanced from its campaign, and that areas of activity slip from its control.
    The first problem with these court cases was that the clerk
registered them under the wrong section of the act.   In addition,
the courts do not recognise organisations as legal entities and so
the summonses had to be issued by individuals citing specific properties.   This meant that the association had to spend a good deal
of time publicising these actions as part of a much bigger campaign,
so that the broader questions of policy were not lost sight of.
    Despite these problems the association won all three cases at the
magistrates' court.   That was early in May 1978.   Later that month
the control of the city council reverted back to the Labour Party.
The Temporary Tenants' Association heaved a sigh of relief.   They
had developed a working relationship with the new chairperson of
housing, Councillor Cairns, and the Labour Party had expressed its
support for the tenants, albeit never in a very public or specific
manner.
    The opening statements from Councillor Cairns, during his first
few weeks in office, were quite promising.   He pledged his support
for their campaign, and promised that the worst of the temporary
homes would be demolished.   The association's response to these
statements was positive but quite rightly guarded.   In a press
statement after the first Housing Committee of the new Council, the
association said:
    We are pleased to see that the punishment policies of the Tories
    are not to be continued.   These policies were based on the
    fallacy that all temporary tenants are in rent arrears - which is
    not true.   The provision of decent housing for all temporary
    tenants, not just single parent families, should be a priority.
    We will accept nothing less than a crash programme of demolition,
    rehousing, repairs and modernisation.   (Coventry Evening Tele-
    graph, 15 June 1979)
Two weeks later, however, the Housing Committee decided to discuss whether there should be a High Court appeal against the magistrates' court findings.   There was uproar in the committee room.
The association turned out some forty of its members to see whether
the council would appeal, and when the committee decided to discuss
it in private the tenants refused to leave.   The committee members
were forced to leave and hold their meeting elsewhere.

The Labour group had decided that there should be an appeal on some complex legal technicality.   This served to enrage the association, firstly because it had expected support from the Labour group and secondly because the process held up the payment of costs to tenants who could ill afford to wait.

At this point the association turned its sights from the Labour group on the council (as it didn't seem likely that it would be able to influence them any more than it had the Tories), and towards the Labour Party and the trade union movement.   It asked to address Labour Party and trade union branch meetings to put its case and to ask for support in getting temporary tenancies abolished and stopping the appeal.

Little by little the association gained support.   In particular, the delegate meeting of the trades council gave its full backing after hearing the tenants' case and seeing the dramatic photographic exhibition of conditions in 'Part 3' housing (produced by the association with help from both Coventry Workshop and Coventry Resource and Information Service).   Indeed the trades council commissioned a pamphlet to tell the story of the temporary tenants' campaign for use with the membership of affiliated trade unions.   Delegates also held a collection to set up a legal fighting fund in the face of High Court injunctions from Councillor Sawdon.   (It was at this time that Sawdon was himself elected as delegate to the trades council from his branch of ASTMS, presumably for tactical reasons.)

Trades council delegates to constituency Labour parties were instructed to move resolutions of support for the Temporary Tenants' Association.   This, combined with the growing pressure from Labour Party branches, committed the party in Coventry to the policies being proposed by the association.   There now opened up a constitutional split between the city party and the controlling Labour group of councillors, which, despite some members' support for the association, dogmatically refused to alter its punitive policy.

This was a busy time for the association.   Preparation for the appeals, making a case to the ombudsman claiming maladministration and injustice on five counts, and maintaining its city-wide organisation requried considerable help from Coventry Workshop, Coventry Resource and Information Service and a group of lawyers and students from the School of Law at Warwick University.   Further pressure was exerted on the Labour group by means of TV programmes (the association took part in a 'Grapevine' programme), the radio and the local press.

The three appeals eventually were heard in the High Court of Justice, Queen's Bench Division, before Lord Justice Donaldson and Justice Hodgson.   Their findings were broadly in support of the association on two of the cases and rather inconclusive on the third. On the whole, the tenants lost little from the exercise, and their costs were paid by the state.

The ombudsman at one time said that she might well have had to set up permanent office in Coventry if she received many more complaints.   She found the local authority guilty of maladministration and injustice in four out of the five cases.   The tenants were awarded costs of between £500 and £750.   These decisions, however, came towards the end of the life of the Temporary Tenants' Association.   By now, the council had to some extent succumbed to their pressure by repairing and improving most of the temporary accommodation, moving people out to more acceptable premises on council estates.   It did not, however, repeal its policy, and still operates along the same lines - not using short-life premises (these are in short supply with the removal of much planning blight by the West Midlands Metropolitan County Council), but using the hard-to-let estates of Wood End and Willenhall to the same ends.

SOME LESSONS LEARNED

Clearly this is not the story of a massive success.   The ultimate aim of the association was never achieved.   However, some very important advances were made.   Firstly, over one hundred tenants have won a significant material improvement in their living conditions representing a substantial investment in housing that would not have otherwise been made.

Secondly, a group of tenants organised themselves, not on traditional neighbourhood lines, but on a basis of mutual interest, across the city;   and they maintained that organisation for a period of about two years in the face of great odds.   They are the poorest group of council tenants, living, without doubt, in the worst conditions, and subject to the most hostile reactions from both the council and media.   They have set an example that has since led to further city-wide action through the formation of a Federation of Tenants' Associations that has taken on the job of representing, co-ordinating and collectivising organised tenants' activity.   This is an initiative again taken by the Trades Council Housing Sub-committee through its role of providing a city-wide framework for housing action, thus enabling autonomous tenants' organisations to be formed.

Thirdly, and perhaps most importantly, the Temporary Tenants' Association has established a political debate about housing in the city.   No other piece of action in recent years has created a level of discussion that has challenged the policy-making structure of the local authority in the way that this campaign has.   In particular the campaign has opened the way for a new form of policy development within the Labour Party, and has mirrored at a local level the constitutional problems facing the Labour Party Conference and the Parliamentary Labour Party.

The issues faced by tenants have for the first time been prominent on the agendas of trade unions and the trades council, and both tenants and trade unionists have joined together in a collective campaign because they have seen areas of common interest.   The Temporary Tenants' Association has established that there is a clear link between unemployment and the economy of the city and poor housing conditions.   As more and more people lose their jobs and are unable to keep up their mortgage payments on houses bought during the boom period of the late 1960s and early 1970s (a period of relatively high wages and house prices), the local authority and the building societies will be foreclosing on these mortgages.   As a result more and more people will be personally punished and thrown into temporary accommodation;   this is a particularly serious situation in a working-class town like Coventry, where about 65 per cent

of homes are being bought on mortgages.   The city has now been
awakened to this problem and therefore owes a great deal to the
bitter battles fought by the Temporary Tenants' Association.

The contribution of the two local resource centres, of the trades
council, local law lecturers and students, should not be underestimated when trying to learn the lessons of this campaign.   All too
often campaigns like that of the Temporary Tenants' Association are
reported as spontaneous developments of working-class organisation,
thus denying or covering up the role and contribution of local resources.   It should be quite clear from this story that had it not
been for the contribution of these agencies this organisation might
not have been formed and its campaign would not have taken place.
However, it is important to know how the organisations have been
working in order to understand this contribution.

These organisations employed a form of work that set out right
from the beginning to help tenants and trade unionists make most use
of the resources, information, and expertise that they have to hand.
It is a form that always had as one of its aims the building of a
tenants' organisation that cuts across traditional barriers within a
community, and strives to be truly representative.   And it is also
a form that intends to be of material use to trade unionists in the
campaigns and activities they have identified.

In particular, the temporary tenants' campaign was able to take
advantage of the way in which the Coventry Workshop's work is constantly held up for internal scrutiny by the whole workshop collective (the full-time workers and others closely involved in the running of the workshop).   This involves a process of bringing
together practice and theory to inform future work, of never being
content with repeating elsewhere any particular piece of work and,
above all, of having a clear set of aims and objectives by which to
judge all work.

There is a clear set of principles that make this educational
approach to our work possible:

to work with people and organisations on the issues they themselves identify;

to work with groups and people within their own experience;

to work with groups and people at their own pace;

to make sure that groups have the space to make their own
decisions;

to make sure that professional services and resources don't
become a substitute for autonomous tenants' organisations;

to make sure that the work we do is unambiguously committed to
working-class campaigns;

to take care not to become professional friends blowing in the
wind without any political direction;   and

to be able to produce the skills required by the campaign, effi-
ciently, accurately and in a way that makes them accessible to
the groups with which we are working.

11 Pooling our resources

The Network of Labour, Community Research and Resource Centres

THE ORIGINS OF THE NETWORK

Since the mid-1970s, attempts at grassroots organisation within the trade union, women's and community movements in localities, regionally and even internationally, have been supported by a growing number of organisations offering research, specialist advice and learning opportunities to working-class people attempting to exercise control over their own lives.

Research and resource centres with this orientation now exist in Bradford, Bristol, Coventry, Leeds, Liverpool, London, Manchester, Nottingham, Sheffield, Tyneside and elsewhere in the UK, Europe, Australia, Canada and the USA.

These centres have a variety of origins. A number in the UK have grown out of part of Britain's poverty programme of the 1970s - the Community Development Project (CDP). Some of the resource centres continue to work from their original CDP bases, while several CDP workers have been involved in the establishment of centres elsewhere.

Not all have direct links with the CDP though. Some have their origins in local labour movement initiatives and community struggles and have continued work begun by tenants' federations, the Workers Educational Association (WEA) or regional councils of the TUC. Others have roots in pilot projects financed by national voluntary organisations or charitable trusts. Examples of these are the more generalist resource centres funded by the Gulbenkian Foundation, Rowntree and the Community Projects Foundation. There are also a small number of centres whose existence can be traced back largely to developments within the women's movement and their work is primarily defined by the needs and struggles of women in the home, the community and the workplace. They also undertake work of the kind tackled by centres with a more traditional labour movement orientation. Leeds Trade Union and Community Resource and Information Centre (TUCRIC) is one example of a resource centre which, from its beginnings, recognised the need to confront issues facing women, arising from their dual, reinforcing, roles as unpaid domestic workers and nurturers in the home and undervalued wage labourers in the workplace. The Lewisham Women and Employment Project arose from the failure of the London Dockland's Strategic Plan to give any weight to women's employment needs. Lewisham's aims were 'to investigate and improve job and training opportunities for women in

the London Borough of Lewisham'.   Emphasis was placed on the needs
of women school leavers and those returning to the labour market
after 'breaks' for child-rearing.

These differences in origin, funding and local circumstances have
resulted in considerable diversity in the priorities and forms of
resource centre established.   Despite this, it has become increasingly clear that they have a core of shared aims and perspectives,
issues tackled and methods of work.   In recognition of this, an
initiative was taken by a number of established centres in April
1979 to explore the potential for closer collaboration in all
aspects of their research and organisational work.   It seemed that
a cross-fertilisation of ideas would add to the work of the individual centres and permit the development of a clearer, more common
analysis of the issues faced by each locality.   After a series of
discussions throughout 1979, a common statement of working aims and
principles was agreed.   A nucleus was constituted for what is now
called the Network (of Labour, Community Research and Resource
Centres).   A group comprising one delegate from each centre undertook to co-ordinate the work of the Network and a grant was obtained
to allow the appointment of a national development officer.

Neither the individual centres nor the Network were established
to pose a fundamental challenge to the official organisations of the
labour movement or, in the case of those with a primarily feminist
perspective, to adopt a 'leadership' role within local women's movement structures.   Nor is there any wish to exacerbate the existing
divisions which weaken working-class organisation.   However, it is
becoming increasingly clear that the traditional machinery of organised labour is not, by itself, adequate to tackle the crucial issues
confronting people in urban communities today: issues affecting
those in waged work affect those deprived of it, and there are other
problems which face everyone, whatever age, gender or race.

The work of centres is largely based in the older industrial communities which face fundamental social and economic dislocation.
The industries for which these communities have traditionally provided labour have been undergoing major contraction and restructuring
and whole local economies have been undermined.

In the case of manufacturing industry there has been withdrawal
or rationalisation of capital investment leading to run-down, reloca-
tion or complete closure of factories.   The rapid introduction of
'new', labour-displacing technology in some has also created job
shrinkage, de-skilling and intensifying of the labour process at the
same time.   In other areas - for instance, where dock work and
dock-related employment has been crucial, processes like containeri-
sation, linked to the drive to maintain profits, have devastated
older dock locations and their surrounding communities.   Sharp
rises in unemployment over the last decade characterise all those
areas within which resource centres are located.   In most instances
expansion of the service sector has only partially compensated for
this job loss and in any case 'skilled' male workers have found
their knowledge and experience to be redundant.   Women workers
derived some initial 'benefit' from the growth in the service
sector, although wages have generally been poor and unionisation
often weak.   In any case, new technology and public sector cuts are
now seriously undermining even this source of employment.

De-industrialisation and the wider economic crisis not only
affects employment.   Local housing, health, education, social and
personal services and the environment also suffer.   Their deterioration has created a severe reduction in the quality of people's
lives in urban communities.   More seriously, divisions between
working-class people have been widened at the same time, between
those with paid work and those without, skilled and unskilled
workers, those working full-time or part-time.   The rights of women
and black people to have paid jobs is being questioned and their
secondary status reinforced by regressive legislation, cutbacks in
essential services and ideological pressure which serve to reinforce
self-help 'solutions' centred around the nuclear family and the
ideology of female domesticity.

Our work with tenants' groups, the unemployed, workers affected
by new technology, communities questioning the state's planning proposals for their areas, women campaigning for more and better childcare provision and black people fighting racism, has led us to look
for the causes of their problems and the interconnections between
them.   We have been led to investigate the political economy of our
areas within a radical economic framework and with an understanding
of differing and conflicting class interests.   But we are also
striving to integrate an analysis and understanding of gender and
racial oppression within our 'political economy' approach.   For
example, one weekend meeting of Network centres was devoted to discussion of how best to further the development and integration of a
feminist perspective in all areas of our work and to formulate priorities according to the needs and demands of women as well as
better organised, often more vociferous, male workers.

All these issues pose a challenge to the limited, often centralised resources of the trade union and wider labour movement.   In
any case, some groups - particularly women and black people - have
fallen outside the orbit of their political and organisational activities.   Through our work we hope to increase the resources available to labour and women's movement groups, helping to strengthen
'horizontal' links between grassroots or shop-floor groups in different neighbourhoods, factories, unions, cities and countries.

We are aware that this 'bottom up' development of ideas and initiatives can frequently place a strain upon the traditionally hierarchical structure of the labour movement.   For instance, a joint
shop stewards' combine committee, developing an alternative workers'
plan for their factory might find it difficult to get support from
officials of all the separate manual and white-collar unions concerned.   In the case of women organising within the workplace,
their demands may pose a different but equally threatening strain on
forms of organisation which have evolved to protect the position of
the male 'breadwinner' whose workplace role has been seen as separate from his family life.

The strength and organisation of trade unions has traditionally
been directed primarily at the protection of wage levels and conditions at the workplace.   Their power has resided in their capacity
to withdraw labour from employers.   The current run-down of industry and high levels of unemployment render this power redundant and
leave the trade unions in a weaker bargaining position, with a set
of unfamiliar problems to tackle.   Factory-level organisations like

shop stewards' committees are now forced to tackle company-wide
issues like corporate restructuring and rationalisation which demand
an inter-factory, inter-union response.   Dealing with new technology requires unusually close co-ordination between manual and white-
collar unions.   Factory closures have a major impact on the local
community and trade unions need close liaison with community-based
organisations.   Redundancy and unemployment confront the unions
with the need for new areas of expertise about social security and
the welfare state and for forms of organisation which are not only
workplace-based.

A reappraisal of even the most radical of analyses and strategies
to meet these needs also has to take account of the location of
women within the labour market and in the home.   To date, forms of
labour movement organisation and strategy have assumed that women's
primary role is a domestic one.   Some Network centres are working
with unions, community groups and women's groups at a grassroots
level on a number of issues from a position which challenges this
view and take as central to their work women's right to equal job
and training opportunities and financial independence from men.

THE PRACTICE WE AIM FOR

It is not simply the issues which centres work on which are important.   We are also trying to evolve a work practice, one which
avoids the use of 'vanguardist' tactics or radical professionalism
or which is ambivalent in its political orientation.   There are
certain underlying principles to the methods of work we employ to
realise our two major aims.   The first of these is to help groups
with whom we work to gain material improvements in their immediate
situation.   The second is to facilitate an understanding of the
underlying causes of their difficulties while trying to change it in
a collective way.   Our emphasis on work with groups should be
clear.   In the main, centres do not tackle individual problems.
Often, where no relevant organisation exists, we help to organise
and strengthen networks of previously isolated people experiencing
similar problems.   We might, for instance, develop a new technology
network between factories, offices and shops in one town, or a city-
wide nursery campaign.

An understanding of problems as structural and the need for collective solutions to them does not mean that relationships between
individuals engaged, through resource centres, in struggles are seen
as unimportant.   On the contrary: recognition of the 'personal' as
highly 'political' has led us to give considerable thought to the
way that we work together as workers in centres, how we work with
groups and how members of those groups relate to each other.

What does this mean in practice?   First of all, most centres
have, or are moving towards, a non-hierarchical and democratic workplace structure in which decisions are the result of collective discussion amongst workers and management/advisory groups.   Pay parity
is a crucial feature of working conditions, as is the sharing of
administrative and secretarial jobs.

The relationship between resource centre workers and groups, as
well as individual members of those groups and the people they

represent, is of equal concern.   The internal and external democracy of the organisation is seen to be as important as any issue and
this means that information has to be shared throughout the membership, regular reports made by delegates and the widest possible participation in all decision-making processes encouraged.   Recognition of the frequent inability of working-class organisations to
involve their members in these processes - and their consequent
failure to capture the imagination and active allegiance of many of
them - informs this practice.

How the 'professionals' relate to groups with whom they work has
long been a subject of discussion for community workers and contin-
ues to be one within the Network.   Certain fundamental principles
are agreed on.   We do not see ourselves as 'outside experts' but
rather as people who are committed to the struggles we become involved in, usually with particular skills to offer.   Our work takes
place alongside groups and rarely do we negotiate on their behalf.
We recognise that whilst we may often be able to offer specialist
knowledge or explanatory theory, both are useless unless matched by
the direct experience of groups we work with.   Traditional 'top
down' research methods continue to overlook key issues facing working-class people because they fail to engage directly with what is
happening on the shop-floor or in localities.   This implies too
that we do not impose issues onto groups who have not identified
them as important areas of struggle.   The starting point for our
work is always an issue regarded as a grievance or priority for
change by that group.   Where the resource centre has identified an
issue as important, workers will initiate contact with people affected to check that they regard it in the same way.   In either case
the interplay between research and action, theory and practice will
inevitably move the dialogue on beyond the original starting point.

People who come together to tackle common problems often have to
overcome years of demoralisation.   However, they discover that
changes can be gained by collective action, confidence grows and new
learning begins, both for the individual and group.   It is vital
that the centre worker shares sources of information obtained with
the group and passes on particular knowledge, expertise or skills
which she or he has contributed.   This is clearly a long-term process in which research and action combine with education to build up
the self-consciousness and self-reliance of the group.

Most of our work, whether workplace, home- or community-based,
has clear political implications.   The response of the resource
centre to an issue should generally be to shift workplace or living
conditions in a direction which benefits working-class people or to
challenge the negative power of existing institutions and intrusion
of capital's influence over everyday life.   However, our approach
is non-sectarian and is governed by our accountability to the groups
we work with and our elected management/advisory committees.   Any
element of political manipulation would be unacceptable.

BUILDING LINKS

We see the building of links and sharing of experience between workplace, community and women's groups as a central aim of our work.
We are trying to develop an understanding of the interconnections

between the issues they tackle.   This may mean linking tenants'
groups with the local trades council, to strengthen support for tenants' campaigns and to deepen the trades council's understanding of,
and involvement in, housing issues.   Or it might involve discussing
with a shop stewards' committee about the effect of new technology
at their factory on job opportunities for women and young people in
their area.   Similarly, an estate-based women's health group might
be brought together with women in a local union branch who are campaigning against health hazards in the workplace.   At a theoretical
level it may mean trying to analyse the impact of the economic and
political crisis upon the life of the city as a whole.   Effective
action to win improvements in the workplace or home environment requires better understanding of the relationship between employment
and the community; the economy and the state; production, reproduction and consumption.

The involvement of resource centres in a national network has
allowed us to extend this linking function nationally and even
internationally.   In some cases this has been crucial to local campaigns.   For instance, in 1979 the Bristol Resource Centre was
approached by the APEX branch of the Bendix-Westinghouse factory to
research the implications of a possible takeover of their jointly-
owned subsidiary by the Bendix Corporation, a giant American multi-
national.   The resource centre was able to make contact with trade
union and research organisations in the USA and in other countries
where Bendix has subsidiaries, and to compile a comprehensive report
on the company's world-wide structure, finances, operations and industrial relations practices.   The Bendix workers in Bristol were
also helped to make contact with workers in other plants making
similar products.

Local campaigns against job loss by groups of auto and telecommunications workers and their unions have led them to develop more
direct links with their counterparts in overseas subsidiaries of the
same firm or industry, sometimes with the help of the Transnational
Information Exchange (TIE).   Trade union delegates and worker representatives from the main European subsidiaries of Massey-Ferguson,
Peugeot-Citroen-Talbot (Chrysler), Ford and Fiat met together with
labour researchers on the industry in Rome in June 1979.   Trade
union representatives and workers from European Peugeot-Citroen-
Talbot and Ford plants have since held a further series of meetings
with background research and organisational support from Coventry
Workshop and other centres.   Nottingham Workshop (now called 118
Workshop) and Coventry Workshop helped to bring European telecommunications workers together as part of the TIE programme.   In Milan,
delegates from resource centres, together with those from GEC,
Plessey and the Post Office Engineering Union, discussed the impact
of new technology on the telecommunications industry with union representatives from Siemens, Phillips and ITT.

To some extent, the informal networks emerging from these meetings overlap with the more formal world councils for trade unionists
like that organised by the International Metalworkers Federation
(IMF).   Yet they have some distinguishing features, reflecting the
way in which Network centres try to work.   Firstly, the informal
networks have included workers excluded from the IMF or which have
chosen not to affiliate.   Secondly, they have been geared very

specifically to the needs of shop-floor representatives from the factories and finally, the form the meetings have taken has been such as to encourage personal relationships between those who attend.   This has strengthened contacts and led to some very direct exchanges of information and support between European car workers.

The strengthening of 'horizontal' links of this kind is as essential as the development of such links at a town or national level. They will be vital in building protection against the growing power of the transnational corporations and developing alternative industrial strategies.

The work that centres are engaged in spans the broad areas of employment, unemployment, planning and housing.   They provide basic services to their users including research, specialist advice of a legal, economic, housing, accountancy or planning nature, libraries of materials useful for local research and campaigns, fact sheets, bulletins and briefing notes on, for example, recent legislation, the local economy and local cuts, and duplicating, typing and media services.   Groups are helped to carry out their own research, produce their own materials and are put in touch with relevant specialist help which centres cannot always provide.

EMPLOYMENT ISSUES

Work on employment issues has been central to the activity of all the centres.   In several cases this work preceded the formation of the Network.   Much of the campaigning and research work in which we have been involved has been documented and published in a variety of forms.   Although publishing in itself is not a central aim of our work, the documentation of particular struggles can provide future campaigns with arguments and strength.   The recording of information on local companies can also develop a general awareness of the power and wealth of local employers which, in itself, stimulates further investigation and greater resistance by local workforces.

There is a great demand generally for Network centres to provide material of this kind and most of them keep files on major employers.   Some centres subscribe to specialist information services, thus offering local versions of national enquiry services like that provided by the Labour Research Department, and most keep microfiche copies of company accounts lodged at Companies House.

In addition to keeping this general information, centres are often asked to carry out more detailed research into a particular firm by a shop stewards' committee or trade union branch.   In Newcastle for instance, the West End Resource Centre prepared a report on the worldwide operations of Berec for workers employed in local Ever Ready subsidiaries.   It highlighted the ability of transnational companies to relocate out of Britain to countries providing cheap labour and low-cost manufacturing opportunities when profit levels are under threat.   They have also undertaken similar studies of Vickers, Caterpillar, Henlys and other transnationals.

It is not possible to detail all such work carried out within the Network, but a few other examples will illustrate its diversity. The 118 Workshop collaborated with NUPE in a study of low pay locally, the Joint Docklands Action Group (JDAG) in London's East

End have researched employment trends over a number of years and have carried out particular studies on the engineering industry and dock-related employment locally.   Trade union involvement in the resource centre has been vital to the centre's understanding of the local economy and the problems facing local people, while JDAG's research capacity has strengthened local struggles around employment.   The Manchester Engineering Research Group (MERG) was asked by shop stewards and union officials locally to carry out research for workers facing redundancy in Massey Ferguson, Royal Pride and Ferranti factories, whilst also monitoring local employment.   Their report on 'The Decline of the Engineering Industry in Manchester' led to a trade union day school on this topic, supported by the north-west regional council of the TUC.

A typical example of a piece of work carried out by a resource centre alongside rank and file manual and white-collar trade unionists was the Coventry Workshop investigation into the machine-tool industry commissioned by the Coventry Machine-Tool Workers Committee.   The research was carried out in close collaboration with workers from Alfred Herbert, Wickmans, Webster and Bennett, and Clarksons International and involved several plant visits and discussions as well as a series of 'teach-ins' with the whole machine-tool workers' committee.   In the course of twelve months of joint research and discussion, the committee developed their own strategy for the industry in order to protect employment and skills.   Their report, published by the Institute for Workers Control, was presented to the TUC and to the NEDO sector working party for the industry.   It was also used as the basis for a national conference for machine-tool workers called by the Coventry committee.   This has led to the formation of a national shop stewards' combine committee for the industry.

The drastic rise in unemployment in recent years has inevitably led to the involvement of several Network centres in campaigns and educational work with the unemployed and claimants.   Several of them have prepared briefing material on redundancy legislation, social security and welfare rights for local groups and trade union bodies.   Others such as TUCRIC, MERG, Tyne and Wear and Bristol Resource Centres have prepared background reports on unemployment, job loss and the local economy for regional TUC conferences, union district committees or local trades councils.   The Lewisham Project carried out a study of women's unemployment since 1975 in their area, illustrating statistical material by interviews with women living on local estates who had lost their jobs with firms nearby.   They also undertook a survey of women registering as unemployed in their area, to detail women's particular experience of unemployment.

Other issues related to women's employment have been a central concern of some centres, in particular Bradford, TUCRIC and Lewisham. Each of these is committed to working alongside and within trade union organisations.   At the same time, recognition of women's dual oppression as unpaid domestic workers at home and undervalued wage workers involves them in issues of reproduction and consumption 'in the community' (such as childcare, health, benefit rights and housing).   The low status of women in the labour market is being tackled by a 'positive discrimination' approach in all areas of work.

Several centres have produced information and fact-packs on sex equality legislation, maternity rights, childcare provision and redundancy rights.   Lewisham produced a handbook of local childcare facilities as part of a campaign for better provision.   Bradford, TUCRIC and Lewisham have undertaken detailed research on their local economies and the particular location of women within them.   The wool, textile and clothing industries have provided the focus for much of TUCRIC's work, while in Bradford women's part-time work was the subject of a conference organised through the women's sub-committee of the trades council.   Lewisham looked closely at the relationship between child-rearing and women's job histories in Deptford through a large-scale survey of women on a local estate. (The results showed the damaging effect of 'breaks' in work on skill and family incomes.)   All three centres are involved in work alongside their local trades councils.   'Women Fighting Back and In the Unions' was the subject of a conference organised by TUCRIC and the women's sub-committee.   In a further meeting on Local Employment Initiatives, they ensured that the needs of women were discussed as a particular issue.   Both Lewisham and TUCRIC are involved in the establishment of training schemes for women and in campaigning for positive discrimination within state training provision.   Lewisham have been involved in a local campaign for childcare facilities, hours compatible with domestic commitments and positive discrimination to break down gender segregation within a newly built local skills centre.   This is proving to be something of a test case for other women's groups involved in the issue of women's training. Links have been established with other women's groups and with a national pressure group - Women and the MSC.

Women and new technology has been a central area of work for both Bradford and TUCRIC, who have both carried out research and education work on the subject.   A West Yorkshire Women and New Technology study and resource group has been formed to co-ordinate work in both areas between centres and women working in industries affected by the introduction of new technology.   (The Equal Opportunities Commission has funded a major research project on the effects of its introduction on women's work in the area.)

Campaigning and education work on workplace issues such as sexual harassment and maternity rights has also been undertaken in some centres, as has trade union education work.   TUCRIC, for example, have played a central role in the establishment of TUC women's bridging courses in Leeds.   In all this work, contact between resource centre workers has been crucial as has their relationship with women affected by these issues.

COPING WITH NEW TECHNOLOGY

The impact of new technology on local economies has been the subject of research, educational and agitational work in resource centres. Many have received a steady flow of enquiries from workers, shop stewards and union officials about specific aspects of new technology arising in negotiations, such as its health hazards, the implications of computer numerical control and new technology agreements. To supplement the growing body of material produced by the trade union movement, some centres have produced briefing notes on such issues as the health hazards of VDUs (TUCRIC) and word processors and office automation (The Centre for Alternative Industrial and Technological Systems - CAITS).   In addition, several long-term projects have taken place: Bristol Resource Centre prepared a detailed case study of the Impact of New Technology on Women and Trade Union Organisation in Banking.   This was carried out jointly with the Banking, Insurance and Finance Union as part of an EEC-financed project, co-ordinated by Ruskin College, Oxford.   CAITS helped the Lucas Aerospace Shop Stewards' Committee to survey the actual and potential impact of new technology across all the factory sites and unions.   This has been incorporated into a Technology Plan for Lucas which is being used as a negotiating document by the unions.   It also contains a Model Agreement covering the introduction of new technology.

Educational work around issues related to new technology has been as important as undertaking research itself.   Some centres have generated innovative educational programmes within the trade union movement in their areas.   Both workplace and public meetings have been set up in Coventry with workers from GEC and Massey Ferguson. A new technology network there has facilitated a fruitful exchange of information between workers from a variety of industries and workplaces which has been helpful to the formulation of union responses to the introduction of computer-based plant.   In Nottingham, the 118 Workshop used film and video in courses on new technology in the home, the office, the public services and the shop-floor, run jointly with the WEA.

One piece of educational work on new technology carried out by Coventry Workshop has raised some interesting questions about the use of information gained through research.   In this case, the study - on the impact of new technology on trade union organisation - followed several years of joint study with manual and white-collar unions at GEC's main telecommunications factory.   Jointly financed by the EEC and Ruskin College, it showed that, whilst at an official level trade unions have developed a sophisticated understanding of the problems posed by new technology, this knowledge had not been used to encourage shop-floor awareness or resistance to its use. Furthermore, a frequent lack of communication between shop stewards and ordinary union members adds to the ineffectiveness of trade unions in the face of the 'new technological threat'.   Although some gains had also been made - for instance, inter-union co-operation was greatly enhanced - Coventry Workshop were left asking how the information gathered could best be used to further its aim of strengthening shop-floor resistance.   One conclusion they have drawn poses the need for resource centres to involve grassroots members in such work as well as worker representatives.

HOUSING WORK

This contribution has so far concentrated on the work carried out by Network centres on employment issues.   As we stated earlier, we give equal weight to issues affecting working-class people in their roles as 'consumers' and 'reproducers'.   For that reason, much of

the Network's activity involves housing issues and tenants'
struggles to improve their living, as well as working conditions.
Understanding the links between these two is seen as vital to our
work.   It is important therefore to describe some of the planning
and housing projects undertaken.   The story of one campaign is outlined in the previous chapter.

The range of housing issues confronting centres and their users
includes dampness, heating problems, rent increases, council house
sales, inadequate repairs and the use of 'distraint' on council
tenants.   The approaches adopted in confronting these issues are
correspondingly varied.   Centres may help tenants to find specialist legal or technical advice or become involved in direct action
in pursuance of tenants' demands.   Whether the approach adopted
involves a rent strike or a court case, a public enquiry or an
estate survey, there are certain principles which underpin the involvement of Network centres.   At a general level these have been
described earlier in this chapter.   What our collective approach
means for housing struggles is that resource centres, wherever possible, engage with tenants in building links, either at an estate,
local, regional or national level.   In Coventry this has meant that
the Coventry Resource and Information Service (CRIS) and Coventry
Workshop have supported the development of a city-wide tenants'
federation.   In the north-east the Tyne and Wear Resource Centre
has helped to organise the North-East Tenants Organisation and the
Newcastle Tenants Federation.   Bristol Resource Centre and Services
to Community Action and Tenants (SCAT) have been involved in the
development of similar groups.

Building links between tenants and workers employed by local
authority housing departments is an important objective.   Not only
is this seen as critical to developing an understanding of the
inter-relationship between housing issues and employment within
local economies, but it is also viewed as crucial for the success of
tenants' struggles and the protection of the jobs of council employees dealing with housing issues.   Housing development will also
have a wider impact on local economies which cannot be overlooked.
Examples of attempts to forge such alliances include work carried
out by SCAT, Tyne and Wear and the West End Resource Centres with
committees of representatives from direct labour organisations and
tenants to examine their mutual problems and find ways of improving
services to tenants and the working conditions of council workers
involved in house repair, maintenance and building.   In Coventry,
a Trades Council Housing Sub-committee has been formed which brings
together workers from a variety of unions, with a range of expertise
and knowledge in the field of housing, whilst SCAT has helped several trades councils to analyse housing policies and formulate local
strategies for better housing.   Together, Tyne and Wear Resource
Centre, SCAT and South Shields Trades Council examined the relationship between the local authority's housing and industrial policies.
They concluded that an expansion of private housing would not
attract industry or jobs and outlined the need for a continuous
public housing and building programme to create jobs in the area.

The educational aspects of housing work are viewed as being particularly valuable.   Whilst education of tenants and centre workers
is a continuing part of our work, there have been attempts,

generally successful, to engage with tenants in more formal education sessions, which have had the added benefit of bringing tenants
together from one city, a region or throughout the country.   CRIS
organised a housing day school which attracted more than forty tenants, and several resource centres have co-operated in running four
educational weekends for tenants from Coventry, Sheffield, Tyneside
and South Wales.   A variety of teaching techniques was used and,
apart from being a valuable learning experience, the weekends generated some informal relationships between tenants which have provided strength and support in subsequent struggles.   SCAT is beginning to develop packs of educational material on housing for wider
use in the housing and trade union movements.

CONCLUSION

This careful, long-term educational and organisational work with
members of the trade union, women's and community movements is
beginning to bear fruit in some areas where defensive action to protect existing jobs or housing conditions has increased confidence
and led people to make positive suggestions as to the sort of work,
housing or public services they *need*, rather than ones they can
expect!   Consequently, some centres are engaged with their users
in the formulation of workers' and residents' plans for their areas.
While some of these may be seen as utopian, the provision of alternative visions for the future can only stimulate wider and more
creative struggles amongst working-class people.   For example,
CAITS and workers in the Lucas Aerospace Shop Stewards Combine Committee have produced the world-famous plan which suggests a conver-
sion by their employer away from the production of military equipment to a range of socially useful goods, such as important medical
equipment.   The strong organisation of workers is crucial to the
success of such plans and CAITS have therefore promoted a Joint
Forum of Combine Committees, bringing together union representatives
from Lucas, Dunlop, Metal Box, Thorn, EMI, Vickers and other major
firms, in order to develop and strengthen similar work elsewhere.
JDAG has been involved for some time in opposing plans for the redevelopment of Docklands which disregard the needs of local people.
They are now working with workers and tenants to formulate a wide-
reaching alternative based on people's needs, rather than those of
industry and the state.   Likewise, SCAT and the West End Resource
Centre are exploring the concept of workers' and residents' plans to
provide better housing and jobs for their areas.
    Much of the work being carried out by Network centres and their
users is in its early stages.   There is scope for more joint work
between centres and expansion of the Network itself.   Problems such
as funding are a constant headache for some centres and planning is
often difficult without the prospect of long-term funding.   What is
clear, however, is that the methods of work we are attempting to
employ are contributing to a growing challenge to those 'leaders',
in whatever sphere of life, who wish to retain a monopoly of knowledge or power, or 'the professionals' who dare not dirty their
hands.   Links are beginning to be forged between working-class
people oppressed in a variety of ways and these people are

strengthening their own understanding and extending their educational and political experiences.   All these issues demand new ideas
and new forms of organisation, which cut across the traditional
divisions within and between the workplace, the home and the community.   The Network resource centres are making a modest but useful
contribution to such developments alongside working-class people.

For further information on the Network, individual centres or the
work they are doing, write to the Network Development Worker, c/o
118 Workshop, 118 Mansfield Road, Nottingham.

Part III Radical developments outside the UK

12 The European Poverty Programme: Why re-invent the broken wheel?

Marjorie Mayo

The EEC Anti-Poverty Programme has been described by one of its critics in terms of the re-invention of the broken wheel. Certainly the parallels with preceding poverty programmes such as the British Community Development Project (CDP) and the US War on Poverty are immediate and striking. So was history simply being repeated, as Marx once suggested, with the first performance as a tragedy, and the second performance as a farce?

In contrast (and less pessimistically), this chapter attempts to demonstrate that despite the similarities, there were also key differences between the EEC Anti-Poverty Programme and its predecessors. And there were positive points of comparison, too; in particular, the projects' own creative uses of the programme and the development of collective inter-project work, at a cross-national level. A brief appraisal of one interesting project, in Giugliano, Naples, which stimulated cross-national work, is included to illustrate this.

THE ORIGINS OF THE PROGRAMME

The direct intervention of the EEC in community programmes, through the Anti-Poverty Programme (launched in 1975) originated, it has been suggested, when the heads of states of the newly enlarged community met in 1972. It was felt that the EEC needed to be presented now with a 'human face' to counteract the widespread view that it was concerned only with economic growth and the Common Agricultural Policy (CAP) resulting, it seemed, only in butter mountains and wine lakes. 'Economic expansion is not an end in itself,' it was argued. 'The firm aim should be to enable disparities in living conditions to be reduced....'

A further explanation that has been offered (1) for the EEC's interest in promoting the Anti-Poverty Programme focuses upon the competition between the different organisations of the EEC itself - the Council of Ministers, representing the member states at the political level, the Commission (the bureaucrats in Brussels) and the European Parliament (originally an advisory, now an elected body) each trying to carve out distinctive roles for themselves. According to this interpretation, the EEC Anti-Poverty Programme could be seen as the thin end of the wedge of increased EEC direct involvement in social policy; poverty represented, after all, an

overtly altruistic set of issues around which the different organs
could press their organisational self-interests.

Although Commission officials tended to refute any such imputa-
tions of empire-building, this would seem to be an increasingly significant area for policy analysis; because, in effect, whether or
not there are further Anti-Poverty initiatives per se, the EEC has
become, over time, more extensively involved in social policy
issues, if only in a minimum regulatory capacity (for example,
around equal opportunities provisions).

The Anti-Poverty Programme can perhaps be seen too in terms of a
longer-term set of pressures around the nature of the EEC itself.
These pressures include possible tensions arising from wider membership by Mediterranean countries, and current demands for budgetary
reform to reduce spending on the CAP and to increase the emphasis
upon regional and social fund spending.   Whatever the reasons, by
the time the programme came towards its end in 1980, it was possible
for the local projects to achieve, in response to a joint lobby, a
broad level of support amongst European MPs from Ian Paisley through
to the Italian Communist Party.

The budget of the programme appeared to be considerable in terms
of the funds available nationally, particularly as the public expenditure cuts proceeded in Britain from the mid-1970s.   However, it
was miniscule in terms of the EEC's own commitments.   The Anti-
Poverty Programme accounted for only a fraction of the Social Fund,
which was in turn barely 6 per cent of total EEC spending in 1975 -
compared with some 75 per cent of the budget devoted to the CAP.
By 1979-80 the programme's budget had doubled but the effect of inflation meant that expenditure had barely kept pace with increasing
costs.

Part of the justification for such a modest input of resources
was that the programme had pilot status;   'it was to test and develop
new methods of helping persons beset by or threatened by poverty in
the community.'   (Council of Ministers' decision, July 1975, quoted
in 'Europe Against Poverty' (2))

Once again, as in other poverty programmes, research, and especially action-research, was to stand in for main spending programmes.
Yet the EEC's own evaluation exercise was not even launched until
1979, when a team based at the University of Kent (ESPOIR) was commissioned to produce a report on the first five years of the programme.   The research input was in practice uncoordinated and inadequately conceived at both the cross-national and the local levels
(despite systematic attempts by the Irish, for example, to learn
from previous experience). (3)   As the Final Report of the Irish
Combat Poverty Programme, one of the participating projects, concluded, (4) 'the difficulties in combining action-research, survey research, and evaluation within the one programme posed a serious
challenge for the management of such a programme' - the very tensions inherent in previous quasi-experimental pilot/action-research
programmes.

Broadly, the EEC programmes which eventually emerged included the
following elements:
(a)   Cross-national studies into poverty, directly sponsored by the
Commission.   These have included a study on the perception of poverty in Europe, which demonstrated, incidentally, that the British

had some of the most punitive attitudes towards poverty, far more so
than the French and Italians who were more likely to blame the
'system', rather than the 'victims'.

Twenty-one pilot projects were also approved and others subsequently added, including the British Area Resource Centres in
London, Glasgow and South Wales, funded until 1980-1 on an 'experi-
mental' basis.

(b) Community action projects (in the UK this included funding for
the Craigmillar Festival Society, Edinburgh).

(c) Service delivery programmes (including welfare rights services
and tribunal representation as in Wolverhampton).

(d) Services for deprived and marginal groups, such as vagrants
(W. Germany) and gypsies (Ireland).

In the broadest sense, all these action projects were described as
being 'community action'.

SOME CONTRADICTIONS

As in other poverty programmes, a number of significant contradictions emerged as projects began to be established. One has been
referred to earlier, the role of research or action-research in projects concerned with social change. In a number of instances,
management evidently found that action-research designed to produce
accessible and locally utilisable findings was particularly problematic. The North Centre City Community Action Project (NCCCAP, part
of the Irish programme) on the edge of Dublin's docklands, for instance, undertook research into levels of unemployment, commissioned
an architectural study of the area, carried out an attitude study
with local residents to measure their views on redevelopment, and
completed a brief review of the principal sectors of economic
activity.

Not surprisingly perhaps, some of the findings proved highly con-
tentious. When the attitude survey found that 80 per cent of local
people wished to remain living in the inner city, for example, in
opposition to the redevelopment plan, it was denounced in the media
as partisan and/or false.

'Your job is over!' was the comment of the then Minister of
Health and Social Welfare, to the NCCCAP researcher. According to
the researchers' perspective, however, the problem was not so much
the incapacity of the researchers to function, but rather of management to handle their product.

The major source of tension, however, was to arise over the projects' definition of poverty and the target groups and strategies
which flowed from it. The notion of poverty which the programme
was eventually to work to was broader than a simple stress upon minimum standards. It was, in some senses, a relative definition,
similar to the definition developed by Townsend in the UK: (5)

Individuals or families may be considered in general to be in
poverty when they have a command of resources so different that
they are excluded from ordinary living patterns, customs and
activities of the Member State in which they live.

In operation at both national and international levels, there
were, not surprisingly, wide variations in the conception of poverty

and its causation.   The Irish programme's Final Report, for
example, comments on the co-existence, in practice, of approaches
which emphasised individual pathology alongside those which stressed
the underlying structural causes of poverty.   The case study from
Naples illustrates the development of project work based upon the
'structural', as opposed to the 'individual pathology' approach to
the definition of poverty. (6)

Similarly, the Irish Combat Poverty Programme itself formally
viewed poverty as an aspect 'of inequality in the social and economic system....'   'Poverty,' the Parliamentary Secretary concluded,
'can only be ended if the structures and institutions of our socio-
economic system are altered profoundly.   This is a policy goal
which is radical and long-term.'   But in practice, there was also
considerable variation in the use of the concept of poverty, even
within participating programmes such as the Irish one.   These included uses based upon identifying the most marginal individuals,
and/or the most marginal communities, in other words, an 'individual
pathology' approach.   The following example, again from NCCCAP,
Dublin, illustrates some of these contradictions in operation. (7)

Within weeks of its establishment, the NCCCAP was confronted with
a major crisis: a plan by the local authority, Dublin Corporation,
to demolish the housing of 5,000 people, relocate them in the sub-
urbs and replace the housing with office blocks, car parks, and
roads.   Before discussion could take place on conceptual definitions of poverty, or the project's brief 'to revitalise the inner
city', the project team were obliged to take a quick decision -
whether to oppose the plan or not.   The team and its board of
management agreed it was imperative to oppose the plan by mobilising
the whole community and by the commissioning of an 'Alternative
Plan'.

Underlying this decision was the assumption that popular participation and radical socio-economic transformations were requirements
of any anti-poverty strategy.   Using architectural, cultural and
sociological resources, the NCCCAP focused city and even, at times,
national attention on this small, tightly knit community.   The Project supported spontaneous initiatives, leafleting of the local
authorities, sit-ins in public buildings, sit-downs on streets,
housing marches, open press conferences.   Cultural initiatives were
particularly well received.   These ranged from a song, (8) recorded
by a local singer about the north inner city, a play by a local
playwright performed in a city theatre, and a photographic exhibition, to a pamphlet of historical reminiscences by a local resi-
dent. (9)   This process of resistance had a limited success, in
that the housing authority revised its plans twice to include housing units for over 150 families in among the office blocks and car
parks.

These campaigning activities tended to eclipse the social service functions which some of the Irish social policy makers considered more suitable for a Combat Poverty project, services consistent
with the work of professional social workers, with the identification of so-called marginal groups in the community, with information
and advice work.   Inherent in the NCCCAP perspective was the prevention of a process of marginalisation of the whole community, by
initiatives to stimulate 'community identification'.

In this sense then, the NCCCAP experience was consistent with a
'structural' rather than an 'individual pathology' definition of
poverty.

But the reality was more complex.   In opposing the redevelopment
plan for the north inner city, (10) the NCCCAP leaned heavily on the
fostering of a sense of united community, stressing the common cultural and historical links of the area with the upsurge of the
labour movement at the turn of the century. (11)   Whilst the proposals of the insurance companies and housing authorities to depopu-
late the district were presented as external elements impinging on a
closed and unchanged community, this was in fact no more than a par-
tial truth.   So by defending the right of local people to refuse
the development plan, to be rigid in their opposition, to 'stay
put', to keep the community demographically and geographically
intact, the NCCCAP may have inadvertently appeared as a conservative
force, opposed to change of all type.

By tending to internalise debate and critical discussion into the
community, rather than outwards, internationally, or at least
nationally to other cities, the concept of poverty was enlarged from
the individual to the level of the community and yet simultaneously
was not situated within a national or an international perspective.
The project team were conscious of these dilemmas, but hampered in
their capacity to resolve them, by the lack of inter-project co-
operation with the programme.

To summarise so far then, the EEC Anti-Poverty Programme certainly did have parallels with preceding national programmes, at
least in terms of the explicit concern with legitimacy, the 'human
face of the EEC'. (12)   There were parallels too, in relation to
the action-research component of yet another 'pilot' programme (13,
14) as a substitute for main-spending programmes.   And there were
parallels in the ambiguities of the overall conception of the Poverty Programme, which allowed for very considerable variety of interpretations, both amongst the different project teams and amongst the
relevant politicians and responsible officials.

A CHANGING CONTEXT

But there were also crucial differences.   And there were certainly
conscious efforts, if not necessarily successful ones, to avoid the
mistakes of previous programmes.   For example, the paper by A.A.
Delperee at the seminar on 'Action Against Poverty' at Gouvieux in
1977 specifically emphasised the need to learn from the US experiences ... to avoid 'the chaotic lines' of the pilot projects, and
the ways in which some 'served as an excuse for hindering social
progress'.   The Irish programme was also particularly aware of the
need to learn from the Home Office's mistakes with CDP.

Apart from such consciousness (or the lack of it) amongst key individuals and organisations, the economic background and the institutional framework for the EEC Anti-Poverty Programme were both significantly different from earlier programmes.   Although the programme was first discussed in the more optimistic climate of the
early 1970s, it was implemented in the harsher climate of the second
half of the decade.   This deteriorating background affected the

programme in a variety of ways, mostly negative.   However, this did
mean that restrictive definitions of poverty in terms of pathologi-
cal individuals were less sustainable, even in the previously successful West German economy.   (The West German government had been
the most reluctant to accept that 'poverty', however defined, might
exist at all within their borders.)

Public expenditure cuts, in Britain at least, affected the projects' own attitudes too.   For example, as it became harder to find
national or local government funding for community projects, EEC
initiatives (in terms of both the Anti-Poverty Programme and of the
Social Fund more generally) took on correspondingly greater potential significance.   And even where, as in Ireland, a national government has committed funds to a further anti-poverty programme,
this has been on a relatively reduced scale.   (In November 1981,
the Fine Gael Party and Labour Party coalition government announced
the creation of a new anti-poverty agency, in fulfilment of their
election campaign promises.   But notwithstanding inflation at 20
per cent, only 1/5 of the former Combat Poverty budget has been
allocated to this new agency.)

In a more general sense too, the overall atmosphere of the inter-
project discussions, which took off in 1979-80, felt very different
from those of the previous decade in Britain.   Although there was
concern amongst some of the projects to develop the more challenging
approaches, at the level of the projects' public dealings with politicians and the Commission, the emphasis was typically low key,
focusing upon the appraisal of mutual 'interests'.   Projects had in
mind the realistic possibilities for renewed funding - as long as
this could be achieved within an organisational and definitional
framework which was not so constricted as to be ultimately counter-
productive.   On the whole, there was not much, if any, interest in
throwing down political gauntlets.

In any case, a multi-national state structure cannot simply be
equated with a national government, in terms of its interests and
spheres of operation.   For example, CDP has been considered in
terms of the development of more sophisticated information feedback
and social control systems, although there has recently been less
emphasis upon this aspect, and more emphasis upon CDP as a way of
promoting social service rationalisation in order to stem the growth
of public expenditure.   In fact, the Giugliano case study illustrates an attempt to redefine precisely these concerns with a local
context and to develop a model of social service integration in
terms of users' needs, rather than in terms of more effective control systems or public expenditure constraints.   But neither of
these two aspects can be simply applied to a multi-national structure, which just does not have comparable direct responsibilities.
Nor would the organisation of political constituencies, a key concern in relation to the US experiences, seem to be directly comparable either; (15) the European Parliament was not even an elected
body when the EEC programme was devised.

WHAT DID THE PROJECTS, COLLECTIVELY, MAKE OF THE PROGRAMME?

The lobbying of European MPs by the projects to obtain further funding, referred to earlier, was, in itself, the trigger to one of the
most stimulating outcomes of the programme as a whole.   Although
there had been occasions when the projects had been called together
by the EEC to exchange experiences, these international gatherings
had been infrequent and relatively formal.

Even within a single national programme, such as the Irish one,
it had proved difficult to promote concerted strategies to tackle
poverty.   For example, it has been suggested that the opportunity
for collective inner city inter-project work was not so much lost,
as handicapped from the outset, by the establishment of community
projects devoid of any vehicle for inter-project research, comparison, debate or meeting, and thus appearing to perpetuate the notion
that the decline of inner city working-class communities is city-
specific and geographically unique.

In the autumn of 1979, however, the different national projects
took the initiative in meeting together, in response to their
common, impending refunding crisis (their funding was to run out
over the following year).   Initially, the focus was upon this immediate financial concern: a joint project organisation, ESCAP, was
set up, and a rigorous lobbying process was set in motion, both at
the European and national government levels.   But, meanwhile, a
process of exchanging experiences was also set in motion, spurred on
by the possibility that the Commission might be interested in funding joint initiatives, to overcome earlier criticisms about the
'hotch-potch' character of the first programme.   (It was indeed a
'hotch-potch', of course, since the projects were selected through
the member state governments, rather than from any inherent reasons
of international comparability.)   Out of these inter-project exchanges certain projects did identify potentially compatible strategies, and these projects developed programmes for comparable work.

Common strategies and programmes of work were agreed in the
summer of 1980, for example, around inner city initiatives on jobs,
housing, health, welfare rights and client self-organisation, on a
cross-national basis.   The case study from Giugliano provides an
example of project work which was discussed in this context, in
terms of developing community health initiatives on a cross-national
basis.   The Giugliano workers themselves played an active part in
these discussions; and there was considerable interest in their
approach in any case, because of new developments in community
health in the UK and elsewhere.   In the event, however, the refunding crisis eventually cut these common work programmes short.

Since then, certain of the projects have been refunded individually through other sources (such as local government, in the case of
the Giugliano project).   In Ireland, in contrast, two teams of project workers, in Waterford and Cork, decided to keep the project
going independently and continued to do so throughout 1981, maintaining their work through fund-raising, concerts, sponsored walks,
co-operation with local trades councils, voluntary contributions and
unpaid labour.   ESCAP too has continued meeting (with private foundation funding), both to exchange experiences and to plan the joint
campaign for further EEC funding.

Clearly, such international exchanges do not necessarily require
an anti-poverty programme;   they can and do take place in a variety
of ways.   But international get-togethers are expensive and time-
consuming too;   direct financial support from the EEC has considerable potential, then, as a means of facilitating exchanges at the
European level, between project workers and community activists
themselves, both of whom, if the ESCAP experience is more widely
relevant, have much in common and much stimulus to offer each other.

The following section provides an example from Italy of a project
which had both these qualities.   Its work was seen to have a wider
applicability and the project workers were anxious to develop it
through cross-project work in an attempt to redefine certain key
concepts within the Anti-Poverty Programme as a whole.

COMBATING POVERTY FROM A CENTRE FOR 'SOCIAL' MEDICINE

The Giugliano Centre for Social Medicine became part of the EEC
Anti-Poverty Programme in 1978.   The goal was preventative medicine in the broadest sense, as well as the provision of particular
services to individuals and groups, both at the centre and in the
community.

The project started, then, from an explicitly critical stance in
relation to certain key concepts in the Anti-Poverty Programme.
'Poverty', in particular, was a concept which they used reluctantly,
because as their Report explains, descriptive categorisations of
'poor people in terms of the priorities of their different needs,
individualise and fragment the poor, failing to take account of the
social processes which produce the phenomenon of poverty in the
first place, whether at international, national or local levels.'
In contrast, the project started from a structural analysis of the
socio-economic contradictions which produce and reproduce poverty;
whilst at the same time emphasising the relevance of a strategy to
combat poverty which combines radical change in the forms of social
organisation at the macro level, with concrete and local action
strategies.

Local action, for us, represents a necessary element in the
struggle against poverty, both because it keeps open the dialec-
tic and the hope of change in the local population (even if this
does also take up a great deal of energy), and because local
action can mark out the concrete forms through which people can
enrich and democratise social organisations, by developing
people's own resources and potential to the maximum, starting
from the base upwards, in the wider process of radical social
change.

One of the most immediate implications of such a structural conception of poverty was that the project defined their target population with reference to the entire local population of 150,000 inhabitants.   The focus was upon meeting needs within the local, and
ultimately the national and international socio-economic cultural
context, rather than upon the identification and thus the stigmati-
sation of the most 'needy' individuals.

A CRITICAL APPROACH TO EXPRESSED 'NEEDS'

The concept of 'need' itself was also problematic for the Giugliano
project.   One of their key concerns was to move away from an essentially passive concept of 'need', associated with traditional, official definitions of problems requiring separate service provision
(services for the elderly, the mentally handicapped, etc.).

    In place of these official definitions the project involved the
local population in a two-part process, consisting of:
(a)   a critical participation exercise involving the creation of
situations in which needs could be expressed;   and
(b)   the critical evaluation of requests for help - a dialogue
between local people, collectively, and the project workers, to dis-
entangle their essential, often underlying needs, from the form in
which their immediate demands were initially expressed.

    For example, the analysis of specific requests for medical inter-
vention often revealed underlying needs of an economic, cultural or
social nature;   hidden needs which would still be unsatisfied if
they were simply treated on the surface with drugs and injections.
The critical analysis, in fact, set out to discover whose ultimate
interests would be served by responding to expressed needs in different ways - the long-term interests of local people or the long-
term interests of the providing agencies and ultimately the interests of the status quo.

    As an example of this process, the project offered the following
story.   Whilst a doctor and a social worker were involved in a project with a school in Melito, a young girl was taken ill;   she wept
hysterically and said that she felt that she was dying.   This type
of hysterical outburst is apparently common amongst women in this
area;   they even have their own particular name, 'i rilasciamenti',
to describe it.   The outbursts are quite dramatic in character and
set up a highly emotionally charged atmosphere.   In this case,
everyone agreed that a doctor was needed to offer diagnosis and to
prescribe tranquillisers (which was what usually happend in such
cases).   The doctor came, and stayed with the girl until she calmed
down.   But he suggested that the problem was not essentially a
physical one requiring medicines;   it would perhaps be more relevant
to try to understand the problems of women and girls which led them
to express themselves through such dramatic outbursts.   The other
girls gathered round and an impromptu meeting took place, with the
sick girl eventually starting to join in the discussion.   They
talked over the socio-cultural pressures on girls and the restrictions which their parents put upon them going out and meeting each
other.   They also discussed the lack of social and cultural facilities for women and girls as a specific instance of their wider
oppression.   Subsequently, the team discussed these problems again
with the girls and their teachers, who decided to organise a demonstration to press for social and cultural facilities.   After two
weeks of planning and preparation the march set out around the town
- a sensational event in a southern Italian town where young women
had never organised a march before, let alone a march for their own
rights.   Out of the ensuing discussions, including a meeting with
the mayor, certain immediate gains were achieved (for example, a
film day for all the women and girls to replace regular programmes

which usually consisted of pornographic films catering exclusively
for the male population).

This, then, was the first phase of a longer-term process of discussions, organisation and collective action amongst the women and
girls of the area, and amongst the team, as they evolved ways of
responding to these 'needs'.

SERVICE INTEGRATION - A HORIZONTAL RATHER THAN A VERTICAL MODEL

As part of their commitment to the de-medicalisation of problems
with socio-economic and cultural implications, the project was also
committed to a horizontal, rather than a vertical model of service
provision and with the whole community, rather than through specific
and fragmented services.   This emphasis upon the integration and
co-ordination of services and structures represented another example
of the redefinition of inherited concepts.

In place of an emphasis upon co-ordination of previous poverty
programmes, in terms of the rationalisation of services, integration
was being approached as a critical and more collective reformulation
of previously fragmented definitions of clients' needs, definitions
which had effectively reinforced the alienation and dependency of
the client.

In organisational terms, the Giugliano project developed multi-
disciplinary teams of three to five staff working from converted
local houses, at neighbourhood level, with preventative health teams
at district level backed up by the full multi-disciplinary team at
the centre, for the commune.

The key focus was the local district level, with specialists from
the centre providing the necessary back-up support.   From the
centre, meanwhile, an overview was mapped out of such socio-economic
causes of ill health as industrial pollution, inadequate housing and
poor living conditions.   The overview also provided a map of relevant local services, local community groups and trade union organisations in the area.   Local organisations were supported and new
groups were called together to develop collective forms of self-
defence in the face of common health hazards, from malnutrition to
industrial illnesses.   There were also special initiatives aimed at
supporting collective organisation by women around the problems of
pregnancy and contraception, and at other groups who tended to be
socially isolated (such as former mental patients, handicapped children, and young people who had been out of work).   In the local
neighbourhood centres political, social and cultural events were
organised, children's events were prepared such as carnivals and
children's theatre, as well as the more overtly health-related activities.   And the experiences of these varying initiatives were fed,
in turn, into the debates about the services themselves, and their
tendency to institutionalise and to individualise their clients and
to fragment the experience of their 'needs'.

The project concluded that a horizontal approach, although central to their strategy, certainly did not, of itself, however,
guarantee that services would be changed, ultimately, in the long-
term interests of the clients.   In fact the horizontal model, they
argued, contained two possible outcomes: it could be orientated

towards the extension and rationalisation of the social control functions of the social services; or it could lead in the opposite direction towards the ultimate goal of collective liberation. (16)

Since the EEC Anti-Poverty Programme's funding ended the project has been locally financed, although it has continued to take part in international debates. Inevitably, a thumbnail sketch of this length and from this distance cannot really begin to evaluate the project's effectiveness in practice, in its own locality. But it is possible to begin to evaluate the contribution which the Giugliano project made to the EEC Anti-Poverty Programme - a contribution which included some of the most stimulating inputs to the inter-project debates. The Giugliano project's experiences have been discussed far more widely too, at least in Britain and France, in relation to the development of radical community-based approaches to health.

AFTER THE EEC ANTI-POVERTY PROGRAMME - WHAT NEXT?

In addition to the project workers' own struggles for refunding, tenants' and residents' groups from the target populations in areas as far apart as southern Italy and south Wales, demonstrated their conviction of the programme's positive potential too, by going to Brussels for a multinational demonstration in November 1981 in support of a renewed programme. For them, at least, the EEC initiatives represented potentially relevant resources, whatever their possible levels of scepticism about the ultimate resolution of 'poverty' through such institutional means. But the prospect of any further programmes seems to have been steadily receding, or at least the prospect of EEC funding for the type of programme which would support community action groups.

The pressures to shift EEC spending away from the CAP towards the Social and Regional Funds have not been receding, though; on the contrary, there is some reason to anticipate increased EEC involvement in social policy issues. But the extent to which any such spending programmes would promote the development of the type of democratically accountable cross-national, action-research projects which local people were demanding is more problematic. So too, of course, is the wider question of the desirability of continued British membership of the EEC at all.

Whilst the final version of this chapter was written by Marjorie Mayo, she would like to emphasise that it is based on the collective work of a number of workers employed within the EEC Anti-Poverty Programme.

NOTES

1 See E. James, From Paris to ESCAP: The European Anti-Poverty Programme 1972-81, in 'Community Development Journal', vol. 16, no. 2, April 1981.

2   'Europe against Poverty: Second Report to the European Pro-
    gramme of Pilot Schemes and Studies to Combat Poverty', 1979.
3   M. Sheehan (unpublished paper), quoted in 'Final Report - Pilot
    Schemes to Combat Poverty in Ireland, 1974-1980'.
4   National Committee on Pilot Schemes to Combat Poverty, Final
    Report, 1980.
5   P. Townsend, 'Poverty in the UK', Penguin, 1979.
6   These approaches were outlined in the earlier reports of the
    British CDP, notably in the Inter-Project Report, CDPIIU, 1974.
7   NCCCAP, Final Report of Project, 1980.
8   D. Baker, 'Inner city sonç', Mulligan Records, Dublin, 1979.
9   M. Corbally, 'Diamond Memories', NCCCAP, 1980.
10 Nathanial Lichfield and Partners, 'A Revitalisation Plan for
    North-East Central Dublin', 1979.
11 'Notice to Quit', NCCCAP pamphlet, 1978.
12 CDP, 'Gilding the Ghetto: The State and the Poverty Experi-
    ments', 1977.
13 J. Higgins, 'The Poverty Business: Britain and America', Basil
    Blackwell, 1978.
14 P. Marris and M. Rein, 'Dilemmas of Social Reform', Routledge &
    Kegan Paul, 1967.
15 F. Piven and R. Cloward, 'Regulating the Poor', Tavistock, 1972.
16 'Progetto pilota di lotta contro la poverta', Final Report of
    the Giugliano Project, 1980.

13 The transformation of community work in the United States

Robert Kraushaar and Barbara Schmidt de Torres

Community work in the United States has always been directly related to industrial growth and urban change. Such early efforts as the Settlement House Movement pioneered by Jane Addams and the ethnic associations of the nineteenth century were organized as a direct consequence of the movement into crowded inner-city neighborhoods of the large numbers of immigrants and minorities needed to industrialize America. From all over the world they came to build canals and railroads, to transform cities into sprawling metropolises, and to increase greatly the economic strength of the nation.

At the same time, the newly formed neighborhoods in which these workers lived were without adequate sanitary facilities, city services were poor or non-existent, and the buildings themselves were overcrowded and in poor physical condition. The immigrants found the transition to an urban setting from a rural environment, the learning of a new language and a strange new culture difficult. Respite was sought, as in England, in 'pub and brothel.'

The response to these social conditions was slow in coming. America was the land of free enterprise and individualism. The culture of capitalism engendered the belief that each man's destiny was his own; therefore, each man's failure was his own. A laissez-faire government policy restricted the scope of social legislation and government intervention. Until the 1930s, 'private philanthropy bore the major burden for community welfare and the relief of poverty and dependency' in the United States. (1)

Major events since then have served to change radically the scope and style of social welfare, of which community work is a part. The Great Depression, the Second World War, the civil rights movement, the riots of the 1960s and the need to 'modernize' urban areas all forced and shaped the involvement of local and national government. All of these events and the programs and policies they engendered have been well documented. (2)

But while the style, scope and tactics of community work have greatly changed over the last century, it is questionable whether its underlying assumptions have progressed much since the philanthropic ideology of the nineteenth century. Simply put, community work still focuses on the adverse effects of industrial change. Poverty, slums and the lack of social integration are still considered unfortunate side-effects of economic development. The underlying theory is that poverty exists because of the limited opportunities and the faults and failures of the poor, rather than because of any defects in the economic and social system. (3)

143

As a result, the focus of community work is usually directed at changing the individual, helping him or her to adjust to society rather than changing society to help the individual.   Ryan defines this as 'blaming the victim' in that it is based on 'the assumption that individuals "have" some problems as a result of some kind of unusual circumstance - accident, illness, personal defect or handicap, character flaw or maladjustment - that exclude them from using the ordinary mechanisms for maintaining and advancing themselves.' (4)   This can be illustrated by examining the major strands of community work that have evolved over the last century: community development, social planning, and community action.

COMMUNITY DEVELOPMENT

The complexity of industrial growth and technological change, coupled, during the Roosevelt years, with expanding international horizons, allowed the concept of community development to be incorporated into American practice.   In its original form, it was a model of development for third-world colonies.   Substantially, it called for informal education as a means of 'bringing the colonies in line with political, economic and social standards as established in the majority of democratic countries.' (5)
    This conception of colonial development was transformed into a model of inner-city redevelopment in industrial societies.   Firstly, the problem in both was defined as a lack of community.   In colonial situations it was usually defined as a lack of modern community forms, a resistance to innovation and a stubborn clinging to traditional organizational forms and methods - notably in farming. In the modern context, it also meant an inability to adapt to modern industrial society, but since traditional structures were diminishing or non-existent, the result was personal disorientation or anomie. (6)   The solution to both was the development of community organizations which allowed the individual to come to terms with the prevailing social order.   At the colonial level, while there was an effort to sensitize the national bureaucracies to local needs, the emphasis was clearly on the integration of the local organizations into the national context.   By contrast, within inner-city areas in industrial societies, national and local bureaucracies were at times seen as a divisive force hampering the development of much needed social cohesion.
    Third, in both instances, there was financial pressure to achieve results at low cost.   Community development, with its emphasis on co-ordination and self-help, seemed a perfect solution.   It was essential to find a method of cheaply integrating alienated individuals into the mainstream of society.
    In the US context, community development has been prominent for a substantial period of time as 'the only valid and legitimate avenue of approach.' (7)   As in its colonial counterpart, it is predicated upon organizing people around a common good or a general welfare 'involving a process of self-guided growth' which heavily emphasizes the 'pro-social' quality of people and minimization of anti-social behaviour or impulses. (8)   Thus, educational objectives and the improvement of problem-solving skills are significant in this

approach; through participation, initiative, and a process of self-
help, the local area can develop important co-operative relationships and democratic skills. The process of creating an indigenous
leadership develops a sense of community necessary to counteract the
effects of alienation from the larger society.

This community work perspective is still practiced in the US, in
urban and rural communities; it also forms the basis of many adult
education programs. On another level, the Peace Corps and Vista
programs, begun in the 1960s, are predicated upon this approach.

The latest development along these lines is the Community Development Corporation (CDC) program created by the Office of Economic
Opportunity (OEO) in the 1960s. While the program evolved as a
response to various contemporary community movements, the concept
itself originated from Robert Owen's co-operative vision. Funding
for the CDC is provided to a great extent by the federal government
and through private foundations - particularly the Ford Foundation.
The CDC operates under an agreement between a poor community (historically this has been predominantly black or hispanic communities), the federal government, and the private business sector.
While the community provides human and physical resources, the private sector participates on the boards of directors, engages in
joint ventures with the CDCs, and supports the sheltered market in
which the CDC can function. (9) Through the CDC program the community is supposed to build confidence while alleviating economic
and social distress through the provision of jobs, increased income,
and greater economic control. (10) As with the community development approach, the intent of the CDC is to 'break the cycle of
poverty...by arresting tendencies toward dependency, chronic unemployment, and community deterioration.' (11) However, as Perlman
notes, the CDC concept contains a built-in contradiction - 'the
attempt to form a capitalist enterprise that is profitable yet
equitable in its distribution of profits in a distressed community.' (12)

SOCIAL PLANNING

A second major strand of community work in the United States is
social planning, which Rothman has defined as a 'technical process
of problem-solving with regard to substantive social problems, such
as delinquency, housing and mental health.' He sees 'rational,
deliberatively planned, and controlled change' as being central to
this concept of community work. (13)

Heskin discusses how social planning evolved from the desire for
a more technical and scientific approach. The emphasis in this
approach is on knowledge, facts, and theory for the solving of
social problems: (14)

In science lay the method of solving all present and future problems...The professionals...saw themselves as the future practitioners of science. They would be efficient; they would plan;
they would determine the public interest.

In an attempt to achieve this, the 1939 Lane Report to the
National Conference of Social Work effectively brought community
organizing into the field of social work. This act signified an

emphasis on social welfare programs and agencies rather than with
the community itself. (15)   The report and its conclusions were an
attempt to professionalize community organizing within the limits
imposed by social welfare agencies.   This can be illustrated by the
channelling of social workers into agency-controlled counselling and
community organizing efforts.   It is in this period that community
organizing virtually became the domain of professionals in which
'planning was used as a *tool* to achieve cooperative and collabora-
tive attitudes in the community.' (16)

Thus the use of professionals and experts is predominant; planners with technical expertise and familiarity with the bureaucratic
process 'represent' the community.   The only community participation stressed as necessary for the implementation of planners'
efforts is approval and assent.   Rein refers to the social planning
approach as a 'consensus of elites' in which this 'consensus is
clothed in strong factual data.' (17)   The technical emphasis of
social planning refers to a predominant concern with the delivery of
goods and services and planning for the arrangement of these goods
and services. (18)

Clearly, then, as Rothman states, social planning is not primarily concerned with 'building community capacity or fostering radical
or fundamental social change.' (19)   It focuses on administrative
and procedural matters - changes in service organizations and in
service systems (20) - not political or economic concerns, something
Mannheim observed was the 'fundamental tendency of all bureaucratic
thought.' (21)   The social planners have 'neither the mandate nor
the tools' with which to influence and/or direct basic political and
economic changes.   They are thus structurally limited in what they
can achieve.   The people who exert greater control over the planners are not the recipients of specific services but those who control the direction of planning efforts. (22)   The planner is thus
relegated to a position in which he or she cannot be concerned with
basic structural changes in the provision, maintenance, and planning
of services.

As a result of the structural limitations and lack of clearly
defined social objectives, Ecklein and Lauffer find that even those
attempts by social planners which have been oriented towards structural changes have resulted in mere corrective effects on the existing system.   Thus it is evident that social planning becomes simply
an intervention concerned with only secondary consequences of social
change and social problems such as 'inadequate housing, poor
schools, inaccessible medical services, etc.' (23)

COMMUNITY ACTION

It was during the 1950s, with the evolution of the Civil Rights
Movement and the government program of redevelopment and urban renewal, that the community action approach gained a foothold in community work. (24)   Racial tensions, unemployment, the rapid growth
of the economy and the social instability of the 1960s led to its
incorporation into government programs and policies.   In all of the
official community initiatives of the 1960s - the President's Committee on Juvenile Delinquency, the Community Action Program of the

War on Poverty, the Model Cities Program - community action became a qualifying and central element. (25)   Its major evolution, though, was an independent community response to, and reaction against, government intervention.

In some ways, community action is the antithesis of social planning.   The aim is not to create an elite of managers and planners, but 'agents of change' advocating for the interests of the relevant community concern.   Its major proponent in the US has been Saul Alinsky who was extremely critical of the more traditional approaches (community development and social planning).   He contended that they lacked an understanding of the relationships between individuals, groups, and the community.   Instead, these approaches tended to focus on the co-ordination of professional agencies which were entirely alien to the community; the result was a rather undemocratic intrusion of these agencies into the community.

Alinksy's initial community organizing efforts grew from a situation of 'scarce' resources for community development.   With his organizing efforts in Chicago in the 1930s, Alinsky became the major pioneer of community action.   Through grassroots organizing which focused on the centrality of the church and its relations to community traditions and institutions, Alinsky advocated the use of conflict and confrontation tactics as a method for achieving economic, political, and social change.

Through these tactics, the 1939 Back of the Yards experiment in Chicago pursued greater citizen participation with the intention of making government and business more accountable to community needs. Alinsky brought together diverse groups within the community to confront outside targets.   For example, church and organized labor were united to obtain community gains from business and local government, such as the enforcement of housing and zoning codes, improvements in physical development and the establishment of credit unions.

Alinsky's conceptualization of organizing was based upon an understanding of the 'cultural - ethnic' relationships within the community - a knowledge of the interrelatedness of local traditions and institutions.   Boyte asserts that Alinsky's work changed community organizing into a 'distinct and developed method of insurgent struggle.' (26)

Yet community action as practised by Alinsky was not a radical approach to community organizing, although it was often perceived as such.   The Alinsky approach did not advocate any radical social transformations.   No structural changes were sought.   The community organizing which Alinsky espoused stressed localism, as evidenced in the parochialism of the Back of the Yards experiment that evolved into organizing around racist issues.   The tendency to organize groups according to their specific interests, effectively strengthened pluralism - consolidating the division among different cultural groups in their community organizing efforts.

In his analysis of Alinsky's tactics, Riessman notes that, as a result of its narrow and introverted perspective, few of the organizations survived.   In fact, he finds no supporting evidence of any significant achievements, and the effectiveness of those efforts seem to be highly questionable.   Thus the radicalism associated with Alinsky is that of rhetoric not of practice;   the 'glamorous tactics' which had particular attractiveness in the 1960s lacked a clearly defined strategy. (27)

Nevertheless, by the end of the 1970s, community action had become the predominant grassroots strategy for community activists as well as for several professionals working within government agencies. (28)

UNDERLYING ASSUMPTIONS

Two questions arise from an examination of these community work strands.   The first is their relevance to the problems they propose to alleviate.   Community work in this context has attempted to help the individual or specific community adjust to the larger society. Implicit is the assumption that it is the individual who is the root of the problem.   Community action varied only in that the blame was placed on institutional malfunctioning.   Even in its more radical forms, community work still contained the underlying tenets of pluralism and reform, thereby rationalizing the political and economic status quo. (29)

Defining the problems as being technical or individual serves to justify the use of community work.   To define inequality, for example, as a by-product of the economic and political structure, as opposed to a necessary part of its continuing operation, means that it is potentially solvable via social reform strategies such as traditional community work.

The second question concerns the present economic context.   A slowdown and imbalance in economic growth has meant that strategies focused on alleviating the imbalances and distributing social benefits have less relevance.   Not only is the US economy experiencing severe problems of structural unemployment and inflation, but entire regions in the north-east and mid-west are suffering economic decline and disinvestment. (30)   In the context of a recession and uneven economic development, the frailty of these assumptions is even more obvious.

NEW DIRECTIONS

Beginning in the early 1970s, a noticeable change with respect to different perspectives and conceptualizations in the literature and practice of community work was apparent.   First of all, the focus shifted from individual and technical defects to economic concerns. Both theorists (31) and activists (32) rallied to the banner of 'economic democracy.'   The main concern was for the transfer of economic decision-making from the few to the many: (33)

For us, the two essential elements of any strategy of fundamental reform in the United States today are: (1) the shift of investment control from corporate domination to the public; and (2) the reconstruction of economic decision making through democratic, worker - and worker/consumer-controlled production.

The second major shift was in coalition-building.   A new consciousness was being developed; Flacks described this as a 'post-industrial consciousness...rooted in a definite class.' (34)   This

change was partly a result of a general disillusionment with the
strategies of organizing throughout the 1960s, but primarily because
of economic conditions.   The conditions of economic austerity,
generated by the concentration of wealth and power in the multi-
national corporations, were in contrast to the apparently more prosperous conditions of the 1950s and 1960s.

There was the realization that this corporate growth was a prime
element in bringing about some of these economic conditions.
Because the economic context had changed, the organizing strategies
of the 1960s were no longer adequate.   What was emerging was a
struggle aimed at challenging the structure of power and decision-
making and the domination of 'corporate, militarist or conservative
interests.' (35)

Greater efforts began to surface at the community and local
levels to unite with regional and national organizing efforts.
This expansion also meant that voluntary structures and institutions
of everyday life, such as religious groups, schools and clubs were
becoming directly involved.   This is significant for these community groupings had previously been the bulwark of the conservatives.
Alliances were formed between the poor, minorities and the working
class over certain issues. (36)

One example of this change is the Ohio Public Interest Campaign.
It is a state-wide coalition of union, church, minority and community organizations formed in 1975 to 'attack the roots of the problems, the structure and behaviour of the giant corporations,
national and global.' (37)   At the moment it is lobbying for a
state law which would require large corporations to give advance
notice of closures, to grant redundancy pay for the retraining and
resettlement of workers, and to compensate the affected communities
for the dislocation caused.

Another typical organization is Massachusetts Fair Share, which
has been able to forge an alliance between blacks and working-class
whites on issues that transcend race.   A state-wide organization,
each local chapter sends representatives to a monthly assembly which
plans overall strategy and policy.   Its strength has been its
ability both to focus on local issues such as street repairs and
housing rehabilitation, and to lobby successfully for state action
to help alleviate local problems.   For example, it was able to
press insurance companies, through protests and organizing efforts,
to pay nine million dollars in back taxes to the City of Boston.
At the same time, it lobbied the legislature in order to have insurance reform laws enacted.   Other victories include a state law
establishing differential property tax rates for residential and
commercial property, and local campaigns against banks that discriminate in their lending practices. (38)

Finally, the Santa Monica Renter Coalition was formed as a reaction to rising rents in Southern California.   With the assistance
of Tom Hayden's Campaign for Economic Democracy, it was able to pass
a strict rent control ordinance and elect a majority to the city
council.   Its political program explicitly focuses on issues of
equity, community control, self-determination and self-reliance.
For example, it has enacted local ordinances to require real estate
developers to make substantial provision for low-income housing and
amenities as a quid pro quo for development approvals.   It has also

promoted the formation of neighborhood organizations and the input
of those organizations into the local decision-making process.
Among proposals being seriously considered at this time is the
establishment of enterprises jointly owned by workers and the
municipality. (39)

CONCLUSIONS

For years, perhaps the most 'radical' theorists of community work in
the United States were Piven and Cloward.   Their work examined the
linkages between social welfare and the needs of the economic system
for surplus labor.   Not only were they highly critical of traditional community work efforts, but also of those 'traditional radicals' who dismissed the new social movements in America - welfare
rights, students, feminists - as not being the 'proper' ones.   The
difficulty with the Piven and Cloward analysis was in its prescription for action.   They concluded that lower class power lies only
in the capacity to effect militant disruptions, a strategy which
'does not require that people affiliate with an organization and
participate regularly.' (40)   In fact, to do so is frequently
counter-productive or results in co-option.

While Piven and Cloward at a theoretical level, and Alinsky at a
practical level, focused on outside events and institutions - the
'enemy' - to create a sense of solidarity, many of the new community
activists turn inward in an attempt to reinforce ties of culture,
trust and community: (41)

  Community stands at the heart of the current activists' vision of
  the future no less than of their plans for the present.   They
  look to community to nurture the ethos and institutions that will
  serve as alternatives to those of corporate capitalism.

At its roots is the native brand of radicalism - populism - which
has a legacy of resisting big business as well as big government.
This is one goal, to shift the present focus in American politics
from the alleged evils of too much government to the pernicious
effects of large corporations.   Many of these activists have their
roots in the 'New Left' of the 1960s and emphasize their pragmatism
(another American trait) over the more ideologically sophisticated
European tradition.   By contrast many of the community activists in
Britain have been more explicitly committed to socialist ideologies. (42)

The outcome of these activities in the United States is far from
clear.   Nevertheless, they are significant in at least two ways.
First, their analysis is more accurate in its focus on economic conditions as the root cause of community and individual problems.
Second, while an older generation of radicals sought to dismantle
local, voluntary and traditional structures, the proponents of the
new model of praxis see in these very institutions and customs the
'capacity and the inspiration for insurgency.' (43)   The danger is
their disregard for the necessity of placing their work within a
wider perspective of society.   The emphasis of action over theory
is, unfortunately, a common feature of community work.   Overcoming
this tendency will be a crucial test for these 'new progressives.'

While the Reagan administration and the New Conservatives would

like to re-emphasize the individual aspects of wealth and poverty, (44) one result has in fact been to direct greater attention to
the broader socio-economic questions.   In the long run, this can
serve to reinforce the community initiatives now in progress, but it
can also lead to a new form of corporatism. (45)   Radical community
work can have a significant impact by giving voice to the 'angers
people feel in their guts' (46) and by helping to direct those
angers towards progressive, as opposed to reactive, policies and
programs.

NOTES

1   George Brager and Harry Specht, 'Community Organizing', Columbia
    University Press, 1973, p. 9;   see also Harold L. Wilensky and
    Charles N. Lebeaux, 'Industrial Society and Social Welfare',
    Free Press, 1965.
2   See, for example, Peter Marris and Martin Rein, 'Dilemmas of
    Social Reform', Penguin, 1974;   Fred M. Cox and Charles Garvin,
    Community organization practice: 1865-1973, in Fred M. Cox et
    al. (eds), 'Strategies of Community Organization', F.E. Peacock,
    1974.
3   Harry E. Berndt, 'The Community Development Corporation as a
    Response to Poverty', paper presented at the 1979 meeting of the
    Midwest Sociological Society, p. 2.
4   William Ryan, 'Blaming the Victim', Vintage Books, 1971, p. 15.
5   Marjorie Mayo, Community Development - A Radical Alternative?,
    in Roy Bailey and Mike Brake (eds), 'Radical Social Work', Pan-
    theon Books, 1975, p. 131.
6   A. Dunham, The Outlook for Community Development - An Inter-
    national Symposium, 'International Review of Community Develop-
    ment', 5 (1960), p. 48.
7   Jack Rothman, Three models of community organization practice,
    in Cox et al., op. cit., p. 38.
8   William W. Biddle and Loureide J. Biddle, Intention and Outcome,
    in Cox et al., op. cit., p. 247.
9   Ibid.
10 Janice E. Perlman, Grassrooting the System, in 'Social Policy',
    7 (1976), p. 9.
11 National Advisory Council on Economic Development, quoted in
    idem., p. 1.
12 Idem., p. 10.
13 Rothman, op. cit., p. 24.
14 Alan David Heskin, Crisis and Response: A Historical Perspective
    on Advocacy Planning, 'Journal of the American Institute of
    Planners', 46 (January 1980), p. 52.
15 Ralph M. Kramer and Harry Specht (eds), 'Readings in Community
    Organization Practice', Prentice-Hall, 1975, pp. 9-10.
16 Brager and Specht, op. cit., p. 10.
17 Martin Rein, quoted in Rothman, op. cit., p. 32.
18 Ibid., p. 24.
19 Ibid.
20 Joan Levin Ecklein and Armand Lauffer, 'Community Organizers and
    Social Planners', John Wiley and Council on Social Work Educa-
    tion, 1972, p. 215.

21 Karl Mannheim, 'Ideology and Utopia', Harcourt, Brace & World, 1952, p. 215.
22 Idem., pp. 218-20.
23 Ibid.
24 Kramer and Specht, op. cit., p. 12; see also James Q. Wilson (ed.), 'Urban Renewal: The Record and the Controversy', Ballinger, 1977.
25 The incorporation of citizen participation and other aspects of community action occurred in several European countries as well. See Tom Miller and Robert Kraushaar, The emergence of participatory policies for community development: Anglo-American experiences and their influence on Sweden, 'Acta Sociologica', 22 (June 1979); also 'Preface to the Second Edition', in Marris and Rein, op. cit.
26 Harry C. Boyte, 'The Backyard Revolution', Temple University Press, 1980, p. 50.
27 Frank Riessman, The Myth of Saul Alinsky, 'Dissent', 14 (July 1967).
28 See Perlman, op. cit.; also Martin L. Needleman and Carolyn Emerson Needleman, 'Guerrillas in the Bureaucracy', John Wiley, 1974.
29 Donald F. Mazziotti, The underlying assumptions of advocacy planning: pluralism and reform, 'Journal of the American Institute of Planners', 40 (January 1974).
30 Barry Bluestone and Bennett Harrison, 'Capital and Communities', Progressive Alliance, 1980.
31 Martin Carnoy and Derek Shearer, 'Economic Democracy', M.E. Sharpe, 1980.
32 Tom Hayden, 'The American Future', South End Press, 1980.
33 Idem., p. 4.
34 Richard Flacks, The new working class and strategies for social change, in Cox et al., op. cit., pp. 229-30.
35 Ibid., pp. 230-1.
36 See Heather Booth, Neighborhood action, 'Social Policy', 12 (May/June 1981); also Boyte, op. cit.
37 Boyte, op. cit., p. 103.
38 Ibid., pp. 97-102.
39 For a more complete listing of organizations and activities, see Boyte, op. cit.; Carnoy and Shearer, op. cit.; Robert Goodman, 'The Last Entrepreneurs', Simon & Schuster, 1979.
40 Francis Fox Piven and Richard Cloward, 'Poor Peoples Movements', Vintage Books, 1979, p. 284.
41 Jeff Lustig, Community and Social Class, 'Democracy', 1 (April 1981), p. 103.
42 See Robert Kraushaar, Pragmatic radicalism, 'International Journal of Urban and Regional Research', 3 (March 1979).
43 Boyte, op. cit., p. 179.
44 The 'best' expression of this is George Guilder, 'Wealth and Poverty', Basic Books, 1980.
45 See Bertram Gross, 'Friendly Fascism', M. Evans, 1980.
46 Lustig, op. cit., p. 111.

14 Radical community development in the Third World

David Marsden and Peter Oakley

There is little need to rehearse the almost traditional critiques of community development which have passed into established literature and resulted in, not only a reluctance to use the term, but also in its perception in many quarters as passé, associated with a discredited epoch of attempted structural transformation in the immediate post-colonial world. (1)   The community development programmes in the Third World during the 1950s concentrated on mass education and the incorporation of largely rural populations into new political entities.   These evolved in the 1960s into a more overt concentration on reaching the 'poorest of the poor' and emphasis shifted to questions of poverty, equity and the nature of 'exploitation', as it became increasingly evident that the benefits of development programmes favoured a relatively small proportion of the population.

This paper aims to provide an overview of developments in the field with particular reference being paid to the work of non-governmental organisations whose contributions to radical practice have assumed important dimensions.   Examples from Brazil and India illustrate the new forms of practice and the new issues which community development is becoming involved with.

CRITIQUES OF COMMUNITY DEVELOPMENT

One might divide the critics of community development programmes into two camps.   Firstly there are the functionalist critics whom in an age which demands tangible results, emphasise the intangible and supposedly inconsequential results of many community development programmes.   They have pointed out the naive idealism which often seemed to inform (or misinform) community development practitioners. Such critics did not fundamentally question the ideological premises and the often ahistorical perspectives which underpinned such programmes, and proceeded to elaborate a sophisticated and comprehensive framework with more fashionable labels (such as 'integrated area development') and seemingly more pragmatic foci.   Emphases have shifted from 'education for independence' to a supposed attack on poverty and inequality, with programmes aimed at target groups - the underprivileged and marginalised sectors of society.   The public rhetoric of the programmes remains the same - an emphasis on 'self-reliance', 'participation', 'grassroots development', and 'self-help' - and the ideological commitment remains rooted in an attachment to liberal democratic values and capitalist forms of development.   Most government-inspired social development pro- grammes, as well as those encouraged by official inter-governmental aid and development agencies were heirs to this tradition. (2)

The more radical critics of community development, on the other hand, insist that, despite more recent attempts to deal with prob- lems of development in a more holistic manner by giving greater pri- ority to social issues, such a framework still leads into a theore- tical and practical impasse, and that the historical dimensions of the processes leading up to particular forms of organisation are not usually dealt with adequately.   Such critics maintain that commu- nity development programmes are little more than neo-colonial tools for the expansion and maintenance of capitalist control in the sup- posedly 'Free World'.   These arguments are supported by reference to the place of community development in the foreign policies of such countries as the United States and the United Kingdom, and the relationships these have to domestic policies, notably those con- cerned with ethnic minorities in the inner urban areas in the 1950s and 1960s.

Community development programmes have been used, together with other instruments of policy, such as land reform (conveniently sepa- rated out in a functionalist analysis) to further capitalist expan- sion and to consolidate a hegemony over recently 'independent' nations.   This resulted in the continued underdevelopment of those countries and the enrichment of those at the 'centre', and increased inequalities both between and within nations.   Critics argue that, while community development programmes publicly espouse decentrali- sation, the actual results are the disenfranchisement and proletar- ianisation of the disadvantaged peasant whose contribution to the developing cash economy is either ignored or marginalised in some 'dualistic' interpretation of social and economic development. (3) By some ideological sleight of hand the causes of underdevelopment are placed firmly at the feet of the peasant, who is accused of ignorance, conservatism and obstructionism in the process of devel- opment, and of being opposed to 'modernisation'. (4)

Such, often explicit, assumptions have traditionally informed social development policies and aid policies generally, whether these be governmental, or voluntary, through theories of modernisa- tion which divorce the analyst from the objects of her analysis. While attempts have been made in more recent years to incorporate into policy planning the ways of thinking of 'indigenous people' so that more appropriate policies might be devised, (5) many would argue that this is no more than a sophisticated co-option by elites, in an age when overt policies of slavery and forced labour are pub- licly unacceptable;   an elaborate disguise to hide the actual nature of exploitation, by clothing it in the myth of good faith in commu- nity, of participation and independence.   This provides a conven- ient means by which the 'expropriators' can ignore their responsi- bilities to those whom they have dispossessed and disenfranchised. Perhaps the most overt example of such a process is to be found in the so-called 'separate development' policies of the present South African government, based on dualistic theories of economic develop- ment and making extensive use of the rhetoric of community develop- ment.

THE SEARCH FOR ALTERNATIVE DEVELOPMENT STRATEGIES

In the face of widening inequalities between sectors of the national
and international community, seemingly supported by development
strategies which only enhanced 'dependent' futures for the majority
of newly-independent Third World nations, there have been renewed
calls for alternative development strategies.   These are reactions
against the dehumanising results of industrialisation and emphasise
rural development.   The emphases on decentralisation, self-reliance
and participation, together with co-operativism, are not new, but
build on nineteenth century romantic and populist traditions. (6)
   Calls for such alternative strategies come from a wide variety of
sources, and various models have been offered which inform the analysis of those involved in a search for a 'New World Order'.   These
include the agricultural and peasant-based socialist strategies
adopted in post-revolutionary China, whose achievements, together
with those of North Korea (which offers another type of model) were
realised as a result of de-linking from the international economic
system.   They also include the socialist strategies of Tanzania and
the humanist strategies of Zambia, as well as the approaches of Pol
Pot in Kampuchea and Khomeini in post-revolutionary Iran.
   In addition, the populist voice, associated with such writers as
Schumacher, (7) Ward (8) and Nyerere, (9) and the idealistic and
often mystical voices of people like Capra (10) and Roszak (11) were
calling for ecologically sound and harmonious development strategies
with appropriate, usually small-scale and rural-based, solutions to
problems of development, in both the rich and poor countries of the
world.   In addition to a threshold being placed on the provision of
basic needs for the poor, it was urged that a ceiling should be
placed on consumption for the rich.   Such views are consistently
argued by, for example, the Dag Hammerskjold Foundation through its
journal 'Developing Dialogue', and through the International Foundation for Development Alternatives and its 'Dossier'. (12)   It is
also the basis of the work of the Commission of the World Council of
Churches on participation in development, (13) as well as by the
Freedom from Hunger Campaign of the Food and Agricultural Organisation of the United Nations and their journal 'Ideas in Action'. (14)
Many such initiatives are in contra-distinction to urban-based (and
urban-biased) government-backed schemes which stress profitability
and productivity in a narrow economistic sense.   The public rhetoric of these initiatives may be the same but they are often anti-
urban and implicitly anti-government, which implies the adoption of
fundamentally different tactics and strategies and divergent relationships with what are often seen as corrupt and nepotistic governments.
   There are those initiatives which insist that reforms achieved
through consensus politics can produce the required changes and
guarantee the redress of inequalities through redistributive measures of one sort or another;   increased co-ordination and centralised control can clear the blockages in the system.   On the other
hand there are those initiatives which demand armed struggle for the
overthrow of corrupt systems;   the strategies that they adopt demand
confrontation with the government and its agencies.
   In between there are a large number of initiatives, voluntary,

para-statal, local and international, which often straddle uneasily
the boundaries of legitimacy and authority as reflected and inter-
preted by those who control the physical and ideological instruments
of state power.   These are the types of initiatives represented by
the case studies from India and from Brazil, described below.

Each government purports to represent all interests within its
jurisdiction, but inevitably the distribution of limited funds will
be determined by the pressure that particular groups can apply, and
by which sectors government is obliged to ally itself to in order to
maintain its position.   Those sectors with the least organisation
and ability will be neglected until such time as they become a
threat to public order.   Such sectors of society have been the
focus for new initiatives as they swell, not only the cities of the
Third World, but also the burgeoning refugee camps.   Areas neglected by formal government involvement provide opportunities for non-
government organisations (NGOs) to initiate schemes aimed at increasing the organisational power and consequently the pressure of
these poorest sections of the community.

Poverty and neglect have traditionally been foci for the activities of non-government and other voluntary organisations in bourgeois society.   As social conditions and relations of production
have changed, the welfare functions of such organisations have also
changed.   In some cases their activities have been taken over by
government in circumstances reminiscent of the expansion of welfare
statism in the West.   Such situations of poverty and neglect have
also given rise to political movements in the form of trade unions
and political parties with a working-class base.

Until the 1970s the major role of most NGOs, including relief
agencies and international voluntary organisations, mirrored the
earlier charitable foundations in the West, being concerned mainly
with disaster relief and with provision for 'outcasts' - the physically and mentally handicapped who still remain the primary objects
of many government welfare programmes in Third World countries.
Unfortunately, the term 'outcast' now applies to many millions, dispossessed and marginalised as a result of the 'modernisation' of
Third World economies.   This increase in the number of marginalised
people has been paralleled by a change in the form and nature of the
contributions of these non-government organisations.

It is necessary to emphasise the relative newness of this change
which has involved a massive increase in the flows of aid to Third
World countries from NGOs as well as a changing emphasis in the uses
to which such aid is put.   Immediately after the war such NGOs were
primarily involved in relief in European countries previously under
German occupation.   This was followed by an early concentration on
refugees - from Palestine in 1948, Hungary in 1956, and Tibet in
1959.   The first major voluntary aid activity unrelated to warfare
was the 1951 famine relief programme to India.   It was only in 1961
that the Freedom from Hunger Campaign was initiated, and only in
1970 that the World Council of Churches' Commission was established,
and support for southern African liberation movements sanctioned.
In the mid-1970s it was the Sahelian drought which occupied major
attention.   In a study of western aid agencies, Lissner maintains
that:

it is possible to conclude ... that the recipient countries -

ceteris paribus - obtain more goods and services per statisti-
cally recorded dollar from the NGOs than from the government
donors.   (p. 51) (15)

While Lissner would argue that such figures are by no means
accurate, they do give some indication of the extent of support distributed through NGO channels.   Conversely they also indicate the
poverty of governmental contributions on both a bilateral and a
multilateral basis, a point emphasised by the Brandt report in its
attempt to promote international Keynesianism. (16)

The work of NGOs in the so-called developing world cannot be
divorced from their work in the developed world.   In both areas an
increasing part of their work focuses on educational programmes,
aimed at increasing the awareness of people to the nature and causes
of international inequality and poverty, and the fundamental, but
often disguised interrelationships which institutionalise systems of
inequality and exploitation.   Both 'here' and 'there' the aims are
to increase people's participation in decision-making.   These are
based on the seminal educational work of people like Paulo
Freire, (17) who remains a major intellectual stimulus for a wide-
ranging number of programmes with an educational dimension, geared
to promoting practical action through organisation.   Through such
action and organisation it is hoped that the inherently unequal relationships which govern social and political life might be de-
mystified and an inherently more just social and political order
initiated.   In combining the ideologies of socialism and Chris-
tianity into a means for combating poverty and inequality he offers
the tools by which the labouring poor can take hold of their own
futures.

ILLUSTRATIONS OF NGO ACTIVITY

The two case studies which follow draw heavily upon the method of
Freire and are characterised by their attempts to tackle the causes
of poverty rather than merely to ameliorate its consequences.
Moving away from government-sponsored programmes one enters a much
more loosely defined and uncoordinated range of community initiatives which, nevertheless, share a variety of common elements.
Practice has remained often unrecorded but informal co-ordination
between NGOs in different parts of the world has provided cross-
fertilization of ideas and methods.   A recent study has, as well as
looking at the origins of such grassroots community action, examined
some of these links. (18)   In terms of more general publications,
the study by de Silva and his colleagues of the Bhoomi Sena movement
in Maharashtra State, India, is illustrative, (19) but a position
paper by Galjart provides us with a succinct conceptual framework
within which such community action might be defined and the case
studies presented.   Galjart defines this community action approach
as 'counter-development': (20)

This approach entails intervention to facilitate the effort of
relatively small local groups in achieving, in a participatory
manner, their development goals, and thus enhancing their members' life chances, in spite of, and in opposition to societal
mechanisms and processes which influence these chances adversely.

Invariably this community action takes place within the context
of a specific project, directed by some external agency.   The general characteristics of such projects include an agricultural economic base which aims at improving the productive capacity of the
group, strengthens collective interest and fosters the kind of non-
material objectives which the project as a whole seeks.   This is
done through the establishment of some form of organisation through
which the group can participate effectively in the process of development.   Associated with this is a continuous educational process
built around the economic activity and the organisational process.
This covers the internal dynamics and the main objectives of the
project.

THE COMMUNITY ACTION MOVEMENT (MAHARASHTRA STATE, INDIA)

This movement covers a number of loosely co-ordinated, but similar
small social development projects throughout the state.   The movement began in Palghar District, just north of Bombay, as part of the
Bombay University Graduate Volunteer Scheme, and soon spread.   The
movement works with small farmers, the landless and tribals - the
'weaker sections' of the Indian rural society whose problems are
identified as being those of powerlessness, lack of organisation,
alienation, indebtedness and dependency.   A recent meeting of the
representatives of the different Community Action Movement's groups
commented on the direction their work should take: (21)
    We have to fight against misery, exploitation and atrocities....
    What is the root cause of these evils?   It is that there is a
    tier system: there are levels of poor, middle class, rich and
    richer.   And the people of every level try to exploit the lower
    level people and strengthen themselves.... So the cause is ex-
    ploitation, or a social structure based on exploitation.
It is obvious that this is not just welfarism, but rather a political struggle based on a class analysis of Indian society and the
organisation of an oppressed majority.
    The approach adopted depends on a team of animators who undertake
social development work in a defined geographical area.   The group
organisation, through economically based projects, such as agricultural credit or improved health care, is reflected in the movement's
characteristics and emphasis is placed on change as a result of a
process of education.   One group of animators stated:
    [We are] ... fully convinced of the value and efficiency of edu-
    cation.   We believe that education can bring about total reform
    in these rural folk making them aware of their rights and duties.
Such education is directed towards creating awareness, instilling
progress, informing people of their rights and duties and organisation, and it is in obtaining substantial results in these areas that
the educational process is to be judged.   While few references in
the movement's documents refer to any theoretical influence in their
educational approach, informal discussions revealed a knowledge of
Paulo Freire and a wish to implement his radical concepts of education.   Workers in the movement emphasised the priority both of such
non-material objectives and of material objectives such as the economic aims of projects.

In terms of synthesising the work of such movements a particularly difficult question is how the teams of animators go about their
work.   Such work is, by nature, lengthy, unamenable to observation
and often not conducive to the demonstration of material results.
Few of the teams keep any kind of continuous record and indeed the
nature of the parameters by which such records might be constructed
have been little explored.   One of the teams explained its work in
terms of four broad stages: firstly, the building of the team's
experience with the project group, leading, secondly, to discussion
of critical issues, culminating, thirdly, in reflection by group
members, and fourthly, action to tackle issues highlighted - a
pattern reflected in the work of other such teams.   To implement
these stages a variety of methods are employed, ranging from group
meetings, usually held on a weekly basis, and providing the major
forum for discussion and decision-making;   adult education classes
which are more formally structured around specific topics (government-sponsored adult education programmes are often used for this
purpose);   public meetings and protest marches focused around a particular campaign;   and drama or cultural festivals which, as community theatre, provide, arguably, one of the more effective and
imaginative instruments in creating general awareness.   While the
above mix will vary according to the situation and the context, the
drama performances would appear to be particularly valuable for the
initial suggestion and spread of critical issues, while the group
meeting is important for consolidating organisation.   Finally, the
protest is useful as an outlet for action and as preparation for the
logical consequences of the process of creating awareness.
    The results of decades of development initiatives which have by-
passed these 'weaker', or, in their own terms, 'exploited' sections
of society, would appear to have resulted in a realisation that if
the poor are to receive a share of the development cake then they
can no longer rely on hand-outs.   Rather they must grasp political
opportunities through effective organisational development, and
maintain concerted pressure on the traditional establishment.

THE FISHERMEN'S MOVEMENT (NORTH-EAST BRAZIL)

The second example comes from one of the poorest regions of
Brazil. (22)   Although agriculture is the dominant economic activity of the north-east, a substantial number of people earn a liveli-
hood either partially or wholly from fishing. (23)   These fishermen
are organised administratively on the basis of government-controlled
colonies which are supposed to facilitate the fishermen's documentation and protect their rights.   In practice the colonies are used
more to tax fishermen, their boats and their beaches.   Few of them
gain any benefit from association with the colonies, which tend to
become vehicles for government assistance programmes to the bigger
fishermen.
    The north-east's small fishermen strive to gain a livelihood
under the most difficult of circumstances.   Most do not own their
own boats;   they rent those of others at extortionate rates.   The
owner of the boat receives 50 per cent of the catch and the fishermen are generally forced to sell the remainder to him.   The

receipts that the owner gives are usually in the form of merchandise
and rarely in cash.   In addition to this unequal exchange a number
of other problems were identified by the Fishermen's Movement.
These include river pollution, encroachment onto beaches by urban
middle-class tourism, a lack of documentation enabling them to take
advantage of government assistance to the colonies, and a total lack
of health or welfare facilities.

These problems collectively reflect the basic powerlessness of
the fishermen's position; official community development programmes
have failed to reach them and the benefits of official government
assistance are captured by a local elite.   The Fishermen's Movement
emerged from a recognition of this powerlessness within a framework
of state control supposedly elaborated to help him.   It was established in 1971 by a local priest, assisted by both lay and religious
animators, and has subsequently been extended into most of the
north-east's nine states.

While the context is different, the work of the Fishermen's Movement is not dissimilar to the work of the Community Action Movement
in India.   The two main elements are an economic programme, orientated to the provision of credit for net and boat purchase, and an
educational programme designed to create an awareness among the
fishermen of the causes of the problems they face, and a commitment
to tackle them.   North-east Brazil is, of course, the birthplace of
Paulo Freire and the place where his adult literacy programmes
began.   As with literally hundreds of similar small-scale community
action programmes in the north-east, the staff of the Fishermen's
Movement use Freire's methodology.   The movement's team is made up
of a co-ordinator, the priest and the founder of the movement, and
six animators.   The movement is very openly linked with the Roman
Catholic Church, which has emerged in Latin America generally as a
major front-line development force through the elaboration of what
has come to be termed 'liberation theology'. (24)

The emphasis in the movement, as in India, is to build organisations to pressurise government.   To date it would appear that considerable gains have been made.   In 1979, for example, the Federal
Brazilian Government enacted legislation on river pollution and in
late 1981 elections will take place for the board of directors of
the fishing colonies, and, for the first time, the small fishermen
will not only be voting but will be presenting a list of candidates
of their own.

As with the Indian example, so in north-east Brazil, there is an
inherent flexibility in the methods adopted.   The tactics for dealing with different local contexts vary, but the broad aims are to de-
mythologise the relationship between the animator and the small
fisherman and to establish a mutually productive relationship
between them.   The Fishermen's Movement, in common with similar
projects in north-east Brazil, explains its methodology in terms of
the process of 'accompaniment', which characterises the nature of
the work of animators with the fishermen's groups.   The animators
work alongside the fishermen providing support and stimulation.
The process seeks to ensure that the fishermen eventually assume
responsibility for their own development.   This is done through
regular group meetings which fulfil the same sorts of functions as

those recorded in India, inter-group and regional meetings, which
have served as powerful tools in co-ordinating a common front, and
the publication of pamphlets and regular bulletins.   Such publications proved particularly effective in efforts to tackle the problem
of river pollution.   The animators lay great emphasis on actually
participating in the lives and activities of the fishermen, but
maintain regular contact amongst themselves to review their work.

CONCLUSION

These two brief case studies, though limited, are illustrative of a
host of, as yet, relatively uncoordinated efforts associated with a
general movement for radical community action.   This movement questions traditional, formal welfare strategies and parallels the development of similar courses of action in the UK and the USA.   Despite often confusing class interpretations of society, and the re-
tention in some instances of a 'modernisation' approach, the efforts
of such non-government organisations are likely to have more far-
reaching effects, because they are relatively scattered and small in
scale.   While formal government-inspired community improvement
schemes still receive a great deal of support, they are usually fet-
tered by an elaborate and often 'corrupt' bureaucracy, supporting a
system of privilege and nepotism which, at least in part, such non-
governmental initiatives are able to bypass through their associations with international aid agencies.
   The contradictions that are presented by such organisations
should not, however, be underestimated.   There are many parallels
with the growth of working-class movements in nineteenth century
Europe and North America and it might be rather simplistically
argued that the struggles which resulted there in the emergence of
working-class political parties and trade unions are mirrored in
these developments within the Third World.   This has very profound
implications for the position of international aid agencies, which
have not gone unnoticed;   the powerful appeal of, for example,
'liberation theology' is in stark contrast to the inherent conservatism of the Roman Catholic Church.   In addition, the success of
such movements implies a major reallocation of resources which in
turn demands structural changes in the forms of government.   In
some contexts government reaction to such movements is overtly hostile;   in others it is, at best, ambivalent.   The results may be
merely the co-option of such community level initiatives coupled
with only marginal changes in the distribution of wealth and power.
Inevitably, however, the conflict between rich and poor takes on
international dimensions as the boundaries which supported the
'independent' nation state are called into question and those boundaries which separate rich and poor are increasingly de-mystified.
In their place emerges an analysis of society in terms of mutually
antagonistic classes.

NOTES

1 See, for example, Marjorie Mayo's article, Community development, a radical alternative?, in R. Bailey and M. Brake (eds),
   'Radical Social Work', Edward Arnold, 1975, and Alpheus Mang-
   hezi, 'Class, Elite and Community in African Development',
   Scandinavian Institute of African Studies, 1976.

2 For a recent overview of the history of government-sponsored
   community development programmes, as well as detailed case
   studies from India, South Korea, Mexico and Tanzania, see R.
   Dore and Z. Mars (eds), 'Community Development', UNESCO/Croom
   Helm, 1981.

3 The term 'dualistic' is here used to illustrate the underlying
   assumption of some development theories that modernisation results in the creation of a 'modern' sector of society which is
   divorced from the 'traditional' sector. These two sectors are
   seen as isolated from each other rather than mutually determined.

4 As an illustration of this sort of approach, see E.M. Rogers,
   'Modernisation among Peasants: the Impact of Communication',
   Holt, Rinehart & Winston, 1969.

5 See, for example, D.W. Brokensha, D.M. Warren and O. Werner
   (eds), 'Indigenous Knowledge Systems and Development', University Press of America, 1980.

6 For a review of such traditions see G. Kitching, 'Development
   and Underdevelopment in Historical Perspective: Populism,
   Nationalism and Industrialisation', Methuen, 1982.

7 E.F. Schumacher, 'Small is Beautiful', Abacus, 1974.

8 B. Ward, 'The Home of Man', André Deutsch, 1976.

9 J.K. Nyerere, 'Freedom and Socialism: Uhuru na Ujamaa', Oxford
   University Press, 1968.

10 F. Capra, 'The Tao of Physics', Fontana, 1976.

11 T. Roszak, 'Where the Wasteland Ends: politics and transcendence
   in post industrial society', Faber & Faber, 1973.

12 The former may be obtained through the Dag Hammerskjold Centre,
   Ovre Slottsgatan 2, S-75220, Uppsala, Sweden. The latter may
   be obtained from the secretariat of the IFDA, 2 Place du
   Marche, ch-1260 Nyon, Switzerland.

13 World Council of Churches, 150 Route de Ferney, ch-1211,
   Geneva 20, Switzerland.

14 Available from FAO, 0100, Rome, Italy.

15 J. Lissner, 'The Politics of Altruism', Lutheran World Federation, 1977.

16 'North-South: A Programme for Survival', Pan, 1980.

17 See for example P. Freire, 'Pedagogy of the Oppressed', Penguin,
   1972, and 'Education for Critical Consciousness', Sheed & Ward,
   1974.

18 P. Oakley and D. Winder, 'The Concept and Practice of Rural
   Social Development', University of Reading, Research Reports,
   1979-80.

19 G.V.S. De Silva, Bhoomi Sena; a struggle for people's power, in
   'Development Dialogue', no. 1, 1979.

20 B. Galjart, Counterdevelopment: a position paper, in 'Community
   Development Journal', vol. 16, no. 2, 1981, pp. 88-96.

21 This quotation and most of the material for the rest of this
    paper are taken from project documentation of the two case
    studies.   Care has been taken to preserve the language of the
    original documents, particularly with reference to the need to
    translate the Brazilian documents.
22 Historically the north-east has constituted a major problem for
    the Federal Government of Brazil.   See S. Mitchell (ed.), 'The
    Logic of Poverty: the case of the Brazilian Northeast', Rout-
    ledge & Kegan Paul, 1981.
23 Mitchell (op. cit.) puts the figures at 100,000.
24 There is a growing body of literature on the church's involve-
    ment in Latin American development.   See for example J. Pitt,
    'Good News for All', Catholic Institute of International Rela-
    tions', 1980.

Index